T0327741

East Asian Development

The Edwin O. Reischauer Lectures

East Asian Development

Foundations and Strategies

Dwight H. Perkins

Harvard University Press
Cambridge, Massachusetts
London, England
2013

Library of Congress Cataloging-in-Publication Data

Perkins, Dwight H. (Dwight Heald), 1934– author.
East Asian development : foundations and strategies / Dwight H. Perkins.
pages cm — (The Edwin O. Reischauer lectures)
Includes bibliographical references and index.
ISBN 978-0-674-72530-0 (alk. paper)
1. East Asia—Economic conditions.   2. Southeast Asia—Economic conditions.
3. Economic development—East Asia.   4. Economic development—Southeast Asia.
I. Title.
HC460.5.P47 2013
338.95—dc23
2013004558

Contents

East Asian Development

Introduction

A half century ago the countries of East Asia bore little similarity to the way they appear to the outside world today.[1] For those familiar with the region, the conditions in these countries could not be more different. Japan was the furthest along, with its economy having recovered fully by 1955, and was well launched on the accelerated growth that was to raise it to first world economic status by the early 1970s. Most Japanese households by 1961 owned television sets and many other consumer durables, but few—less than 5 percent—owned automobiles, and the total number of four-wheeled vehicles in use (including buses and trucks) was only around 2 million. Tokyo and Japan's first skyscraper, the Kasumigaseki Building, at 30 stories, was not built until 1968. Hong Kong and Singapore, at the same time, had per capita incomes only a little below that of Japan (see Table I.1) but income inequality was high. The hillsides and large areas of Hong Kong Island and Kowloon were covered with shack housing for the tens of thousands of refugees who had flooded in from the Chinese mainland, housing that was subject to large-scale destruction from mud slides and fire. The Hong Kong government's massive public housing program was well under way by the early 1960s, and the shacks disappeared, to be replaced by large concrete apartment blocks that had running water and toilet facilities, but of a very basic sort, at least initially. Singapore, like Hong Kong, was still a British colony, having just emerged from the Communist insurgency in Malaya that officially ended with Malayan independence in 1957, and was about to be involved in an undeclared war with Indonesia that went on from 1962 through 1966, during which period Singapore first joined Malaysia (in 1963) and then was expelled from it (in 1965). Labor strife was common in Singapore in the early 1960s, and there

1

Table I.1. Per capita GDP in 1961 and 2010.

	GDP per capita (PPP$) (2005 prices)		GDP per capita 2010/1961 ratio
	1961	2010	
China	623	7,746	12.4
Indonesia	696	3,966	5.7
Japan	6,231	31,453	5.1
Vietnam	554*	2,779	5.0
Philippines	1,508	3,194	2.1
Thailand	983	8,066	8.2
Republic of Korea	1,703	26,614	15.6
Taiwan	1,915	32,118	16.8
Malaysia	1,519	11,962	7.9
Cambodia	1,045*	1,890	1.8
Hong Kong	3,366	38,688	11.5
Laos	564*	2,620	4.6
Singapore	4,514	55,839	12.4
Mongolia	1,756*	3,523	2.0
Brunei	59,273*	44,543	0.8

Data source: Alan Heston, Robert Summers, and Betina Aten, *Penn World Tables 6.3* and *7.1* (Philadelphia: Center for International Comparisons of Production Income and Prices, University of Pennsylvania, August 2009 and July 2012).

Note: Purchasing power parity estimates of GDP and GDP per capita are estimated by recalculating GDP product by product and service by service, using a consistent set of international (mainly U.S.) prices rather than the actual prices of the country whose GDP is being estimated.

* Data for 1970.

was little evidence of the economic dynamism that has characterized the country since the late 1960s. Malaya, soon to be Malaysia, in 1962 was relatively prosperous thanks largely to rubber and tin and the relatively good infrastructure (for the time) left by the British. The Philippines also had a per capita income similar to that of Malaysia, but political strife was soon to produce the election and then dictatorship of Ferdinand Marcos and long years of economic stagnation.

Taiwan in 1961 had made the policy changes the previous year that were to inaugurate its three-decade boom, although there was little physical evidence of the prosperity that was to come. My first opportunity to visit

South Korea was not until the winter of 1969, when its boom was in its sixth year, although again a visitor saw few signs of increasing wealth. The hotel we stayed in with roughly 10 floors was one of the tallest buildings in Seoul, and there were few cars on the streets. Even in 1972 when I worked at the Korea Development Institute helping the Institute get its research program started, there were still few cars. When the North Koreans sent a delegation to Seoul that summer, for example, the Institute was asked to drive its fleet of cars continuously while the delegation was in town to give the impression that there were far more vehicles in the South than was actually the case. More relevant to actual living standards for the poorer parts of the population, rural infant mortality in the early 1960s was over 60 per 1,000 live births,[2] a figure that would put rural South Korea in the bottom fifth of all countries in the world today in this category.

At the other end of the spectrum were Burma, where a coup in 1958 brought to power the junta that has ruled the country ever since and, until recently, stifled economic growth as well as open dissent, garnering what surplus there has been for the privileged few, mostly in the military. Vietnam in 1962 was for all practical purposes already in the midst of its long civil war. Saigon had the appearance of a quiet French provincial town, but only one or two roads outside but near the city that were safe to drive on and then only in daylight. What one saw were "strategic hamlets," villages surrounded by barbed wire that were supposed to cut off contact between villagers and the insurgency. Laos was also already involved in a civil war of its own. Cambodia was in the calm before the storm of the spillover of the Vietnam War and the Khmer Rouge.

Indonesia was still ruled by President Sukarno, who was focused on international posturing while the Indonesian economy steadily deteriorated. All of the Indonesian economic indicators were negative year after year except for prices, which were rising rapidly. On the policy side, the Indonesian rupiah was massively overvalued. An acquaintance of mine in Hong Kong had offered to exchange dollars in Hong Kong for rupiah delivered to my hotel room in Jakarta at a rate that would have made our time in Indonesia almost free of charge, but the possibility of this leading to time in an Indonesian jail led me to decline the offer. The only new buildings in Jakarta were the sports stadiums built by the Soviet Union for the Asian Games. Most Jakarta residents other than the well-to-do lived in kampongs that were fenced off from the road so that visitors to the country would not see them on the ride from the airport to their hotel.

And finally there was China. Americans could not visit the country in the 1960s. The Chinese would not give them a visa, and the United States would have confiscated one's passport or worse if somehow one had obtained a visa and had visited the country. Hong Kong was as close as I could get, but research for my Ph.D. thesis was facilitated by the famine that engulfed China in 1959–1961 after the failure of the Great Leap Forward. During a brief period in early 1962, the Chinese government stopped enforcing its prohibition of border crossings (except for a small number with permits) into Hong Kong, and there was a flood of refugees into the colony, a few of whom I interviewed. At the time we did not realize that nearly 30 million people had died during the past three years, because those making it to Hong Kong and Macau were the healthy ones. When I finally made it to China for the first time in 1974, China's per capita income was still lower than that of any other East Asian economy a decade earlier (at 641 purchasing power parity [PPP] dollars in 2005 prices). In Beijing and Shanghai bicycles were the main means of transport within the city, and cars were only for very high cadres and foreign visitors. Few buildings in either city had been built since the 1950s.

Fast-forward to 2012, a half century later. There are still countries in East Asia where much of the population is below a poverty line of US$2.00 per day. The list includes Myanmar (Burma), The Democratic Peoples' Republic of (North) Korea, Laos, Cambodia, and Mongolia, but even in the latter three, incomes on average are double what they were a half century ago.[3] For the other 10 economies that are the focus of this study (11 if Japan is included), the rise in incomes and changes in the way of life has ranged from respectable to spectacular. Japan, Hong Kong, and Singapore are among the richest countries in the world. The Republic of Korea in the 1990s became a member of the Organization of Economic Cooperation and Development (OECD), the club of first world economies, and Taiwan would be a member if it were recognized as a separate independent country. Skyscrapers in the cities of these five economies are ubiquitous, the streets and highways are jammed with automobiles, and large majorities of the populations in each consider themselves to be "middle class." Farm households are either virtually nonexistent (Singapore) or make up well under 10 percent of the total population, and poverty is defined by poverty lines that are well above the World Bank's two-dollars-a-day standard.

But it is not just the "four tiger" economies plus Japan that have witnessed profound change. Indonesia, Vietnam (since 1989), Thailand, and

Malaysia have all experienced four- to eightfold increases in per capita income. Their cities are also dominated by skyscrapers, and the roads are clogged with automobiles, although a larger share of the population is still in the countryside, and those in poverty are a much larger share than in the richest five economies. Among the countries that were relatively well-off by the standards of 1961, the Philippines, where incomes have only doubled over the past half century, is the main laggard. And then there is China, whose per capita income has risen more than seventeenfold during the most recent three-plus decades beginning in 1979. China has risen from being substantially poorer than much of the rest of East and Southeast Asia to having caught up or passed most of the more successful economies of Southeast Asia, except for Singapore and Malaysia. The most advanced cities of China are even richer. The per capita GDP of Shanghai's 19 million people in 2009 was US$11,800, converting GDP in renminbi into U.S. dollars using the official exchange rate, or nearly double that figure (over $20,000) in PPP terms.[4]

The questions I shall try to answer are: why have several of the economies of East and Southeast Asia achieved rates of growth seldom witnessed elsewhere in the world (with a few exceptions), why have some of the economies in the region done better than the others, and why have the richest economies eventually all slowed down? I will spend very little time on those economies that have not grown at all or have grown only very slowly. There is nothing mysterious about why Myanmar and North Korea have done so poorly. Countries that channel most of their funds to the military either for weapons or to support the lifestyle of the officer class are not likely to experience much if any increase in GDP.

To try to answer these questions, it is helpful to first look at per capita GDP growth rates for the economies in the region rather than per capita dollar GDP figures. The GDP growth rates are presented in Table I.2. There are several things to note about the data in this table. There are 10 economies in East and Southeast Asia that have achieved two or more decades of rapid growth, defined as growth of 4 percent per capita or higher. The economies that did not achieve sustained periods of high per capita growth were, for the most part, economies that were engulfed in war or political chaos (Laos, Cambodia), were part of the Soviet empire until recently (Mongolia), or had closed themselves off from the outside world (Myanmar and North Korea). The one country that performed poorly for much of the latter half of the twentieth century that was not engulfed in

Table I.2. East Asian GDP per capita growth rates.

	1955–1960	1961–1970	1971–1980	1981–1990	1991–2000	2001–2011
China	4.2	1.0	4.3	7.7	9.3	9.7
Hong Kong	NA	7.7	6.9	5.4	2.3	3.6
Taiwan	3.4	7.0	7.9	6.4	5.7	3.9
Japan	7.3	9.8	3.3	4.0	0.9	0.5
Republic of Korea	1.6	5.7	5.4	7.5	5.1	3.6
Mongolia	NA	NA	3.4	4.2	-0.8	5.8
Indonesia	NA	1.8	5.4	4.4	2.7	4.1
Vietnam	NA	NA	NA	NA	5.9	5.9
Philippines	3.0	1.8	3.1	-0.9	0.8	2.8
Thailand	2.6	5.1	4.3	5.9	3.5	3.0
Malaysia	1.3*	3.4	5.3	3.1	4.4	2.7
Cambodia	NA	NA	NA	NA	NA	6.6
Singapore	NA	4.4	7.2	4.9	4.6	3.2
Laos	NA	NA	NA	NA	3.5	5.6
Brunei	NA	NA	13.5	-1.2	2.3	-0.5

Data sources: Most of the 1970–2010 data were derived from World Bank, World Development Indicators, http://databank.worldbank.org/ddp
/home; the 1955–1970 data were derived from the Alan Heston, Robert Summers, and Betina Aten, *Penn World Tables* 6.3 and 7.1 (Philadelphia:
Center for International Comparisons of Production Income and Prices, University of Pennsylvania, August 2009 and July 2012), as were the data for
Taiwan, except that the 2001–2009 data were derived from the Penn World Tables together with data on growth rates in 2008 and 2010 from Taiwan's
Council for Economic Planning and Development, *Taiwan Economic Forum* 10, no. 12 (December 2012), p. 98. The fact that the methodologies used
in estimating GDP in the Penn World Tables and the World Development Indicators are not the same no doubt produces some differences in the
growth rates estimated, but the differences are not likely to be large and certainly not large enough to influence conclusions reached using these data
in this study.

Note: "NA" indicates that the data were not available or too unreliable to be used.

* Data for 1956–1960.

war or political chaos or extreme repression was the Philippines. I will pay some attention to the experience of the Philippines, but that country's story has much in common with the weak performers of so much of the rest of the developing world: overemphasis on import substitution as the main goal of development and a political system that brought to leadership politicians more interested in pursuing rents than development. Brunei is a small petroleum-based sultanate whose economy goes up and down with the price of its one product.

My main focus, however, is on the 10 economies that achieved a substantial degree of economic success. These economies fall broadly into three groups. The first group includes Japan, South Korea, Taiwan, Hong Kong, and Singapore. These five economies all grew rapidly until they reached over $13,000 per capita (in PPP 2005 prices) and then slowed down but continued to grow and close the gap between them and the highest income economies. As of 2011 all had a per capita income over $30,000 (in current PPP prices). Japan, Hong Kong, and Singapore, in fact, have fully closed that gap and are among the highest income economies in the world. The second group includes Malaysia, Thailand, Indonesia, and Vietnam. These economies have achieved sustained periods of high growth that have raised per capita incomes from five to eight times but have run into economic difficulties that have slowed growth. Malaysia is at the high-income end of this group with a per capita income in 2011 in 2005 PPP prices of over $13,000, but its economic performance particularly during the past decade has been sluggish. Vietnam is at the low end in per capita income terms and because of its decades long civil war only began its rapid rise in 1989 and appeared in 2010–2012 to be making economic choices that jeopardize continued rapid growth.[5] All of these countries are in Southeast Asia but there are significant differences as well as similarities among the four.

Finally there is China, which is a group unto itself in part because it is larger than the other nine economies taken together (nearly twice as large in terms of population). China's GDP growth has been more rapid over a longer period (more than three decades), but China started at a much lower per capita income than the others and has not yet achieved PPP income per capita above $15,000 except in a few of its richer cities. Sustaining such a high growth rate during the past decade, because of China's unusual economic structure on the demand side, has required an unprecedented state-led investment effort that may be capable of sustaining China's rise to high-income status over another two decades. It is noteworthy,

Table I.3. East Asia income distribution.

	Year	Gini	Top 10%	Top 20%	Bottom 20%	Bottom 10%	Top 20%/ Bottom 20%
China	2004	46.9	34.9	51.9	4.3	1.6	12.1
Hong Kong	1996	43.4	34.9	50.7	5.3	2.0	9.6
Taiwan	2003/2009	33.9	NA	40.3	6.4	na	6.3
Japan	1993	24.9	21.7	35.7	10.6	4.8	3.4
Republic of Korea	1998	31.6	22.5	37.5	7.9	2.9	4.7
Mongolia	2002	32.8	24.6	40.5	7.5	3.0	5.4
Indonesia	2002	34.3	28.5	43.3	8.4	3.6	5.2
Vietnam	2004	34.4	28.8	44.3	9.0	4.2	4.9
Philippines	2003	44.5	34.2	50.6	5.4	2.2	9.4
Thailand	2002	42.0	33.4	49.0	6.3	2.7	7.8
Malaysia	1997	49.2	38.4	54.3	4.4	1.7	12.3
Cambodia	2004	41.7	34.8	49.6	6.8	2.9	7.3
Singapore	1998	42.5	32.8	49.0	5.0	1.9	9.8
Laos	2002	34.6	28.5	43.3	8.1	3.4	5.3
Brazil	2004	57.0	44.8	61.1	2.8	0.9	21.8
United States	2000	40.8	29.9	45.8	5.4	1.9	8.5
Sweden	2000	25.0	22.2	36.6	9.1	3.6	4.0

Data sources: World Bank table 2.7, http://sitesources.worldbank.org/DATASTATISTICS/Resources/table; *Key Indicators for Asia and the Pacific 2011* (Manila: Asian Development Bank, 2011), p. 147; *Taiwan Statistical Data Book 2011* (Taipei: Council for Economic Planning and Development, 2011), p. 87.

Note: "NA" indicates that the data were not available or too unreliable to be used.

however, that there is no real precedent one can point to as a guide to China's likely future long-term performance. I will return to this topic in the final chapter.

This study, as I have said, is focused on explaining the high GDP growth rates of much of East Asia. As many analysts have pointed out over the years, a high GDP growth rate does not necessarily mean that the great majority of the people in these countries have benefited from that growth. One often hears phrases whose gist is that growth only benefited the already rich and powerful. In East Asia that was not the case, however. Several of the countries in the region started growth from a relatively egalitarian base largely because of the impact of war and revolution. That list includes Japan, Korea, China, Vietnam, and Taiwan, and two of these, Japan and Taiwan, have maintained a low level of inequality to the present. At the other end of the spectrum are countries such as Malaysia and the Philippines where insurgency and political change left unequal property ownership with incomes from that property largely intact and inequality higher.

Starting out with a low level of inequality did not always ensure that the country continued at a low level. Income distribution data for recent years are presented in Table I.3. China by the twenty-first century had become one of the more unequal countries in the region, although not as unequal as such extreme cases as Brazil. Singapore and Hong Kong probably also experienced a rise in inequality, and all of the countries in the region were substantially more unequal than Sweden with its strong social welfare programs and progressive taxes. No attempt will be made in this study to estimate quantitatively the changes in inequality in these economies over time. The data on income distribution are notoriously subject to biases, and precise estimates of changes in inequality are not important for the arguments made in this study.

Even the countries with which this study is concerned that experienced a major rise in inequality over the five decade period saw most of their poorest citizens receive large benefits from the growth in GDP. In China, for example, the rise in inequality was probably the largest in the region, and yet the 20 percent of the rural population with the lowest income experienced a fourfold increase in their real income per capita between 1978 and 2011. The real per capita income increase for the bottom 20 percent of the urban population over three decades of reform was over sixfold.[6] Average rural incomes in the two poorest provinces in China, Guizhou and Gansu, rose fivefold, while average urban incomes also rose fivefold in the case of Gansu and eightfold in the case of Guizhou. In looking into the sources of the high rate of GDP growth, therefore, one is also analyzing how these economies and societies transformed the living standards of most of their citizens.

In the analysis that follows, we shall try to understand what these 10 relatively high GDP growth rate economies have in common (other than being at the eastern end of the Asian continent) and where they differ from much of the rest of the developing world. The remainder of the discussion is divided in the following way. The first chapter focuses on the historical foundations of modern economic growth in these 10 economies. In many studies of East Asia's rapid growth performance the Confucian heritage is cited as an explanation for their high growth, and certainly Confucian values are present in all of the more successful economies. A majority of the populations in six of these economies shares a Confucian heritage, and the other three have large minorities that have similar values. These minorities have played an important role in the development of Indonesia, Thailand, and Malaysia. But what is it about Confucian values that may be relevant? Scholars in the past have argued the opposite point, that Confucian values actually retarded growth. And clearly Confucian values are not the only historical forces at work in these economies. There are major differences in these societies' interactions with Europe and North America during the nineteenth and twentieth centuries—interactions that ranged from outright colonial control by European countries and Japan (and the United States in the case of the Philippines) to countries that never were outright colonized (Japan, China, and Thailand). The Cold War, which lasted from the end of World War II until the collapse of the Soviet empire beginning in 1989, brought other kinds of interactions. Even the most casual review indicates that history has had a major influence on development in East and Southeast Asia, as their different histories have so influenced much of the rest of the developing world.

The analysis then turns, in Chapter 2, to a review of what we can learn that is relevant to the East Asian experience from the various quantitative studies of economic growth, much of it involving cross-country comparisons of all of the world's economies, at least those for which relevant economic data are available. Two kinds of methodologies are relevant to this search: the cross-country econometric studies of Robert Barro and many others that have received much attention during the past two decades, and the cross-country patterns of growth analysis pioneered by Simon Kuznets and Hollis Chenery. This study is not the place to systematically review all of the major works in this cross-country quantitative comparisons genre, there are too many, but we do need to ask what these findings tell us about East Asia. Does this literature tell us something that is new about development that we did not see before, or does it basically confirm what has often been suggested but never backed up with statistical tests?

Moving beyond these analyses of history and quantitative data, Chapter 3 looks at how the 10 economies were managed. Specifically, I focus on the role that government played before, during, and after the periods of high rates of GDP growth. A metaphor sometimes used to describe the role of government in development in the region is the "flying geese pattern." In this metaphor Japan with its state interventionist industrial policy is seen as the lead goose, and the other nations form the V shape of the followers. Japan's industrial policy has had a major influence on some of the countries of the region, and I will spend some time reviewing the experience of South Korea and Taiwan and the degree to which an interventionist industrial policy was central to their success, but it had little to do with Hong Kong's success and not much to do with Singapore's. I shall also look at how state intervention worked in Malaysia, Thailand, and Indonesia. In these three countries state intervention in the economy worked substantially less well than it did in Northeast Asia. In Indonesia in particular an activist state industrial policy was mostly a disaster, and this was recognized by the economics ministers who dominated important parts of economic policy during much of the era of President Suharto. Given Indonesia's heritage and limited human capital, the Japanese/Korean approach to economic development was particularly inappropriate.

Chapter 4 takes up the cases of China and Vietnam. Their development strategies have much in common with the other economies in the region, but they began their high-growth periods from a very different starting point. They had first to dismantle the economic system they had adopted from the Soviet Union. Furthermore, they were carrying out their development programs in a world that had changed in major ways from the international economic system that dominated the world economy in the 1960s and 1970s when the flying geese pattern was in its heyday.

The three chapters on the actual experience of the different economies of East Asia make no attempt to cover all aspects of their development during this high-growth period. The focus is on industrial policy as it evolved in each, because industrial policy played the central role in driving high-speed economic growth. The development of the agricultural sectors in these countries is dealt with only briefly. Agriculture was of great importance largely because the agricultural sector was where most of the people in these countries lived, at least at the beginning of their high-growth spurt, but in only a few cases were changes in agricultural policy significant in triggering high growth. The exceptions, where agricultural growth initially was central to high growth rate performance, were China and Vietnam during the first phases of their market-oriented reform programs. For similar reasons, I will not spend much time on social welfare policies or the lack of strong ones in many of these economies. This deficiency and the later gradual efforts to introduce a social safety net for the people of East Asia is a major topic in its own right but was not central to triggering the high-growth period. Some would argue that holding down welfare expenditures and suppressing labor union activities was important for growth because it allowed for a higher rate of savings and investment, but for the most part this study argues that the explanation for high rates of saving and investment lies elsewhere.

The final chapter explores when and why these periods of rapid catch up growth have come to an end. This chapter begins with an analysis of why and when high-growth periods have come to an end, looking first at those of all high-income countries and then at those of Japan, Korea, Taiwan, Hong Kong, and Singapore, and whether that slowdown was unique to East Asia or is in fact typical of all economies when they reach what the World Bank defines as high middle income status. Considerable effort is then devoted to trying to understand one of the biggest issues for the immediate future—when will China's high-growth boom come to an end?

Finally, a brief statement is in order here on the kinds of evidence used in this study and the nature of the analytic approach. The historical and quantitative analyses draw on scholarly works and occasionally on discussions with scholars particularly knowledgeable about one issue or another. The discussions of industrial policy also draw on scholarly works, but in many cases they also rely on interviews with major actors in the economic programs of the countries described. These chapters also draw on my direct experience in working with governments in the region. I have been a professor most of my adult life, but for substantial periods I was also heavily involved in working on economic policies with governments in developing countries, particularly in East Asia. Much of what I know of the economic policies and performances of several of these countries comes from this participant observation. I was a bit player in the process, but I was working at times with some of the most important players in the East Asian economic development drama and had a unique vantage point from which to observe their contributions.

The overall analytic approach of this study is historical and comparative. The historical experience is described for the economies of the region, and attempts are made to discern common patterns or the lack thereof in this experience. I describe the institutions that existed and the policies pursued and the outcomes, good and bad, that appear to have resulted from those policies and institutions. No attempt is made to test the statistical significance of statements that infer causality. The sample is much too small. The historical approach allows for a much richer look at just what these countries did, why they did it, and how it worked out in the end.

— 1 —

The Historical Foundations
of East Asian Development

One cannot understand economic development in East and Southeast Asia unless one also understands the historical foundations on which contemporary development efforts are built. A feature that all of the countries in the region have in common, those that succeeded in achieving sustained periods of economic growth and those that did not, is that they began their development efforts at similar very low levels of per capita income. Nations and colonies, of course, did not have statistical bureaus that estimated GDP in the nineteenth century—the concept of GDP was not even invented until the 1930s, but various attempts were made to construct GDP per capita in Asia in the nineteenth century.[1] The best known estimates are those of Angus Maddison, reported in Table 1.1. They indicate that per capita income in East Asia was roughly half of that in western Europe in the early nineteenth century, when most European countries had yet to begin to achieve sustained modern economic growth.

When one moves beyond per capita income similarities in the region, however, there are significant differences among the economies. In broad-brush terms, these differences break down between the economies of Northeast Asia and Southeast Asia, although there are significant differences within the two regions as well. To begin with, most Southeast Asian countries were colonies of European powers (except for Thailand) whereas much of Northeast Asia was never colonized, except for Japan's brief colonial foray into Korea and Taiwan in the first half of the twentieth century. Northeast Asian countries all shared a tradition based to an important degree on Confucian values whereas most of Southeast Asia did not, although again there are exceptions (Vietnam, and the Chinese minority populations in Southeast Asia). This cultural difference accounts in part

Table 1.1. European and East Asian GDP before modern economic growth.

	Per capita GDP (in 1990 international dollars)	
	1820	1870
Western Europe	1,202	1,960
Japan	669	737
China	600	530
Other East Asia	568	594

Data source: Angus Maddison, *Contours of the World Economy, 1–2030 AD* (Oxford: Oxford University Press, 2007), p. 382.

for another large difference, the emphasis on education even in premodern times in Northeast Asia, in contrast to the lack of much formal education in most of Southeast Asia prior to modern times. Northeast Asia is entirely in the temperate zone while Southeast Asia is entirely in the tropics. Partly because of this geographical difference but also because of differences in governance, Northeast Asia was very densely populated while much of Southeast Asia in premodern times (with the notable exception of the island of Java) was not.

The remainder of this discussion will be devoted first to the differing nature of governance in the region, followed by the differences in education levels and in population density, and ending with a brief discussion of the degree to which development of local commercial and industrial businesses in the nineteenth and early twentieth centuries laid a foundation that modernizing governments could later build on.

Experience with Self-Governance

The first thing to note about governance in the region is the fact that China and Japan were self-governing, unified states for hundreds or thousands of years, depending on how one measures unity. Tokugawa Japan unified the warring feudal states of Japan in the early seventeenth century, and the existence of a single emperor for the whole country goes far back before that, although effective rule was located in feudal domains called *han*. China, first unified in 221 BC, was divided mostly by northern invaders from time to time in several subsequent centuries but then was unified under Han Chinese rule in 1368 and has been unified ever since, except for periods of civil war. Korea unified three states within its current borders for the first time in the seventh century, and except for invasions by Mongols and Japanese and direct Japanese colonial rule from 1905 (formally from 1910), through 1945 it was governed by Koreans as a unified state, until its division by the allied powers at the end of World War II in 1945, after which it was self-governing as two separate states. Taiwan was ruled by the Japanese from 1895 through 1945 and Hong Kong by the British from 1841 through 1997, but these economies were otherwise part of China and China's governance traditions. British influence on the way Hong Kong is governed to this day was and is profound, and Japanese influence and the fact that Taiwan has been self-governing since 1949 gives the two territories a substantially different experience from the rest of China but one that today is still rooted in large part in Chinese culture.

Parts of Southeast Asia were also self-governing throughout most of their history, but other parts were the creation of European colonialism. Thailand has been self-governed by the Thai people for centuries, although its borders fluctuated substantially depending on success or failure in wars with Burma and the Khmer. The Burmese ruled Burma during these same centuries until the British, after victory in the Anglo-Burmese wars (1824–1852), made Burma a province of India and ruled it until it regained independence in 1948. Vietnam was ruled by China for a millennium but gained its independence from China a thousand years ago and was self-governing until the French took it over (and Cambodia and Laos) in stages, beginning in 1858 and continuing through 1887, when French Indo-China was formed. French rule ended in 1954 after the battle of Dien Bien Phu. Colonial rule in Burma and Vietnam, therefore, lasted two to three times longer than the Japanese rule of Korea and Taiwan. Neither French nor British political institutions survived for long after independence was restored, however. A coup in Burma in 1962 brought a military government to power, where it remains to this day,[2] and the Vietnamese forces under Ho Chi Minh set up a single-party Communist dictatorship, first in the north in 1954 and then in the rest of the country in 1975, a form of government that had more in common with the Vietnamese monarchies of the past than with anything that could be attributed to French traditions (other than the authoritarian nature of French colonial rule).

Finally there was Spanish rule (followed by a half century of American rule) of the Philippines; Dutch rule of what became the nation of Indonesia, which began in the early seventeenth century and ended in 1949 with Dutch recognition of Indonesian independence; and British rule of what today is Malaysia and Singapore, which began in key parts of the region (notably Penang and Singapore) in the early nineteenth century. Prior to being taken over by the European colonial powers, these areas of Southeast Asia were ruled by a number of kingdoms or sultanates whose territories and populations shifted with the tides of political-military contests between them. Starting with indirect rule through these kingdoms, the colonial powers gradually consolidated their control, leaving very limited power to the sultans in the British-controlled areas, even less to the Jogyakarta sultans, and nothing at all to the indigenous rulers of the area that is now the Philippines.

The reason for this very brief recitation of history is to make a simple point. Governance in Northeast Asia, with the brief interlude of Japanese rule of Korea and Taiwan, was by local rulers working through indigenous institutions. Whether working in the interests of the local populations or against them, whether competent or incompetent, the experience gained was by local people governing their own people. Furthermore, in Northeast Asia the people in each country shared a common culture and saw themselves first and foremost as part of that culture, whether Han Chinese, Korean, or Japanese. Unity of these states within reasonably well-recognized borders was thus the norm. Invasions and civil wars occurred from time to time, but no breakup of these countries into various parts was sustainable. The tension caused by the division of the Korean people into two separate states is simply a contemporary manifestation of this powerful drive to match a shared culture with shared rule. On a more positive note, none of the rulers of these states has had to contend with major efforts backed by a large part of the population to break away and form a separate state, as happened to Pakistan and Ethiopia and has led to countless civil wars and attempts to break away elsewhere, particularly in Africa.[3]

Those with political aspirations in Northeast Asia thus had the opportunity to test their governance skills if they could pass the necessary examinations (imperial China and to a degree Korea), had the right pedigree and skills (pre-Meiji Japan), or were involved in a movement capable of seizing power in all or part of the country (the various political forces in post-1911 China). In Southeast Asia, in contrast, there were few such opportunities for local elites to become involved in governing their own people. In the Dutch East Indies there were effectively no such opportunities much above the village level. In British-controlled Malaya and Burma there were more low-level government jobs for the local population, but most such jobs involved following the orders of British officials who made all of the important decisions. When there were not enough British citizens to staff sensitive jobs or the jobs were too low level (ordinary workers on the rail-roads and the police for example), the colonial government often brought in people from elsewhere in the empire (Indians for the Malaysian rail-roads for example). The French role in Indo-China was not much different. Most government jobs involving any degree of discretionary authority were held by the French. In short, the only way an indigenous person could gain experience in politics and governance was through rebellion, and the rebellions were vigorously suppressed until it was no longer possible to do so. At that point the colonial power withdrew, and the newly independent country got a ruler who had led the rebellion (Sukarno, Ho Chi Minh). In Malaysia, the British withdrew in 1957 after suppressing a Communist rebellion, but before doing so they made sure that most senior political, military, and police jobs would be in the hands of Malays rather than Chinese or Indian Malaysians (the rebellion was almost entirely led by Chinese Malayans, many from the Hakka minority).

The starkest contrast between the governance experience of Northeast and Southeast Asia, however, is not within these two regions taken together but between the East Asian region as a whole and much of Sub-Saharan Africa. In Sub-Saharan Africa the colonial powers eliminated virtually all local governance institutions and replaced them with colonial constructs. To slightly oversimplify they then drew boundaries around "countries" that bore little if any relation to the ethnic, linguistic, or precolonial governance structures on the continent. In West Africa Islamic nomads were put together with Islamic settled farmers and Christian producers of cocoa for export, not to mention a variety of ethnic and linguistic groups.[4] The result has been a long series of civil wars and other forms of ethnic conflict.[5]

There is nothing fully comparable to this African colonial heritage in Southeast Asia, although Indonesia comes closest. The Dutch East Indies encompassed a wide variety of ethnic groups and some differences in religion and language that had limited connection with each other prior to Dutch colonialism. There was in fact a rebellion of the outer islands against Java in 1958, but it had more to do with the division of Sumatran oil revenues and the Cold War than with ethnic differences. The lack of any long-term historical basis for many of the boundaries aside from the fact that they had been drawn by the colonial powers also played a role in Indonesia's Konfrontasi with Malaysia, when the British colonial territories of northern Borneo were added to Malaysia. Indonesia's military actions to take the western half of New Guinea from the Dutch in 1962 and its takeover of East Timor in 1975–1976 also resulted from conflicts over where the borders of the Indonesian state should be drawn. In effect, the lack of widely recognized borders gave President Sukarno before 1965 and the Indonesian army after 1965 a basis for using military action to redraw the country's borders and create instability in the region, instability that most of all distracted Indonesia itself from efforts to develop its own economy.

For the most part, however, unlike the case of much although not all of Africa, the colonial powers of Southeast Asia had been there for a century or more, and large majorities of the population in each country shared a common cultural heritage[6]—and, with the exception of Indonesia and to a lesser degree Burma, a common linguistic heritage.[7] Indonesia solved the linguistic problem early on after independence by accepting as the national language Bahasa Indonesia, a trading language spoken by relatively few Indonesians in contrast to Javanese, but one that all Indonesians could and did accept. The Philippine archipelago prior to the Spanish had a population that spoke a variety of Malay languages, and many people still do, but the national language is based on Tagalog, which is an amalgam of Spanish, Malay, and other languages including English and Chinese, and most Filipinos also learn English. Most Filipinos, with the notable exception of Moslems in the south, are Christian.

In summary, at this level of generality, the nations of Northeast Asia do not have major border issues or fundamental conflicts over ethnicity and language, and their borders are well established for the most part because of a millennium or more of a shared history, culture, and language. Among other things, this shared history and culture made it easier, once systematic economic development efforts began, for large parts of the populations of these countries to see development efforts as benefiting the country and people as a whole rather than one ethnic group or region over another.

The northern part of Southeast Asia (Thailand, Vietnam, and to a lesser degree Burma) is more like Northeast Asia in terms of culture and language, but its borders are partly the result of decisions made by European colonial powers. The Cold War division of Vietnam at the seventeenth parallel in

1954, however, had the effect of engulfing Vietnam and the rest of Indo-China in war and making sustained economic growth impossible.

The Malay archipelago, which in a sense stretches from Malaysia through Indonesia and up through the Philippines, has borders that were completely the product of European colonial decisions but for the most part were made centuries ago. The region has widely diverse languages but nevertheless at different stages, as already noted, has established common languages with which to communicate across ethnic groups and common heritages (Islam in Malaysia and Indonesia and Catholic Christianity in the Philippines) shared by a majority of the population. Still, territorial issues disrupted development efforts in the early stages of Indonesian development and continue at a low level to plague development in the southern Philippines. Large ethnic minorities within Malaysia, as we shall see, have also had a major influence on the country's development strategy, often in a negative way, and are an ongoing disruptive problem in Myanmar that, among other things, has provided an excuse for continued military dominance of the society to the detriment of development.[8]

Governance and Development in East Asian History

Having experience with self-government (Northeast Asia plus Thailand), accepted borders, and a common language and culture (most but not all of the rest of East Asia) simplifies the tasks facing leaders attempting governance of a country, but these conditions have been no guarantee that these countries would choose an appropriate path to sustained development either in historical times or more recently. Furthermore, the differences in cultures between and within Northeast and Southeast Asia have had an important influence in shaping how these countries and their governments have approached the challenges of development. This can be seen initially in how East Asian governments responded to the challenge of Western imperialism.

One of the important questions of nineteenth- and early twentieth-century East Asian history is why Japan and not China was the first to enter into a sustained period of modern economic growth beginning around 1900.[9] In the early nineteenth century China was not only much larger but appeared to Western eyes a much more promising venue for commercial development. Japan had a tiny trade with the Dutch based in Nagasaki, but European and American trade at Canton was much larger. Commodore

Matthew Perry of the U.S. Navy and his "black ships" did not appear off Japan's Izu Peninsula until 1854, more than a decade after the British and China had fought the first Opium War (1839–1842), which established British control over Hong Kong and opened up a number of ports on the Chinese coast to international trade.

But it was the Japanese who almost from the start fully recognized the magnitude of the Western imperialist challenge and took action to deal with it. Unlike China, they did not fight Commodore Perry or the other Western powers. Understanding that Western naval might was superior to theirs, they instead negotiated diplomatic recognition and an opening up of trade with the West. More important, they overthrew their Tokugawa rulers and not just the rulers—they overthrew the entire feudal system of daimyo and samurai (lords and upper-class warriors) that presided over the feudal domains (*han*). This was a revolution from above in that leadership of the Meiji period remained in the hands of the existing upper classes even though they, the daimyo and samurai, lost their feudal stipends and their role of running and defending their local domains. The Japanese then set out to adopt those Western ways that seemed to be central to the West's military power and economic prosperity. The army was among the first institutions to be reorganized and by 1895 was able to easily defeat China. In 1905 it defeated the Russian fleet and consolidated Japanese control of Korea and laid the foundation for the gradual takeover of northeast China (Manchuria), although that was not completed until 1931. Finance Minister Matsukata Masayoshi reformed the tax system and then began a policy of severe fiscal restraint in 1881 known as the Matsukata deflation that caused hardship for many but laid the foundation for Japan to join the international trading system based on the gold standard and to introduce a modern monetary system. Japan's government also supported the development of a handful of modern industrial enterprises, although not with much success, at least initially. The Japanese even tried top hats and ballroom dancing, presumably on the grounds that these were common in the West and might have something, however remote, to do with Western wealth and power.

There have been various explanations for why Japan was able to lay the foundations in the late nineteenth century of what became a modern industrial economy in the first four decades of the twentieth century. Many of these explanations have fallen by the wayside—the fact that Japan, like Europe, had primogeniture whereas China did not, that the former feudal domains were used to competing with each other and that promoted innovation, for example. There are two explanations, in my opinion, that go to the essence of why Japan succeeded. The first is that Japan from the start had some intellectual understanding of the magnitude of the challenge posed by the West and knew they had to make fundamental changes in their political and economic systems to meet it.

The second is that they were able to make the many radical changes required while maintaining unity and stability in the country. After the Meiji Restoration in 1868 there was only one rebellion by the old feudal system, a revolt that came to be known as the Satsuma Rebellion after the domain that initiated it. It was an effort to defend the old ways, and it was put down. The Satsuma army was totally destroyed in a series of battles with the modern imperial army over several months in 1877. The Satsuma defeat proved the superiority of a Western-style army (with Gatling guns), but that is not a complete explanation of why there was only one such rebellion. A part of the explanation must be that the feudal system of stipends and traditional military roles and governance may have been destroyed but its basic values continued intact. It was not a radical departure from the past to transfer the unquestioned loyalty samurai gave their lords into unquestioned loyalty to the emperor and the new imperial system. Loyalty was to the person, in this case the emperor, not to the feudal system. That extraordinary level of loyalty in the form of loyalty to the emperor persisted right through to the surrender of Japan to the Allied Forces in 1945.

China's history beginning in the nineteenth century and carrying through the first three decades of Communist Party rule could not have been more different with respect to both of these explanations for Japanese success. To begin with, the Chinese government decided to go to war to stop the Western incursions. They lost two wars to the Western imperialist powers in 1842 and 1860, forcing them to sign treaties that opened a large number of ports and gave special rights to foreigners in China. (The Japanese also signed such treaties but without a war because they knew at the time that they were too weak.) Prior to the second Opium War, rebellion broke out in southern China in 1850 and spread to many of the richest provinces on the Yangtze River, threatening the very existence of the Qing Dynasty. The Taiping Rebellion was finally put down by 1864, but as many as 25 million Chinese people are believed to have died from the direct and indirect effects of the war, and China's population may have fallen by two or three times that amount.[10]

China then enjoyed nearly three decades of relative peace, to which we shall return below, but peace ended with China's defeat by Japan in 1895, which led to Japan imposing a large indemnity on China that put a major strain on the limited financial resources of the dynasty.[11] In 1900 the anti-foreign Boxer Rebellion, encouraged by informal support from the imperial court, attacked the foreign legations in Beijing and was put down by a combined Western and Japanese military force, with the ruling empress dowager fleeing to Xian. The Qing Dynasty stumbled to its final collapse in the Republican Revolution in 1911. Yuan Shikai, a former Qing Dynasty general, soon replaced Sun Yat-sen as president and then tried and failed to make himself emperor. He died in 1916, and China descended until 1928 into what came to be known as the Warlord Period. In 1928 the Guomindang army under Chiang Kai-shek marched north, conquering large parts of the country and making deals with local warlords for control of the rest. The suppression of the Communists, former allies of the Guomindang, by Chiang that same year began the Guomindang-Communist civil war, which lasted until the Communist victory in 1949. In 1931 Japan formally took over China's northeast and in 1937 began its invasion of the rest of the country, soon controlling most of the cities and coast of the eastern half, the most advanced economic part of the country. The Guomindang retreated to Chongqing in relatively backward but defensible Sichuan in the southwest, and the Communists began to spread out from their remote base in Yenan in northwestern Shaanxi Province.

I recite this well-known history to make one point. During the 111 years between the beginning of the first Opium War in 1838 and the Communist victory in 1949, China fought what amounted to five foreign wars, losing most of them. In 1850–1864 and between 1916 and 1949 it was engulfed in a variety of civil wars between different movements and parties and warlords. Imagine being an investor in China during this period, either foreign or domestic. The surprising thing is that there was some investment despite all of the turmoil and uncertainty, but clearly many people were also discouraged from doing so. According to the best estimates available, GDP rose during the first decades of the twentieth century but only at around 1 percent per year.[12] Compare that history to Japan between the arrival of Commodore Perry in 1854 and the Japanese invasion of China in 1937. The Tokugawa shoguns were overthrown without a fight, the Satsuma Rebellion was put down quickly, and Japan was involved in three wars two of which it won easily without significant damage to either the homeland or its military forces and a third (World War I) in which its role was confined mainly to attacking German raiders in the Pacific and taking over German colonies in the region. Japanese investors, and they were mostly Japanese because Japan was hostile to foreign investors then and later, did not have to worry about the security of their investments. The period after 1937, to be sure, was a very different matter. Ultimately most of urban Japan was burnt to the ground by American bombing, and recovery to prewar levels was not achieved until 1955, but by 1937 the institutions of modern economic growth were well established, and recovery once the war was over was, with the advantage of hindsight, a foregone conclusion.

The reason for China's lack of modern economic growth prior to 1949, however, is not just a story of political and military chaos and an insecure investment climate. As already mentioned, there was a period from 1864 through 1894 when China enjoyed peace in most of its territory. Japan in that amount of time laid the foundation for sustained economic growth after 1900. China did not. China instead had the Tongzhi Restoration, whose objective was not to change the governing system but to restore the vitality of China's traditional approach to governance.[13] That approach involved rule by a government bureaucracy whose members were selected on the basis of their performance in a three-tier examination system. The exams themselves tested one's knowledge of the Confucian classics, and the classics themselves looked not to the future or to events outside China but backward to idealized times when Confucian style governance was seen as having been at its best. There was nothing about industrialization or modern Western-style military organization on these examinations.

Individual provincial governors (Li Hongzhang, Zhang Zhidong) tried to promote particular industries, but their resources were limited, and they received no support from the conservatives who dominated the government in Beijing. There were also efforts by Chinese intellectuals to translate and make available to Chinese audiences some of the major works on development such as Adam Smith's *Wealth of Nations*,[14] but the dominant view among intellectuals and government officials in China was that the West had some useful technology, particularly in the military sphere, but for everything else the traditional system was superior. This conservative view had a thousand years of history to back it up, and government officials had devoted decades of their personal lives to studying traditional values and practices, both to pass the examinations and to govern once in office. They believed in the traditional system and were loyal to it. Even after the humiliating defeat by Japan in 1895, major modernizing efforts by the young emperor, with the guidance of the reformers Liang Qichao and Kang Youwei (the "hundred days' reform"), were quickly overthrown by the empress dowager in alliance with court conservatives and parts of the Qing military. The emperor was in effect put under house arrest until his death in 1908 and completely removed from being able to exercise power of any kind. Japan in 1868 experienced major reform in the context of a restoration of the emperor; China three decades later in 1898 experienced the overthrow of the emperor in a coup that left the traditional system still presiding over a weakened and rapidly declining dynasty. It is hard to imagine a more stark contrast.

For the next five decades there were many changes in the Chinese system of governance, but political leaders were mainly preoccupied with obtaining or holding on to political power against formidable challenges at home and from abroad. When the Communist Party finally won the civil war and gained control of the government of a unified China (except Taiwan), it enjoyed eight years (1950–1957) when economic and political stability was restored and the economy radically transformed to fit the Soviet economic model, which was seen by many around the world at the time as the most effective means for achieving a rapid increase in economic growth and power. The appeal of the Communist Party to large numbers of Chinese and the decision initially after 1949 to adopt the Soviet model of development were themselves in part a product of China's perceived humiliation by the West and Japan over the previous century.

China's civil war also brought to power a paramount leader who was well read in Chinese history and highly skilled at mobilizing the Chinese people but who had little knowledge and almost no direct experience with the world outside China. Mao Zedong could mobilize hundreds of millions of people to build traditional irrigation systems on an unprecedented scale, as he did during the Great Leap Forward (1958–1959). He could mobilize hundreds of millions of others in an attempt to perpetuate revolutionary values and to create a fundamentally different kind of society, as he did during the Cultural Revolution (1966–1976). He also could promote a view that peasants often knew more about technology and technological progress than well-trained scientists. In a very real sense Mao was perpetuating the view that China was different and that it had little to learn from the outside world, although Mao, unlike the nineteenth century conservatives, was actually opposed to a conservative bureaucracy either of the Confucian or the Communist Party variety.

Some scholars have attempted to discern an effective economic development strategy from Mao's writings and actions, but the evidence that he ever had a coherent one that had any chance of being effective is lacking. Mao, like most leaders of revolutions, was a master politician and political strategist—not an economic strategist or manager. Not until Deng Xiaoping was restored to power in 1978 did China get anything like what happened in Japan in the late nineteenth century. Deng's view that "it does not matter whether the cat is black or white, but whether he catches mice" is not unlike the views of the Meiji reformers. "Step by step crossing the river from stone to stone" and catching mice (doing what works and dropping what doesn't step by step) is as good a start on an effective development strategy as has occurred anywhere in the world.

When one turns from the historical foundations of Japan and China's governance to those foundations elsewhere in Northeast and Southeast Asia, much of the story is about the colonial legacy. This study is not the place to attempt to explain and compare the different colonial policies of the Spanish, French, British, Dutch, Americans, and Japanese. For the most part the core goal of all colonial governments was to maintain stability and control in the colony and to develop the infrastructure needed by colonial merchants, plantation managers, and mine owners to build their businesses. The Japanese colonists had the largest and most broad-based development efforts, first in Korea and Taiwan and later in their puppet state of Manchukuo, but Japanese development in the colonies was fully integrated with the nearby Japanese home islands and was mainly for the benefit of those home islands and Japanese colonists.[15] In Korea, for example, there is quantitative evidence that the standard of living of most Koreans actually fell during the colonial period even though GDP was growing at an annual rate of over 3 percent.[16]

Building physical infrastructure, establishing rubber plantations, and opening mines in colonial times contributed to development after independence was gained, except in Korea, where most of the infrastructure was destroyed by war, and in Indonesia, where it was allowed to fall apart. India, for example, began independence in 1948 with a railroad system far more extensive than the one that existed in China in 1949 or for some years thereafter. But overall the colonial development effort was on too modest a scale to provide a solid foundation for sustained development either under colonialism or afterward under independent governments. The exceptions were Singapore and Hong Kong, which before the 1960s had a full range of infrastructure and institutions required by a modern commercial city. The argument that colonial governments in Asia drained off the economic surplus in these economies and shipped it back home does not stand up to quantitative analysis, but none of the colonial powers had a program to provide a framework for the development of local entrepreneurs, a skilled workforce, or anything other than what was required to maintain political control and a stable and profitable environment for the colonists' businesses, few of which were in manufacturing.

The colonial experience in Southeast Asia also shaped the kind of governance that the countries in the region had once independent governments took over. Where the colonial government resisted independence militarily, as in Indonesia and the countries of Indo-China, independence brought to power revolutionary leaders who, like Mao Zedong, had shown considerable talent in mobilizing military action against the colonial power but whose talents did not translate well to the new situation, which required systematic development efforts. President Sukarno presided over 17 years of continuous economic decline. Ho Chi Minh died before Vietnam was reunified in 1975, but his immediate successors devoted much of their energy after 1975 to restructuring the southern part of the country along Soviet lines while perpetuating a Soviet-style economic system in the North that might have been suitable for a country at war but proved incapable of sustained development once peace was achieved. Not until the late 1980s, after the death of the key political leaders promoting these policies, the collapse of the Soviet economic system in Europe, and the economic success of Vietnam's northern neighbor, did Vietnam shift direction under new leadership toward a very different and ultimately more successful development model.

The former colonies of Malaya and Singapore fared much better. The Communist insurgency was defeated, and Malay elites came to power in Malaya (later Malaysia) and English-speaking, educated elites in Singapore. The Peoples' Action Party in Singapore was avowedly socialist, but by independence its definition of socialism involved making sure that the benefits of growth were widely shared while achieving development based on the inherited foundation of good infrastructure mostly built and run by the state with private foreign investment for manufacturing and commerce. Malaysia, rich in natural resources, started independence with a political alliance of elites, dominated by the United Malay National Organization, that continued to promote a relatively open economy where ownership was mainly in the hands of private foreign and Chinese enterprises, although this was to change substantially in 1969.

Thailand, the one Southeast Asia country that never lost its independence, came out of World War II relatively unscathed, with a government that soon had a new king (King Bumibol Adulyadej was crowned in 1950), was centralized in Bangkok, and was dominated by an urban elite with the military in the lead. While there was substantial official discrimination against Bangkok's large Chinese-Thai population in the early years, this ethnic Chinese population, whose members dominated the Bangkok business community, increasingly integrated with the urban Thai elite. Development policy was thus a product of rent-seeking generals and entrepreneurial Chinese-Thai businessmen, presided over by a popular constitutional monarch. The advent of elections in 1973 did not lead to change in the makeup of the ruling elites until decades later a populist reaction against the Bangkok elite sprang up at the beginning of the twenty-first century. That together with the fact that Thailand was neutral during World War II (although until 1944 it cooperated with the Japanese) helped make Thailand a favorite destination for later Japanese foreign direct investment.

Finally, the Philippines also gained independence without having to fight for it, unless one includes the Philippine guerrillas who fought with the United States against the Japanese in part because the United States had promised independence to the Philippines once the war with Japan was over. The form of governance in the Philippines after independence in 1946 was based on the U.S. model, but the substance of governance was a product of a society structured by more than three centuries of Spanish rule that had put a landed aristocracy firmly in charge. Elements of this aristocracy, much as in parts of South America, soon discovered how government in the name of development could be used to generate large rents for themselves. Import-substituting industrialization behind high state-imposed trade barriers, state manipulation of banks to promote favored interests, often at the expense of portfolios full of nonperforming loans, marked the nadir of this approach under President Ferdinand Marcos, but many features of the Filipino approach to development in the early years have persisted to this day. There was a Communist-led rebellion, mainly in the earlier years, that did not succeed, and the hopes of a large portion of the population who are not rich have turned instead to populist politicians who oppose the old aristocracy but have proved equally adept at rent seeking.

The colonial heritage in Southeast Asia, therefore, was a mixed but mostly negative bag. In no cases other than possibly Malaysia and Singapore can one say that the colonial experience prepared the region's new governments for managing and leading modern economic growth once independence was gained. In two major areas encompassing well over half of the region's population, war and economic mismanagement made development and rising incomes impossible until new kinds of governments came to power later. Burma's traumatic experience with independence began with various insurgencies mainly in the north and east of the country, followed by a decade of democratic political instability and ending in the coup that brought an inward-looking military who increasingly took control of the nonfarm economy mostly for their own benefit. In the Philippines, the four-century colonial heritage had some positive influence outside the governance sphere, but within that sphere governance of the economy has been a consistent drag on performance. In Malaysia, British defeat of the insurgency put a Malay elite in charge that initially was friendly to both foreign and Malaysian-Chinese business and to a relatively open economy, but with major unresolved ethnic divisions that after 1969 came to dominate development policy, although they did not stop growth. Singapore's government after 1965 set out on a systematic path that produced rapid economic development with a central role for the state. Thailand's politics remained in the hands of an elite who also began to develop a viable development strategy after 1960 and gradually a more open political system after 1973. In no country in the region did the end of World War II and the advent of independence immediately produce rapid economic growth.

Japan, therefore, remained the one and only example in East Asia of modern economic growth right through the 1950s.[17] Governments in the region up to then, only partly through no fault of their own, were not capable of maintaining a stable environment for development investors because of war (the entire region in the 1940s), civil war (China during the entire first half of the twentieth century, Korea in the 1950s, Vietnam, Cambodia, and Laos from 1945 through 1975, Burma/Myanmar more or less continuously since independence in 1948, Indonesia in the late 1950s), or a major insurgency (Malaya including Singapore until 1957). When governments came to power capable of maintaining reasonably stable control of the country, too often they were headed by individuals who were charismatic politicians but had little interest in or ability in designing an effective development program (Mao Zedong in China until his death in 1976, Sukarno in Indonesia until his loss of power in 1965, Le Duan in Vietnam until his death in 1986, Syngman Rhee [Yi Seung Man] in South Korea until his overthrow in a student revolt in 1960, Kim Il Song and Kim Jong-il in North Korea continuously from the end of the Korean war in 1953 to 2011). In the Philippines internal instability, partly in the form of a high level of violent crime plus an ongoing Communist insurgency, led to martial law under the presidency of Ferdinand Marcos, who (1965–1986) ran the economy into the ground through rent seeking. Political instability in Burma/Myanmar in a variety of forms led to the military coup that brought General Ne Win to power in 1965 and continuing economic stagnation ever since. In short, throughout East Asia from the global depression of the 1930s through World War II and for more than a decade after most countries in the region gained independence and, in a few cases, a degree of political unity, there was either war, civil war, major insurgencies, or political leaders with little interest or ability to formulate and implement an effective development strategy.

This record of chaos, depression, and inappropriate leadership (except in Japan) began to come to an end in East Asia in the early 1960s. Only from that point on were countries in the region able to take economic advantage of their history of comparative cultural and linguistic unity within well-established geographic borders. In many, though by no means all, areas of East Asia stability was achieved, and new government leaders came to the fore who were capable of and interested in leading a successful effort to achieve modern economic growth. This happened first in the four "Tigers," as they came to be known (South Korea, Taiwan, Hong Kong, and Singapore) but soon thereafter in other parts of Southeast Asia (Malaysia, Thailand, and Indonesia) and considerably later in China (1978) and Vietnam (1986).

Finally, it should be noted in this discussion of war and instability, there was one element of the Northeast Asian heritage of war and civil war that had a positive influence on governance once the fighting had ended and development-oriented leadership had replaced earlier revolutionary leaders. Japan, Korea, Taiwan, and China began their development efforts with a low level of inequality. In Japan and Korea war had totally destroyed most urban property and had reduced almost everyone to low incomes but also low inequality. In China the revolution that brought the Communist

Party to power had a similar effect, and most mainlanders who fled to Taiwan brought little material wealth with them. Thus by international standards inequality was very low throughout these countries. A plausible hypothesis is that it is easier to govern and carry out development programs in a society where incomes are not highly unequal. Where incomes are highly unequal the higher and lower income groups often have different and conflicting development agendas. In Southeast Asia, with the exception of Vietnam, neither war nor rebellion had much impact on the distribution of income. High-income elites for the most part remained in place after independence, and this affected how subsequent development efforts were perceived, particularly in the Philippines and Thailand and in a different way in Malaysia. Cross-country comparisons with data from large numbers of countries tend to confirm that lower inequality relates to more effective governance and hence higher rates of growth.[18]

Education

In the field of education and literacy, the differences in the historical heritage between Northeast Asia and most of Southeast Asia are more pronounced than in the case of governance. On the one side were Northeast Asian economies (plus Singapore, Vietnam, and the overseas Chinese communities in Southeast Asia) that all shared a Confucian reverence for education going back more than a millennium. This was often reinforced by indigenous commercial development at a level that further encouraged the need for literacy. China (and to a lesser degree Korea, as well as Vietnam prior to the arrival of the French) also selected government officials on the basis of exams testing their educational attainments.

We do not have a completely reliable picture of the nature and extent of education and literacy in China, Japan, and Korea in the first half of the nineteenth century, but the basic outline of the situation is reasonably clear. Probably the best evidence of the level of literacy in an East Asian country comes from Japan in the mid-nineteenth century. In the early Meiji period a survey was done to measure the level of literacy by age cohort. Based on the literacy of the older age cohorts—that is, people who would have acquired literacy before the modernization efforts of early Meiji—the data indicate that roughly half of all Japanese males were literate at a basic level.[19] By premodern standards this was a very high level, especially since literacy involved knowing a good many Chinese characters (kanji) as well as Japanese phonetic systems (hiragana and katakana). This level appears to have placed a solid foundation under later Meiji efforts to greatly expand education at all levels after 1868.

If a country wishes to raise the level of education among its citizens it needs teachers who are educated to a substantially higher level than their pupils. Why Japan had such a high level of literacy is more difficult to understand. Part of the explanation is probably that Japan was a highly commercialized society with large numbers of businesses that would have required a basic ability to do accounts and convey written messages. Another part no doubt is that Confucian values were as important in Japan as elsewhere in East Asia, despite the fact that education played little role in premodern Japan in determining high positions in government (daimyo and samurai were inherited positions). In addition, there were many lower positions that needed to be filled by individuals who could read and write.

China, of course, was the original home of Confucian values, and education in the classics was the basis for appointment to the central government's bureaucracy.[20] The three-tiered set of examinations that one had to pass to enter officialdom required long years of study not materially different from the amount of time it takes scholars today to get a Ph.D. and all of the prior education leading up to that degree. In the nineteenth century there were roughly a million men with the *shengyuan* (or *xiucai*) degree and perhaps another million who took the degree exam but did not quite reach the level needed to pass.[21] The numbers fell off sharply as one moved up to the *juren* and *jinshi* degrees, passage of the latter being the required ticket for entrance into government office. Clearly there were several million people in China in the nineteenth century who could be considered highly educated, most of whom would have been men. That is a large number, but it was only around 1 percent of the population of China at that time.

More difficult to estimate is the extent of much lower levels of literacy in China: a level that would have been adequate for reading basic messages and keeping accounts and a higher level that might have been adequate for reading a newspaper. Most villages or market towns, at least in the more developed regions of the country, had professionals who could provide for the writing and reading needs of the local illiterate or semiliterate population. Literacy would have been much more widespread in the cities than in countryside, and in cities in the late nineteenth century there were newspapers that had circulations in the thousands and readerships perhaps 10 times that number. China was also a highly commercialized economy with large-scale long-distance trade and long-distance financial transactions that would have required literacy among their participants. The one serious effort to estimate the extent of literacy in China based on a wide review of the nature of education during the Qing Dynasty suggested that male literacy may have been in the 30–45 percent range whereas female literacy was much lower, at 2–10 percent.[22] A careful critique of this estimate, however, suggests that it may be biased upward and a figure for male literacy of around 25 percent may be more realistic.[23] Whatever the correct figure, literacy by the 1930s had probably risen in the cities of China, with much of the urban population having attended school for at least a few years and having attained a rudimentary level of education, and a substantial number who had the ability to read newspapers and write letters and simple essays. The best estimate of rural literacy that we have for that time is the estimate of John Lossing Buck, whose rural survey suggested that male literacy in the Chinese countryside was around 30–45 percent.[24] Discounting for the likely upward bias in the Buck survey and putting the rural estimate of literacy together with a plausible estimate of urban literacy (up to 80 percent had received some schooling),[25] perhaps a third of the total male population, or around one-fifth of the total Chinese population, including females, had a basic level of literacy by the 1930s. This figure is similar to that of India at the time of Indian independence in 1948, although possible differences in how literacy was defined in the two countries suggests caution in comparing estimates of this kind. At the upper end of the education spectrum, by the 1930s in China there were on average over 40,000 students enrolled in universities, and over 10,000 of those were in engineering and sciences. By the 1940s there were perhaps 174,000 living graduates of Chinese universities, some of whom would have left the country in 1949 but a substantial number who did not leave.[26] Again one needs to emphasize that these were high levels of literacy and of university-level educational attainment by the standards of all low-income countries in the nineteenth century and earlier, not by the standards of the latter half of the twentieth century.

With the advent of Communist rule and political stability in 1949, therefore, China had an education system at all levels that provided a foundation for the rapid expansion in education. It was not just the quantity of education that expanded. China after 1949, with the notable exception of the Cultural Revolution years (1966–1976), was in a position to steadily raise the quality of that education. China did not have to rely primarily on those with a lower secondary school education to teach primary students or those with a high school diploma to teach in higher secondary schools. By the twenty-first century all but a few students were completing the compulsory nine years of formal education, and tertiary enrollment had reached 21.45 million.[27] The number of students in universities abroad reached 229,000 many of them dominating the most difficult scientific and engineering programs in the United States and elsewhere. At lower educational levels, particularly in the richer areas such as Shanghai, students scored among the best students in the world on international tests. Because there was a foundation to build on and the government set out systematically to do so, China (like Japan in an earlier period) was able to achieve by the beginning of the twenty-first century near universal education through lower secondary school for nearly all of its younger population and world-class university education for hundreds of thousands of its very best university students.

I am not aware of any comparable studies for Korea prior to the Japanese colonial period. Confucian values were as strong as anywhere in the region, and education in the Chinese classics (in classical Chinese) was part of the criteria used in selecting government officials (but inherited aristocratic status played a larger role than in China). Commerce was probably less developed in Korea than either China or Japan, but Korea did have a phonetic writing system (*hangul*) in addition to a system using Chinese characters. The occasional foreign visitor to Korea during the Yi Dynasty sometimes remarked on the fact that even in the villages there were people who could read and write.[28]

At the other end of Asia's historical education foundation was Indonesia. The Dutch colonial administration for centuries did virtually nothing about education for the indigenous population. The only education of any kind that most Indonesians received prior to the twentieth century was in Koran schools that taught students to recite verses in Arabic, even though few Indonesians spoke Arabic. By the 1930s the Dutch had finally concluded that they needed to do something about educating the non-Dutch non-Chinese population in the country, and roughly 2 million students at that time were enrolled in primary schools,[29] roughly one-fifth of those of primary school age at the time. There were Sino-Dutch high schools for the Chinese but virtually none for the Indonesians, except for a tiny elite, some of whom went to Holland. There were no universities, although the University of Indonesia can trace its origins back to tertiary-level medical education in the late nineteenth century. Gadja Mada University was founded in 1949, and the Bandung Institute of Technology traces its history back to 1920, when the Dutch established a program to train a local cadre of technically skilled personnel (President Sukarno was its best known graduate), but its formal founding as a technology university was not until 1959. In short there were no recognized universities in what is now Indonesia until after independence. There are no reliable figures on the numbers of Indonesians who had university degrees from somewhere at the time of independence, but the number was probably in the hundreds for a population of roughly 80 million.

Since independence, of course, the education system of Indonesia has expanded rapidly, at least in quantitative terms. The quality of that education is another matter. In the early days after independence there were a handful of individuals educated in Indonesia who acquired an education there and then went on to perform at the highest level in some of America's graduate programs. Professor Widjojo Nitisastro, about whom I will have more to say later, was such an individual. He received his Ph.D. in economics from the University of California at Berkeley along with several other Indonesians and, according to his professors there, could have gone on to a tenured professorship in a top American research university if he had so chosen. Instead he went home and was the central figure in Indonesia's three decade growth spurt under President Suharto. But such individuals were rare. In the 1980s and 1990s the Harvard Institute for International Development worked with the Ministries of Finance and Planning in Indonesia to identify younger officials who had a sufficient educational background to make it through graduate economics and management programs, mostly in third-tier American universities. All of these younger officials had bachelor's degrees from Indonesian universities and had passed through a rigorous selection process in order to join these elite ministries, but only a minority were able to reach a level needed to do reasonably well in these American programs. English was generally not the problem, but skills in mathematics and related topics were.

Indonesia's educational system is improving, but one cannot create a first-class education system in a single generation, especially at the university level. There simply are not enough well-qualified teachers at any level to staff more than a handful of elite institutions in a country where in the mid-1980s there were over 140,000 primary schools with over 1 million teachers and more than 26 million primary students. At the high school level the numbers tailed off markedly, but there were still roughly 7,000 high schools with nearly 200,000 teachers and more than 2 million students (roughly 15 percent of all children in the high school age cohort). The drop-off continued at the tertiary level. In 1985/86, Indonesia had 620 universities (most of them private) with 42,000 teachers and just under 1 million students.[30] The majority of these were more akin to diploma mills than university-level educational establishments.

There were no Indonesian universities in the London *Times* ranking of the top 200 universities in the world in 2010. The list is dominated by the United States and the United Kingdom, but Japan had five, Korea three, China six, and other areas dominated by ethnic Chinese (Singapore, Taiwan, Hong Kong) eight.[31] In 2010, also, no Indonesian universities were on Jiaotong University's list of the 500 best. Japan had 25 in the top 500, China 20, South Korea 9, and other ethnic Chinese areas 14.[32] In the QS World University Rankings, however, the University of Indonesia is ranked at 236 in 2010, Gadja Mada is at 321, and the Bandung Institute of Technology and Bogor Agricultural University are both ranked in the top 600 world universities. In other parts of Southeast Asia five universities were ranked in the top 600 in the world in both Thailand (Chulalongkorn University was 180) and Malaysia (the University of Malaya was 207), and four in the Philippines. In Vietnam none was ranked.[33] In short the cultures with strong Confucian influences in Northeast Asia (plus Singapore and with the exception of Vietnam) have produced a substantial number of world-class universities, in China's case despite the massive abuses to the university system during the Cultural Revolution. Southeast Asia, minus Singapore, has seen a rise in the quality of universities in the region but is far behind Northeast Asia overall.

One gets similar results by reviewing various measures of school performance at the primary and early secondary school level. Indonesia, to its credit, has participated in international rankings of student performance, but the results bear out the view that it has a long way to go before its students rank with Northeast Asian students in areas such as science and mathematics. In the Trends in International Science and Mathematics Study, Indonesian eighth graders ranked thirty-sixth in math and thirty-seventh in science of the 48 countries participating in 2007, ahead of most countries in the Middle East and the only two Sub-Saharan African countries participating but far behind the students of Northeast Asia. Taiwan, South Korea, Singapore, Hong Kong and Japan were ranked 1–5 in math and 1–4 and 9 in science, and the United States was 11 in science and 9 in math. In Southeast Asia Malaysia ranked at 20 and 21 in math and science and Thailand at 29 and 22. The other Southeast Asian countries did not participate.[34]

These current educational quality measures clearly result from more than recent efforts by the education systems of the various countries to raise student educational quality. They also reflect the educational heritage at the time of independence. Reliable school enrollment data for the period immediately after World War II are not available for most of the countries included in this study, but we do have data for 1960 (see Table 1.2). Data for 1975 are also included to indicate how rapidly enrollments were increasing at that time under the mostly newly independent governments. The contrast between the Northeast and Southeast Asian educational levels is pronounced, particularly at the secondary school level. Ninety percent or more of the youth in the relevant age cohorts of Indonesia, Burma, Thailand, and Cambodia did not attend secondary school in 1960.

As a share of the relevant age groups, enrollments in secondary school in Northeast Asia, even excluding Japan, were roughly three times the share of the Southeast Asian countries, with the notable exception of the Philippines

Table 1.2. Number enrolled in school (percentage of relevant age cohort).

	Primary school		Secondary school	
	1960	1975	1960	1975
Burma	56	85	10	26
Cambodia	64	38	3	9
Indonesia	67	81	6	18
Malaysia	96	93	19	41
Philippines	95	105	26	56
Thailand	136	78	8	25
Hong Kong	91	120	24	69
Japan	103	100	74	95
South Korea	94	109	27	59
Singapore	112	111	32	53
Taiwan	67	NA	37	NA
United States	118	104	64	91

Data source: World Bank, *World Development Report 1978* (Washington, D.C.: World Bank, 1978), pp. 110–111.

Note: "NA" indicates that the data were not available or too unreliable to be used.

and to some extent Malaysia.[35] The one clearly positive element of the Philippines' colonial experience was that education received vigorous promotion during the period of American colonial rule. Because the expansion of education was not matched by equally effective efforts in other areas related to economic development either during the colonial period or since, however, this emphasis on education has not been accompanied by rapid GDP growth. That in turn explains why the Philippines became and remains a large exporter of its educated labor. Table 1.2 does not include China (it was not in the UN at the time) but other data indicate that China was not completely similar to either Northeast or Southeast Asia. Even in 1953, just after the Communist Party had come to power and political order had been achieved, over 82 percent of the primary school age cohort but only 6 percent of the secondary school age cohort were in school. By 1964 these figures had risen to 96 and 18 percent, respectively.[36]

In education, therefore, most of Southeast Asia, with the notable exceptions of the Philippines and Singapore, lagged far behind Northeast Asia in the early years after independence, both in terms of enrollments and in the quality of the education received.[37] Enrollments could fairly easily be rapidly expanded, and that was the case at both the primary and secondary levels. But the quality gap was much more difficult to close and clearly had not been closed even by 2012.

The Commercial and Business Heritage

Northeast Asia's historical foundations were fundamentally different from those of Southeast Asia in one other important respect. Commerce in China and Japan was highly developed long before Western merchants arrived on the scene in great numbers. Initially at least, the opening of China and Japan to foreign trade led to an influx of foreigners to manage trade with Europe and America. Chinese merchants initially knew next to nothing about European and American markets. But by the same token Western merchants knew next to nothing about the internal workings of the Chinese domestic market. Western merchants did not set up their own trading networks throughout the country for the most part, even when they were allowed to do so. They relied instead on Chinese merchants called compradores who purchased the tea and silk from the interior and delivered them on Chinese vessels to the coastal ports, where the cargos were loaded on foreign ships. Over time Chinese merchants gradually learned about international markets and shipping, and by the late nineteenth and early twentieth centuries much of the foreign trade of the region as well as the domestic trade was in Chinese hands.

Involvement in commerce in China was not confined to wealthy Chinese merchants in the coastal ports. Chinese farmers sold a large share of their output on the market and bought many of their nonfood necessities there as well. Chinese farmers were familiar with the gains to be had from moving a good from one market with low prices to another with higher prices and with other market practices. Many, as I have shown, also had some basic literacy and familiarity with contracts and other business procedures. The relevance of this experience to Southeast Asia is straightforward. Many of the more adventuresome but poor farmers in China's southeastern provinces of Fujian and Guangdong migrated to jobs in the Southeast Asian countries in the nineteenth century. Initially they might work as miners or plantation workers and in other low-level jobs, but as soon as they were free of their obligations to their initial employers and had acquired a small financial stake, they went into business, mostly commercial businesses, for themselves. By the nineteenth century large merchant enterprises in Southeast Asia were mostly in the hands of European colonial businessmen, but at the next level down of commerce, trade was mostly in the hands of the overseas Chinese. By the time independence was achieved from the colonial powers after World War II, Chinese merchants in Southeast Asia were no longer confined to the lower levels of the marketing structure, and by the latter half of the twentieth century they dominated commerce at all levels.

The most obvious initial impact of the rise of overseas Chinese business in the markets of Southeast Asia was that it meant that the local populations for the most part gained very little experience in anything other than farming. The Dutch, the British, and the French monopolized the upper reaches of commerce, and the overseas Chinese monopolized the lower reaches and then moved up the ladder to gradually take over the foreign businesses, although that came for the most part well after independence. Partly as a result there were strong feelings against these overseas Chinese among the Malay, Indonesian, and Vietnamese populations, and only in Thailand and to a lesser degree the Philippines did the overseas Chinese fully integrate with the indigenous people, and that was not until long after World War II had ended.

When the governments of the newly independent countries in Southeast Asia needed money beyond what their limited taxing ability provided, or for political and personal purposes that were less than legal, however, who could they turn to for help? For the most part the answer was the more successful Chinese merchants. When decisions were made to promote particular industries or other development efforts, who had the experience to carry these projects out successfully? As I will show, they could and did turn to government officials to carry out some of these projects, but with consistently bad results, because the government officials, almost entirely from the indigenous population, had no relevant experience. That left either foreigners (Europeans, Americans, and Japanese) or local Chinese. Overseas Chinese thus used their experience with business in the commercial sphere to take the lead in businesses elsewhere in the economy.

We don't know if local entrepreneurs would have risen up among the indigenous population if the overseas Chinese had not already had a dominant position in modern businesses of all kinds in Southeast Asia. There is little evidence in the colonial period that the indigenous population were trying to compete with Chinese businessmen for these tasks.[38] That would change after independence, but even then the choice a government leader faced was often whether to promote local indigenous business development efforts or get the job done efficiently and on time. Even today, the overseas Chinese still dominate large parts of the private business sector in Indonesia, Malaysia, Thailand, and the Philippines.

The one place where the entrepreneurial spirit and business acumen of Chinese was not readily apparent after the end of World War II and before 1978 was China, but that is not difficult to understand. The Soviet economic system that the Chinese adopted in the 1950s called for an economy run entirely by government bureaucrats. That together with the fact that the Communist leadership distrusted and disapproved of capitalist businesses and capitalist businessmen as a matter of principle meant that no private businessmen were allowed to exercise their talents. The same can be said about Vietnam after reunification (and before as well in the North). In fact many of the "boat people" who fled Vietnam after reunification were overseas Chinese who saw little future for themselves in a centrally planned command economy. The Vietnamese government did not really open up to private local business (as contrasted to foreign direct investors) until the beginning of the twenty-first century. In China at least, however, the post-1978 reforms unleashed entrepreneurial efforts that made it clear that Chinese in China itself had not lost their entrepreneurial spirit.

Commercial legacies of this sort are another form of human capital, a form that is obtained through observation and experience rather than formal education. This form is similar in a broad sense to the industrial organization and management human capital legacies in Europe and Japan that made it possible for those countries to recover so rapidly from the almost complete destruction of their physical capital during World War II. The differences between Northeast and Southeast Asia with respect to the legacies of experience in commerce and business or lack thereof is thus fundamental to understanding many of the differences in the development programs in these two areas in the half century between 1960 and 2012, and I will return to this important underlying theme later.

Other Differences Relevant to Development

There are other aspects of the historical heritage that also have some bearing on development in recent decades. Japan, of course, had a well-developed industrial economy prior to World War II. But China also had many factories, half or more of them owned by Chinese businessmen, in cities such as Shanghai and in other treaty ports. There were also the many factories in Manchuria in China's northeast set up by the Japanese but with substantial Chinese participation, at least at the labor force level. Korea also had industries built and run by the Japanese, but few Koreans managed anything but small businesses, and most of Korea's industrial structure was in the north and, physically at least, was totally destroyed in the Korean War.

In Japan after World War II the industrial base of the country was rapidly rebuilt and operations restored. In Japan as in western Europe, it was the knowledge of what needed to be done in the industrial and other spheres and the organizational capacity to do it that mattered far more than the physical infrastructure and machinery. Something similar can be said about the economically most advanced parts of China at the same time. Shanghai was the commercial and industrial center of China before World War II and remained the center of China's most sophisticated industries right through the first three decades of Communist Party rule (1949–1978) despite being starved of investment and tax revenue and forced to share many of its ablest technical people with the rest of the country. Industrial development in Hong Kong got its start after 1949 largely from the influx of Shanghai industrialists. Again, as in Japan, it was the knowledge and organizational ability that mattered, since these Shanghai industrialists brought little of their physical infrastructure and machinery with them. Taiwan to a limited degree had a similar experience. Most of the consumer goods industries in Taiwan in the 1960s and

1970s were started by local Taiwan-born businessmen, but the early phase, beginning in the 1970s, of Taiwan's heavy industry drive was led mostly by engineers and others from the Chinese mainland, many of whom had been employed by the mainland China Petroleum Corporation.

There was nothing really comparable in the industrial sphere in Southeast Asia. Modern business organizations there mainly consisted of commerce, plantations, and mines mostly run by Europeans and at lower levels by overseas Chinese. As already discussed, it was the overseas Chinese initially who had the experience to move up and take over many of these businesses as the Europeans began to withdraw. Non-Chinese local businessmen in the first decades after independence more often than not required substantial help from government to move up the business ladder in terms of scale and sophistication. Many of the industrial enterprises were owned and managed directly by the state, particularly in Indonesia.

There are many other differences between Northeast and Southeast Asia. The most obvious difference is that all of Southeast Asia is in the tropics and all of Northeast Asia is in the temperate zone. There is a clear correlation with countries that have low per capita GDP and low GDP growth rates and are in the tropics, but it is not at all clear why this should be the case. The usual explanation typically attributes the difference to the prevalence of tropical diseases, but life expectancy in Northeast Asia in the eighteenth and nineteenth centuries was not much different than in Southeast Asia. Prior to colonial times, the population of Southeast Asia (outside of Java) was very small; governments often controlled limited areas, and the frequent fighting between them, together with disease, helped keep the population low. A small population with lots of potential arable land meant that agriculture did not have to be very sophisticated to produce enough food. The population of Northeast Asia, in contrast, grew very large relative to the amount of arable land at a much earlier date, and this was made possible by an increasingly sophisticated agriculture with crop yields much higher than in Southeast Asia. There was also considerable crop specialization in Northeast Asia and increasingly sophisticated commerce that made it possible to specialize in something other than food crops. Even poor peasants in Northeast Asia were familiar with how to make money by exploiting the small differences in price between one region and another and were familiar with written contracts and many other accoutrements of a more complex society.

The Chinese peasants who left their homes in Southeast China for tropical Southeast Asia took this knowledge with them, and they had one other characteristic: they were risk takers par excellence. Leaving imperial China was a criminal offense, and these people, mostly men, knew they might never see their homes and families again. Some idea of the risks they were willing to take can be seen in such examples as the early development of Malaya's tin mines. Chinese entrepreneurs and miners were the early developers of these mines most of which were deep in the jungle where malaria and other diseases were rampant. Malay workers were not willing to go into the jungle for tin for good reason, but the Chinese who came to Malaya were willing, and many of the earlier miners died of malaria. But those who survived saved money and left the mines and became small merchants, filling a need in the economy that the local population was not providing. Most small merchants worked long hours, some began to make enough money to expand, and a few even at the end of the nineteenth century became very wealthy. A century later the descendants of these merchants dominated the trade (and much of the industry) of Southeast Asia both internally and with the rest of the world.

There have been various attempts drawing on psychology and other disciplines to explain why minorities such as the Chinese in Southeast Asia rose to such economic prominence, but all, like the discussion here, are highly speculative. Clearly there is something this minority (and the South Asians in East Africa, the Lebanese in West Africa, etc.) brought to the task that made them a dominant commercial force in their societies. The suggestion here is that it may have been the greater knowledge of more sophisticated societies plus a willingness, perhaps out of desperation and hence a readiness to take large risks, that is part of the explanation. There was also the fact that the local populations, at least initially, had little interest, or perhaps ability, in competing with them in their commercial endeavors.

The Historical Heritage

There were some similarities but also significant differences, therefore, in the historical experiences of countries in Northeast Asia when compared to those in Southeast Asia. Chinese and Japanese governed China and Japan within fairly well-established borders for centuries before and during the challenge posed by the imperialist pressures emanating from Europe. Korea had a similar experience except for the 35 years Koreans were ruled by Japanese. The way these societies were governed was rooted in traditions, institutions, and values that were their own. Some of these traditions, institutions, and values were not compatible with the requirements of modern economic growth or of warding off the imperialist threat from abroad, and they had to be changed, but the change was carried out by Chinese, Japanese, and, after 1945 at least, Koreans. In the case of Japan the changes proved relatively easy to introduce. Many of the institutions of the Tokugawa era could be thrown out without threatening other core Japanese values of loyalty and obedience to higher authority.

In China, in contrast, the loyalty of the ruling elites to traditional institutions that were not compatible with achieving modern wealth and power proved to be much more difficult to overcome. It took China over a century to first abandon the imperial bureaucratic system and then replace it with something that was compatible with attaining wealth and power on modern terms. When they finally established a new unified government, it had many features that were not all that different from the way the country was ruled in the past—a society with a large government bureaucracy managing a wide range of activities overseen by a single party that shared a common ideology. Initially that new government did not work well in economic terms, largely because it had taken nearly three decades of civil war for a new government and new leader to emerge. Like so many others with similar backgrounds, he proved to be neither skilled at nor interested in doing what modern economic development required. Later, when China got another new leader, the economic boom began. On Taiwan there was a different government, but initially it grew out of the same traditions and the same civil war as the government on the mainland. That government failed in the civil war but was able, partly because of that failure, to more quickly make the transition to what modern economic growth required.

Korea at first tried to ignore the Western imperialist challenge and hold on firmly to its traditional ways and lost its independence to neighboring Japan as a result. Independence was then given to it by the Allied victors of World War II but in a truncated form, with the country divided between two hostile forces, more or less guaranteeing a civil war in a Cold War–dominated world. In the end, despite the imposition by the United States of the first president of the country and later U.S. pressures to institute a Western-style democracy, Korea got a government that for better or worse was designed by Koreans, the Korean military in particular. That government then designed and carried out the changes needed to achieve modern economic growth, something that many outside observers thought would not be possible.

In Southeast Asia independence was achieved by the decisions of the colonial powers to withdraw (in some cases after suppressing an anticolonial rebellion) in the Philippines, Malaya, and Singapore. The initial Japanese defeat of the colonial powers in the region had permanently undermined the credibility of the colonial powers' capacity to rule the local populations. These powers had a role in picking the initial postindependence leaders, but governance in the three countries quickly evolved into something more rooted in these countries' own traditions—domination by a Spanish-style landed aristocracy in the Philippines, Malay interests and values in Malaysia, and Chinese traditions and values in Singapore. In the three countries of Indo-China and in Indonesia, in contrast, independence had to be won through military action, and the first postindependence leaders were mostly men who knew how to lead a revolution but knew little about building a wealthy and powerful society. New leaders with very different views finally gained power in Indonesia in 1965 and in Vietnam in 1986. Still, despite the fact that these societies were governed by Europeans, for centuries in many cases, they were able within a few decades to establish reasonably effective governments capable of designing and implementing constructive economic development programs. Myanmar in the respect was a notable exception.

Looking within the region, therefore, there are significant differences in the way modern leadership came to power in each country, and it took some longer than others to gain legitimacy and to design effective development programs, but the similarities in governance (mostly highly authoritarian during the first periods of accelerated economic growth) were greater in many respects than the differences.

When one leaves the area of governance, the differences between Northeast Asia and Southeast Asia become sharper. Northeast Asia is clearly far ahead when it comes to education. In terms of enrollments the differences have closed over time particularly at the primary level where near universality is the norm throughout East Asia. The differences are much greater at higher education levels, particularly at the tertiary level. In South Korea nearly 100 percent of the relevant age cohorts now go on to universities or other tertiary institutions. Much of the region, north and south, is moving today toward universal education at the secondary level, and all of the countries have universities, more than 150 in Myanmar and over 500 in Indonesia. It is in quality where the difference is marked. Northeast Asia has built on historical traditions and values that emphasize education and has achieved universal education or close to it at the primary and secondary levels, except in some of the poorer regions of China. At their best these Northeast Asian education systems compete favorably with the education systems of the richest countries of Europe and North America. They are off the charts when compared to much of Africa, and they achieve that high level for a much larger share of the population than does much of Latin America.

The education systems of Southeast Asia are another matter. None of the countries in the region is in the same league as the Northeast Asian systems. Most of the schools in the region do not participate in international comparison tests, and the ones that do score well below their Northeast Asia competitors. Only a handful of universities in Southeast Asia even make it into the international rankings, and the ones that do are mostly far down the list of 500 or 600 universities. Even in Vietnam, a country where Confucian values are strong, no universities receive recognition in the formal rankings. Vietnamese who have migrated to the United States often end up at the top of their high school classes and go on to elite American schools. In Vietnam itself, most have to go abroad to get a first-rate education. The situation is if anything worse in Indonesia, where most of the universities are little more than diploma mills. Malaysia, Thailand, and the Philippines have more quality schools at all levels, but none can compete with the best in Japan, Korea, and China. In the elite graduate programs in the United States, tens of thousands of Chinese, Koreans, and Japanese (and Indians) can compete with the best American and European students. The number of Southeast Asian students who can compete at this level is probably a few thousand, although I know of no survey that would verify this.

Northeast Asians, particularly Chinese, also have clear advantages when it comes to organizing to do business. They acquired rich experience in commerce in the past, and they have built on that experience ever since. Southeast Asians other than the overseas Chinese had no such foundation to build on. With the help of their governments they have been trying to catch up, but experience in state enterprises, the vehicle in many of these countries for promoting indigenous business persons, is a poor substitute for independent private entrepreneurship, as I will show in Chapter 5. In this respect Southeast Asia is more like Sub-Saharan Africa, where minority immigrants (South Asians in the East, Lebanese and others in the West) dominate private business and poorly run state enterprises are the vehicle of choice for raising up indigenous entrepreneurs.

Finally, and most controversially, because it is difficult to find hard evidence to verify the personal impressions held by so many, Northeast Asians work harder and longer hours on average than most other people.[39] There is more to this than just that they were on average poorer than much of the rest of the world and thus have had to work harder to get ahead. I believe it is also probably a product of their heritage that is more deeply ingrained than the Chinese saying about from rags to riches back to rags in three generations implies.[40] Hard work when combined with more experience with modern commerce and with dedication to becoming better educated is a formidable combination.

Northeast Asians together with overseas Chinese, therefore, at the time of independence from colonial rule clearly enjoyed advantages not possessed by most non-Chinese Southeast Asians. I shall look at how these differences across the East Asian region have played out in policies and performance in these countries' efforts to achieve high-income status. Before that, however, I will briefly review what formal quantitative analysis can tell us about East Asian economic development.

— 2 —

Understanding East Asian Growth

In recent decades economists have tried to move beyond historical explanations of high and low GDP growth rates by using econometric techniques to test the significance of different causes of high and low growth. I have already cited several of these studies that are broadly consistent with our conclusions about the impact of political inequality and ethnic diversity on growth. In this chapter I focus on studies that attempt to explain all or most of the major elements that determine economic growth. The statistical samples used have been all of the countries for which reasonably reliable data are available. Two of the earlier and better known efforts of this sort are summarized in Table 2.1. The results are one way of testing whether the major East Asian advantages and disadvantages discussed earlier apply more generally to developing countries as a whole. Put differently, do the findings of these econometric estimates tend to confirm or contradict the foregoing historical analysis?[1]

For statistical reasons, the econometric estimates of the variables that explain growth are measured at the levels existing at the beginning of the growth period being observed, typically the early 1960s.[2] Thus for the countries this study is concerned with (other than Japan), these estimates measure conditions a few years before or at about the time when the growth rate in many East Asian countries began to accelerate. In Table 2.1 the level of per capita GDP at the beginning of the period in both equations would fit this description, as would the variables measuring education and natural resource abundance (measured as the share of primary product exports in GDP in 1971). Certain fixed (i.e., time-invariant) effects are also in the models—notably the geographic variables in the Sachs-Warner-Radelet equation and the region dummy variables (Africa, Latin America, etc.) in both equations.

It should also be noted that the two estimates of the sources of growth presented in Table 2.1 are two among literally hundreds of other estimates using different variables and alternative specifications of the equation. These estimates in turn have led to studies testing the robustness of the various variables identified as significant by one author or another. Levine and Renelt, for example, use an Extreme Bounds procedure to identify variables whose estimated parameters are robust and conclude that almost

Table 2.1. Cross-country explanations of the GDP growth rate.

Dependent variable (real GDP per capita growth rate, 1960–1985)*		Dependent variable (real GDP per capita growth rate, 1965–1990)**	
Constant	0.0447 [0.0119]	Initial output per worker	−2.14 [−8.34]
GDP per capita, 1960	−0.007 [0.0009]	Schooling (log)	0.21 [1.43]
Secondary education, 1960	0.0004 [0.0084]	Natural resource abundance	−2.22 [−2.04]
Primary education, 1960	0.015 [0.0063]	Landlocked	−0.55 [−2.01]
Public domestic investment/GDP	−0.094 [0.024]	Coastline distance/ land area	0.27 [2.30]
Revolutions	−0.0146 [0.0059]	Government savings rate	0.12 [4.83]
Assassinations	−0.0179 [0.0149]	Openness	1.67 [4.58]
Value of investment deflator (deviation from sample mean)	−0.0106 [0.0052]	Quality of institutions	0.29 [3.22]
Fertility (ages 0–4 mortality rate)	−0.0028 [0.0013]	Life expectancy	0.31 [2.55]
Africa	−0.0104 [0.0035]	Life expectancy squared	−2.00e-03 [−2.01]

(continued)

Table 2.1 *(continued)*

Dependent variable (real GDP per capita growth rate, 1960–1985)*		Dependent variable (real GDP per capita growth rate, 1965–1990)**	
Latin America	−0.0104	Growth of working age population	0.98
	[0.0028]		[2.20]
		Growth of total population	−0.6
			[−1.22]
		East and Southeast Asia	−0.21
			[−0.42]
		South Asia	−0.82
			[−1.58]
		Latin America	−0.35
			[−0.82]
		Sub-Saharan Africa	−0.84
			[1.59]
R^2	0.66	Adjusted R^2	0.86
Number of countries	98	Number of countries	78

Data sources: Robert J. Barro, "Economic Growth in a Cross Section of Countries," *Quarterly Journal of Economics* 106, no. 2 (May 1991), pp. 407–443, and Steven Radelet, Jeffrey Sachs, and Andrew Warner, "Economic Growth in Asia," in Asian Development Bank, *Emerging Asia: Changes and Challenges* (Manila: Asian Development Bank, 1997), p. 330.

Note: GDP growth rates used in these regressions are the PPP GDP growth rates taken from various editions of the Penn World Tables.

* Figures in brackets: standard deviation.

** Figures in brackets: t statistics.

all of the variables used by others are "fragile."[3] Using a somewhat lower standard for robustness, Xavier Sala-i-Martin identifies 17 variables that appear to be strongly related to growth.[4] Many of the variables in the discussion that follows were among those 17, but some were not, and the precise definitions of the variables in Table 2.1 are similar to but somewhat different from the 17 considered to be strongly related to growth. Furthermore, many of the variables strongly related to growth in Sala-i-Martin's calculations are difficult to interpret. The "Confucius" variable, for example, is one of the most robust but is more likely to reflect a wide variety of advantages possessed by East Asian economies where Confucian values are strong than anything about the "religion" per se. The discussion that follows uses the Barro and Sachs-Warner-Radelet estimates as the starting point whether or not these estimates are statistically robust. This study's concern is whether the variables they identify as important are consistent with this study's more historical analysis.

The first thing that these equations and virtually all of the many other econometric estimates of this type tell us is that countries with lower per capita incomes have the potential to grow more rapidly than those with higher incomes. This is the convergence hypothesis: that nations lagging behind have the potential to begin to catch up with those ahead of them in terms of GDP per capita. But convergence is conditional on having certain other variables already in place such as a higher level of education or better standards of health. This certainly fits the East Asian experience. Japan started modern economic growth after Western Europe and North America and grew at a rate more rapidly than those other two regions, fell behind because of wartime destruction, and then made up for lost ground with accelerated growth in the 1950s and 1960s. Taiwan and South Korea, together with the city economies Singapore and Hong Kong, started their growth somewhat after the first part of Japan's second wave of high growth and grew much more rapidly than Japan had grown in the prewar period. Several Southeast Asian nations joined in this growth spurt in the 1970s or earlier.

China did not start its growth spurt until after 1978 and began from a lower per capita income than was the case in the four tiger economies. An interesting question for which no answer is yet available is whether China's later start into accelerated growth and lower initial per capita income explains why China, relative to other successful East Asian economies, has grown at a somewhat higher rate for a longer period. The fact that China started with a lower per capita income is consistent with the convergence hypothesis that states conditionally that the lower the per capita income, the higher the growth rates. It is also consistent with the view that a country with a very low per capita income can grow rapidly for a longer period since at the start there is a longer way to go before the country catches up to the point where it must begin to develop its own technology and its own unique approach to economic growth. In addition, the later a country starts on a high-growth path, the larger is the backlog of existing technology and experience that a country can adopt in its own growth program. Japan's modern economic growth, for example, began around 1900, and that arguably allowed Japan to grow more rapidly than the United Kingdom or the

United States, which began their growth rates earlier. The potential rate of growth due to the backlog of technology and experience was much larger in 1960, when several other East Asian economies began sustained economic growth, and their growth rate was much higher than that of Japan in the first three-plus decades of the twentieth century.

Most of these econometric growth equations, including the two in Table 2.1, also confirm the importance of education (for East Asia and for all other countries) as one reason for higher growth rates. Northeast Asian countries also "benefited" from having few natural resources. South Korea and Japan (plus Hong Kong and Singapore) had hardly any natural resources, and Taiwan and China consumed more natural resources than they produced. The Southeast Asian countries were richer in natural resources than Northeast Asia, and although their level of natural resource wealth was modest compared to the Middle East or parts of Sub-Saharan Africa, they experienced problems. The idea that natural resources can be more of a curse than a blessing has been part of the development literature for a long time.[5]

East Asian economies for the most part were not landlocked (except for Laos and Mongolia) and had long coastlines relative to their land area, although it is difficult to understand the mechanism at work that related these geographic facts to later economic performance. Presumably it has something to do with being more exposed to trade, technologies, and ideas from western Europe and North America, since these flows largely came by sea in the nineteenth and twentieth centuries, as contrasted to, say, the twelfth through the fourteenth centuries, when the main route between Europe and Asia was over land (the Silk Road), or today, when ideas move through publications, student exchanges, and the internet. Countries isolated from the outside world, whether physically isolated by geography or self-isolated by government action (e.g. Myanmar) have many features that can have a negative impact on economic growth. The negative coefficients for the regional variables simply say that there is something else about the poorer performance of, say, South Asia or Sub-Saharan Africa that we have not yet been able to understand or measure.

The political variables in the Barro equation in Table 2.1 also have significant negative coefficients, and that is certainly consistent with the foregoing review of East Asian history. One problem with political variables is that there are so many ways governments can create an unstable environment for investment and hence slow growth. As I have pointed out, China alone had five foreign invasions and two or more civil wars, depending on how one counts, and had a government that opposed changes that were needed for growth (the Tongzhi Restoration) and a government led by an individual who launched two major disruptive movements (Mao Zedong with the Great Leap Forward and the Cultural Revolution). And it was not just the number of major disruptions from war and political upheaval, it was their length. In China's case the Taiping Rebellion lasted for fourteen years, the same as the Japanese invasion of China if one sets the beginning date in 1931 when the Japanese seized Manchuria. Getting all of this political/ military disruption of the investment climate into one or two simple variables is difficult, and the Chinese experience by no means encompasses all the ways governments can create an unstable environment for investment. Other econometric studies have focused on the many ways instability induced by politics and military action inhibits growth.[6] Suffice it to say here that many of these studies show a clear correlation between various forms of political/military disruption and growth. What none of these econometric estimates explains is the principal mechanisms whereby political instability, however defined, influences growth. For that one must look at concrete historical experience.

Finally there are what for a lack of a better term I will call the policy variables in these two equations. What do the estimated coefficients of these variables tell us about East Asian growth? In the Barro equation, public domestic investment as a share of GDP has a negative impact on growth, while in the Sachs-Warner-Radelet equation government savings has a positive impact. Large inappropriate public investments clearly had a negative impact on Indonesia and no doubt are one of the many problems facing Myanmar (the construction of a lavish new capital at Naypyitaw for example). On the other hand, public investment in Japan prior to World War II was a major part of its economic success, and China since the late 1990s through the first decade of the twenty-first century, with one of the largest public investment programs ever, sustained economic growth of over 9 percent per year and avoided the global recession of 2008–2009. On average, large public investment programs have a negative impact on growth because so many countries manage such investments in ways that are corrupt and inefficient, but at the same time few developing economies, Hong Kong being one of the rare exceptions, have achieved rapid sustained growth without large-scale public infrastructure investment.[7]

Government savings measured as the difference between government current revenues and current expenditures is basically a measure of whether fiscal policy is prudent or not. Numerous other studies have shown that macro-instability in the form of high inflation has a negative impact on growth;[8] and the experience of East Asia is consistent with this result. The successful economies of East Asia during their high-growth periods have avoided high levels of inflation or seriously overvalued exchange rates. In the periods before high growth started in countries ranging from Indonesia through 1965 and South Korea in the 1950s, rates of inflation were high or currencies were heavily overvalued, or both. Bringing inappropriate macro-economic policies to an end was an essential component of these countries' later success, as I will show later.

Openness to foreign trade is clearly a major part of the East Asian economic success stories. Openness in East Asia, however, did not involve adherence to what has sometimes been called the Washington consensus. Imports in the early stages of growth in some of the success stories (South Korea, Taiwan) were tightly controlled, for example. I shall return to this topic when I look at the policy experience of these economies in much greater depth in the next chapter. It should also be noted that openness to foreign trade (or at least to exports) had a positive impact in the latter half of the twentieth century in large part because of the liberal trade policies of Europe and North America at that time. When South America began its industrialization programs prior to World War II, in contrast, war and the global depression made an export-oriented development strategy difficult to implement.

The variable using the deviation from the sample mean of the investment deflator is basically a measure of price distortions (deviations from free market prices) caused by government interventions in the economy. Extreme distortions in prices are often associated with policies that inhibit growth such as excessive dependence on protective barriers to imports. I shall defer my discussion of whether or not East Asian development got prices right to Chapters 3 and 4.

Finally, there is no question that strong institutions are related to growth and that parts of East Asia had strong institutions, although not necessarily the ones used in constructing the institutions variable in Table 2.1.[9] Except for Singapore and to a lesser degree Hong Kong and Malaysia, for example, none of the countries of Northeast and Southeast Asia had strong legal institutions when growth began, and many have very weak legal institutions today.[10] One of the more imaginative quantitative efforts to link institutions to modern economic growth, by Daron Acemoglu, Simon

Johnson, and James Robinson, suggests that countries with strong institutions today acquired them in part through their colonial heritage. In broad-brush terms, European colonists settled in areas where mortality was lower than elsewhere and created strong institutions in the process, and these have carried over to the present. Thus there is a correlation between settler mortality centuries ago and economic performance today.[11] This imaginative hypothesis fits the story of Hong Kong and Singapore and, to a lesser degree, Malaysia fairly well but does not appear to have much explanatory power for Indonesia or Vietnam. Japanese colonies are not part of the sample in this study, and Japan, China, and Thailand are not included because they were never colonies of a European power.

Acemoglu and Robinson more recently have attempted to do the historical analysis to back up their earlier speculation mainly based on econometric regressions.[12] Using many historical examples, they argue that nations fail to achieve sustained economic development because they possess "extractive" as contrasted to developmental institutions and those extractive institutions persist because it is in the interests of the powerful in many societies for them to persist. Thus to achieve development, there must be a political process that pushes the extractive oligarchy aside, replacing it with inclusive institutions based on inclusive politics such that the interests of a broad spectrum of a country's population is served.

Extractive regimes have certainly been an important element in some of East Asia's poorest performers, notably Myanmar and the Philippines, particularly during the rule of Ferdinand Marcos. Indonesia and several other nations in Southeast Asia had regimes that had important extractive elements but still managed sustained economic growth, although not at a rate comparable to what happened in Northeast Asia. The argument that inclusive politics and societies led, in contrast, to successful sustained development, however, fits the East Asian experience poorly. In effect it is an attempt to apply the European experience to Asia, and it doesn't fit very well. The governments of South Korea and Taiwan, not to mention Hong Kong, during their first decades of high growth were hardly politically inclusive, and the transition to democracy in these two cases was much more a result of economic growth than a cause. China on the other hand is no more an extractive state than South Korea and Taiwan prior to or even after democratization, although the authors of the study suggest that it is. This book is not the place to pursue the nature of politics and government in East and Southeast Asia, but the one thing that one can say is that all of the governments in East Asia that have achieved sustained development have pursued policies that were designed to benefit most of their people, whatever the level of participation of those people in running the government.[13]

Overall the findings in this book are broadly consistent with the major findings of these econometric studies. At the same time, however, the objectives are different. The econometric studies are basically attempting to find fundamental underlying truths about economic development that apply to all countries through all time. Their method is to use measures of underlying contributors to development and statistical tests of significance to establish that the derived relationship is unlikely to be random. Because many of the variables are not easily reduced to numbers (institutional variables in particular), the data used to obtain these estimates are inevitably crude estimates of what is being measured. As others have pointed out, one result of the use of these crude measures is that these econometric exercises have not proved very useful in the design of concrete development programs and policies.[14]

The goal in this study, in contrast, is to try to understand in much greater depth what explains economic development in specific countries, the countries of East Asia. Underlying fundamentals are important, and I have said that those fundamentals (e.g. education, absence of political instability of certain kinds) are consistent with what is happening elsewhere in the world. But we want to understand in greater depth just how East Asia accomplished sustained economic growth or in some cases failed to do so. Were there consistent patterns and policies across the region or not? And can the experience of Asia provide anything of value to countries elsewhere in the world trying to develop their economies and societies? There are not enough countries in the region to test our conclusions using statistical tests of significance, and bringing in large numbers of countries from other regions of the world inevitably introduces many other possible explanations of economic performance. Here I try to tell a story of what happened that is consistent with the facts about what is known about East Asian development practices and their likely impact on economic performance.

Before turning to an in-depth look at how the East Asian countries managed their economies, another kind of quantitative economic analysis can provide a guide to what needs to be understood. Accounting for the sources of growth began with Robert Solow's analysis of the American economy showing that total factor productivity (TFP) was a far more important explanation for U.S. growth than capital accumulation, which had previously been considered the primary explanatory variable.[15] Hundreds if not thousands of growth accounting estimates for the United States and many countries have been done since Solow's original article, together with a large number of critiques of the variables, the measurements of those variables, and the underlying theory used to construct these estimates.[16]

In my view, growth accounting is mainly useful as a way of sorting out whether growth in a particular country in particular periods was driven mainly by a concerted effort to raise the rate of savings and investment or was driven more by increases in the productivity of that investment and of other inputs, notably labor. In a sense it is arbitrary to separate the contribution of productivity from the contribution of capital because many sources of productivity increase typically require capital investment in new equipment. However, there is a kind of capital formation that does not involve any increases in productivity, and China in the prereform years, 1957–1978, is a case in point. More generally the Soviet economic system, whether in the Soviet Union, eastern Europe, or East Asia (China, Vietnam, North Korea) produced growth primarily through large increases in the capital stock with little in the way of TFP growth. In contrast, there are also increases in productivity that were not embodied in new capital investment, and Chinese agriculture during the early reform period in 1979–1984 is one of several illustrations of that fact. Other examples of East Asian TFP growth without much capital investment can be seen in the early reform and high-growth experiences of South Korea and Taiwan (see Tables 2.2 and 2.4).

Much of the discussion in this book is directly or indirectly focused on explaining the steps taken by the various countries in East Asia to accelerate growth through reforms that raised TFP. To demonstrate quantitatively the important role played by TFP in the accelerated growth of East Asian economies, however, one must organize the analysis in a way that relates quantitative estimates to the fundamental policy and institutional changes. These policy reforms typically occurred at the beginning of the high-growth periods and, in some cases, at later times as well. Too often growth accounting estimates simply present the average contribution of capital, labor, and TFP over the entire period or decade by decade without trying to relate the results to the changes in policy and institutions that were going on at the time. In many cases, usually because the data are of

Table 2.2. South Korea: growth accounting decomposition (in percentages).

Period	Aggregate GDP growth rate	Contributions to aggregate GDP						Labor income share
		Capital	Human capital	Employment	Labor hours	Total factor productivity		
1964–1966	9.20	3.87	0.59	1.89	NA	2.84		59
1967–1971	9.54	7.35	0.27	2.10	NA	0.18		59
1971–1982	7.44	3.71	0.29	4.02	0.00	0.58		66
1982–1989	9.48	3.98	0.44	3.85	−1.00	2.05		69
1989–1997	7.32	3.22	0.41	2.76	−0.47	1.40		74
(1989–1998)	5.86	3.02	0.54	1.82	−0.58	1.06		74
1998–2005	5.75	1.61	0.37	1.91	−0.20	2.06		74

Data source: This table was derived from two tables in Barry Eichengreen, Dwight H. Perkins, and Kwanho Shin, *From Miracle to Maturity: The Growth of the Korean Economy* (Cambridge, Mass.: Harvard Asia Center, distributed by Harvard University Press, 2012), p. 11.

Notes: "NA" indicates that the data were not available or too unreliable to be used. Data for 1964–1971 include the agricultural and mining sectors; data from 1971 on exclude those two sectors in the calculations. Labor hours figures are also not available for the pre-1971 period.

lower quality, no attempt at all is made to measure what happened during the critical transition period from low to high growth rates.

Tables 2.2 to 2.4 present estimates that I, together with others, have made following for the most part the methodology and detailed data used by Alwyn Young, with one important exception. We account for growth in the entire economy whereas Young excluded agriculture. The years covered in our analysis also differ in some cases, as well as does our analysis of the results.[17] I start with the growth accounting estimates for South Korea and Taiwan to illustrate the principal point. The Korean data are presented in Table 2.2. The quality of the data is much better for later periods than for the 1960s, but unlike in many other studies of the sources of growth in Korea, the 1960s are included because that was the critical period when high growth got underway.

Korea's accelerated growth began after the military coup that brought President Park Chung Hee to power in 1961 followed by a series of major economic reforms that were well under way by 1963. The growth rate of GDP jumped from 3.9 percent per year in 1961–1962 to 9.2 percent per year in 1963–1966, and the rate of investment rose, but only from 9.7 percent of GDP in 1961–1962 to an average of 15.3 percent in 1963–1966.[18] The domestic savings rate was even lower—it rose from 3.0 percent to 9.2 percent over this same period, the difference between savings and investment being made up by foreign borrowing and aid to Korea.[19] The enormous jump in the GDP growth rate, therefore, was the product of a substantial jump in TFP and a large increase in the productivity of capital as well. In later years the investment rate would rise markedly (the average rate in the 1970s was 27.9 percent of GDP), and TFP fell to negligible levels. In the 1980s Korea once again began a series of major economic reforms, this time in the direction of an economy more open to imports with less government intervention, and TFP once again rose for a time.

The direction of causation of these results almost certainly ran from economic reforms to increases in productivity that expanded good investment opportunities, which in turn led to increases in investment. Only in the case of Korean government infrastructure investment can one make a plausible case that the causation went first from a government decision to increase investment helped in part with financing mainly from U.S. and Japanese aid (including Japanese reparations) and the World Bank. Much the same appears to be true for the acceleration in TFP in the 1980s and after the financial crisis of 1997–1998. The investment did not rise significantly in the

1980s as liberalizing reforms were introduced, but the GDP growth rate rose. After 1998 TFP increased, but the investment rate actually fell.

Much the same phenomenon can be observed in the Taiwan data (Table 2.3). There was a substantial increase in TFP in the first years after the major reforms of 1960 were introduced and again in the 1980s, particularly the latter half of the decade, when Taiwan, like South Korea, began a series of liberalizing economic reforms. In between these spurts in TFP, productivity slowed down, and growth depended mainly on increases in investment (and in the labor force and the education of the labor force).

Arguably the most dramatic change involving a rise in TFP was what occurred in China when in 1978 it began the process of dismantling its Soviet-type economic system and replacing it with what the government now calls a "socialist market economy." The data are presented in Table 2.4. By 1955–1956 China had installed a complete Soviet-style centrally planned command economy with collective agriculture. Beginning in 1958 it introduced a radical crash program to catch up with the West (the Great Leap Forward, 1958–1960) and a radical political movement (the Cultural Revolution, 1966–1976). A high rate of investment caused the growth rate of fixed capital to exceed the growth rate of GDP. Throughout the years 1958–1978, TFP was negative. Then came the reforms initiated by the Third Plenum of the Eleventh National Congress of the Chinese

Table 2.3. Sources of growth on Taiwan (annual rates of growth in percentages).

Period	GDP	Labor input	Capital input	Total factor productivity
1952–1955	9.00	3.51	5.70	4.83
1956–1960	6.70	4.87	6.04	1.47
1961–1965	9.50	4.75	7.78	3.84
1966–1970	9.37	10.43	12.76	−1.77
1971–1979	9.55	5.57	13.48	1.95
1980–1985	6.59	2.43	9.31	2.36
1986–1990	8.74	2.74	7.91	4.62
1991–1994	6.57	2.22	8.87	2.68

Data source: Dwight H. Perkins and Lora Sabin, "Productivity and Structural Change," in Li-min Hsueh, Chen-kuo Hsu, and Dwight H. Perkins, *Industrialization and the State: The Changing Role of the Taiwan Government in the Economy, 1945–1998* (Cambridge, Mass.: Harvard Institute for International Development, 2001), p. 152.

Communist Party in 1978. The investment rate in the next decade did not rise above the rate achieved before 1979—in fact it fell slightly in the early 1980s—but the growth rate doubled from 4.9 percent per year (1965–1978) to 9.7 percent in 1979–1985.[20] There was a slowdown in both GDP and TFP growth in the late 1980s as inflation and a limited return to more state controls after June 4, 1989, brought more conservative political leaders to the fore. Deng Xiaoping's famous trip to the south in 1992 then reignited the reform process, bringing about a major rise in the GDP and TFP growth rates in the early 1990s. Since the early 1990s, however, the rapid growth story has increasingly been driven by high levels of capital formation. This was especially the case in 2009–2010, when the rate of gross capital formation reached 47.7 and 49 percent of GDP, respectively, fueled by a massive increase in housing and state public infrastructure investment.

One can also see major economic and political reforms leading to large jumps in the GDP growth rate in Singapore and Indonesia. In Singapore growth during the period 1961–1965, when Singapore was engulfed in political turmoil—connected in part to first becoming a part of Malaysia and then being driven out of Malaysia—averaged 5.8 percent a year. It jumped to an average growth rate of 12.9 percent per year over the next five years (1966–1970). During this growth spurt in the late 1960s TFP was also high, but it was negligible thereafter.[21] There is no comparable jump in Hong Kong's GDP and TFP performance, or to put it differently, the major policy and institutional changes in Hong Kong occurred in the immediate aftermath of World War II and the Communist victory on the Chinese mainland, followed by the Western embargo on China during and after the Korean War. At that time the Hong Kong government did not yet calculate national income estimates. When Hong Kong began calculating its GDP there were few significant changes, since its economic system relied almost entirely on free market forces (except for real estate and land prices). There is thus no reason to expect that there would be a large jump in GDP or TFP growth, although Hong Kong's GDP growth rate fluctuated along with external conditions.

Another economy that experienced a sudden major change in both economic policy and political governance was Indonesia in 1965. There is little doubt that the changeover from the disastrous economic policies of President Sukarno to the pro-economic-growth policies under President Suharto led to a major improvement in Indonesia's economic performance. In the

Table 2.4. China: supply-side sources of growth.

Period	Growth rate (%)				Contribution to growth (%)		
	GDP	Fixed capital	Educated labor	Total factor productivity	Fixed capital	Educated labor	Total factor productivity
1953–1957	6.5	1.9	1.7	4.7	12.7	14.9	72.4
1958–1978	3.9	6.7	2.7	−0.5	73.7	39.7	−13.4
1978–2005	9.5	9.6	2.7	3.8	43.7	16.2	40.1
2006–2011	11.0	14.4	2.1	2.1	72.0	8.6	23.1
1953–2005	7.0	7.7	2.6	2.1	47.7	21.4	30.9

Data sources: Estimates for 1953–2005 are from Dwight H. Perkins and Thomas G. Rawski, "Forecasting China's Growth to 2025," in Loren Brandt and Thomas G. Rawski, eds., *China's Great Economic Transformation* (Cambridge: Cambridge University Press, 2008), p. 839. Estimates for 2006–2011 used the same basic methodology. Educated labor and fixed capital figures were done by Zhang Qiong, Central University of Finance and Economics, Beijing, using the same methodology as the earlier data; I am grateful to her for sharing these estimates. GDP and raw labor data were taken from National Statistical Office, *Zhongguo tongji zhaiyao* (Beijing: Statistics Press, 2012), pp. 24, 43, and National Statistical Office, *Zhongguo tongji nianjian 2011* (Beijing: Statistics Press, 2011), pp. 60, 112. Because the share of labor income in gross national income has fallen steadily and was a low 45 percent of income in 2010, the share of labor and capital used to compute the total factor productivity residual was 0.45 and 0.55, respectively, whereas the labor and capital income shares in national income for the earlier years were 0.53 and 0.47, respectively.

Sukarno years GDP growth per capita as well as TFP growth must have been sharply negative, but the quality of Indonesian statistics in this period was so bad that the magnitude of the economic decline is difficult if not impossible to measure. One study that provided estimates of GDP and TFP growth throughout the Sukarno and Suharto years (1951–2000) came up with an average GDP growth rate for the entire period of 1.75 percent per year and a negative TFP figure of −0.65 percent per year. This implies that growth in years up to and including 1965 must have been strongly negative, since Indonesia grew at 4.1 percent per capita from 1966 through the year 2000.[22] Depending on the methodology used, estimates of the GDP and TFP growth in the Suharto years range from strongly positive to little growth of TFP at all during much of the period.[23]

The Philippines never has had a high-growth period, and not surprisingly TFP has been negative most of the time since 1960. Malaysia and Thailand have enjoyed periods of fairly rapid GDP growth, and TFP has made a positive contribution to that growth, but there has been no one period of rapid policy and institutional change except for the introduction of the New Economic Policy in 1969 in Malaysia, after which TFP fell but was still slightly positive.[24]

The one other economy that experienced a rapid and major change in its economic policies and institutions was Vietnam. The political changes that made possible these economic reforms occurred in 1986, but the economic policy and institutional changes really began in 1989. The Vietnamese experience before and after 1986 or 1989 is much like that of China before and after 1978, although we do not have reliable data in an appropriate form for the pre-1986 period. In the years 1989–1996, TFP accounted for well over half of Vietnam's 7.2 percent growth rate. In those early years, the rate of investment was actually quite low. After 1996, the rate of investment rose substantially, and TFP fell to less than half its contribution to growth in the earlier period.[25]

To summarize this brief presentation of the growth accounting results for East Asia, many of the economies of the region (South Korea in 1961–1963, Taiwan in 1960, Indonesia in 1965, China beginning in 1978, Vietnam in 1986–1989, and to some degree Singapore in 1965) experienced major changes in economic policy and institutions, underwritten in many cases by a fundamental change in the political sphere. In all of these cases changes were accompanied by a major increase in the rate of GDP growth that initially was driven to a substantial degree by an equally sharp rise in

TFP. In Malaysia the major political economic change was the introduction of the New Economic Policy after 1969, which probably slowed GDP and TFP growth modestly. There does not appear to have been any comparable rapid and profound change in Thailand and Hong Kong, at least not for a period when the data needed for a growth accounting exercise are available. The Philippines has yet to enjoy a sustained period of high GDP growth, and TFP growth much of the time has been negative. If we had reliable data for Myanmar, GDP growth would be negligible, and TFP growth would no doubt be substantially negative.[26]

Finally, there is the question of the contribution of education to growth as revealed by growth accounting methods. Most of the more detailed growth accounting estimates attempt to measure the contribution of increases in education to growth, and that is true for most of the estimates referred to here. However, there is a serious problem with the way growth accounting measures the contribution of education in countries in the early stages of economic development. The growth accounting approach estimates the contribution of education by multiplying the increases in the education of the labor force by the increase in the marginal productivity of labor (measured by differences in wage rates) for different levels of education. For a high-income country with a well-educated labor force this approach is defensible. For a developing country at low per capita incomes where levels of education can vary from countries with high levels of illiteracy and low levels of poor quality education for much of the population to those (in Northeast Asia for example) with much lower levels of illiteracy and higher levels of higher quality education, this method almost certainly understates the contribution of education. To take an extreme example, if South Korea had had a population that was 100 percent illiterate and uneducated prior to 1960 and then proceeded to increase education to the levels actually achieved in 1974, growth accounting would say that this massive increase in education increased the growth rate from 6.7 percent a year to 8.4 percent a year during this period. This would be a substantial contribution (1.7 percent) to the growth rate, but no sensible person believes that Korea could have achieved a rate of growth of 6.7 percent a year with a 100 percent illiterate population.[27] Basically the growth accounting equation incorrectly specifies the contribution of education for low-income countries. There are other formulations of education in growth equations, but there is no literature measuring those equations for a large number of countries.[28]

In what follows, the main task will be to try to understand just what it was that these economies and governments did that made possible the high economic performance of so many of them. I will be looking not so much at what explains their high rates of investment as, mainly, at what could explain the rise in TFP. In high-income countries, TFP growth is driven mainly by technological change, but this has had very little to do with TFP growth in East Asia, except in Japan and very recently in South Korea, Taiwan, and Singapore. instead TFP has been driven by other kinds of fundamental change: the shift in labor out of low productivity agriculture to higher productivity urban jobs, the transformation from closed to open economy strategies, the increased reliance on market forces over government commands, and other changes that promoted more efficient use of resources and stimulated entrepreneurship. Most generally, high growth in East Asia has resulted from improved policies and major reforms in economic institutions.

— 3 —

Government Intervention versus Laissez-Faire in Northeast Asia

Earlier I outlined the historical advantages and disadvantages some of the countries of East Asia have possessed. I did this first by reviewing the differing historical experiences within the region and then by observing to what degree attempts to explain economic growth using aggregate growth equations and econometric techniques are consistent with my historical analysis. I then laid the foundation for what follows in this lecture by using growth accounting techniques to show that policy changes and better economic management played a central role in the rapid growth that occurred. Growth was not just a matter of raising the rate of savings and investment, although higher rates of investment were important. The direction of causation, however, went more from policy changes and better economic management to higher rates of investment, not so much from capital formation or high rates of investment to economic reform measures.

In the following chapters I shall attempt to explain just what those changes in policy and management were, why the leaders of these economies chose these policies, and how they worked out in practice. I shall focus first on the most successful economies, the Republic of Korea, Taiwan, Hong Kong, and Singapore. I will then turn to economies that achieved more mixed results, often with similar policies, notably Malaysia, Thailand, and Indonesia and to a lesser degree the Philippines.[1] I shall later review the experiences with economic policy and management of China and Vietnam. The major focus will be on the differing industrial and trade policies pursued by these economies, but I will also discuss where appropriate the degree to which policies toward agriculture and income distribution influenced the differing economic decisions and outcomes.

In this chapter I will focus most of all on the Korean experience because that is the experience I know best and because industrialization in Korea occurred almost entirely in the post–World War II period, which is most relevant for other countries wishing to learn from the Korean experience. Before turning to the Korean experience, however, we need to briefly review how Japan approached its successful industrialization effort. While no country simply copied what Japan did, it was Japan that pioneered an approach to industrial development in which government institutions played a central role, so a brief description of those institutions is in order.[2]

Japan began its industrialization effort in the late nineteenth century with the creation of a number of state-owned enterprises, an effort that for the most part was unsuccessful. After the turn to the twentieth century, industrial enterprises were mostly private, but the state continued to play a very active role in their development.[3] Much of the investment in infrastructure was by the state, with the state accounting for over half of gross fixed capital formation in the modern sector during most of the period before Japan invaded China in 1937.[4] The state also supported the rapid expansion of the education system and much else. Industry, however, was divided between a large number of small and medium firms and a smaller number of very large conglomerates, known as Zaibatsu, that came to produce over half of all industrial output. The Zaibatsu were groups of industries in which each group had a bank at its core that was controlled through cross-shareholding by a few families. From the outset, however, there were very close relationships between the Zaibatsu and the government and the government-owned portion of the banking sector. Government provided a significant part of the demand for Zaibatsu products, particularly as the Japanese military expanded, but more important, government provided leadership and guidance to the private firms across a much wider spectrum.

The bombing and submarine blockade of Japan during World War II destroyed virtually all of Japan's industrial and transport fixed capital, but it did not destroy many of its key economic institutions, even though the U.S. occupation of Japan that ended in 1952 tried to do so. In the 1950s and 1960s a modified version of the prewar industrial organization reappeared, with large conglomerates of related companies centered on a main bank, the Keiretsu. Ties between the Keiretsu and the government were close, with the Ministry of International Trade and Industry, taking the lead in industrial policy. Through this ministry and others, the government played an active role in guiding Japanese industry during these early postwar decades.[5] The instruments of government influence included its tight control over what was then a limited supply of foreign exchange, together with considerable government control of banking finance through state-owned banks and the close relations between those banks and private sector banks. Imports, particularly imports that competed with potentially vulnerable Japanese industries, were tightly restricted, largely through the use of foreign exchange licenses. Foreign direct investment was discouraged and was never an important element in Japanese industry.[6]

Close ties between business and the Ministry of International Trade and Industry and other ministries were fostered by, among other things, the *amakudari* system (literally "descent from heaven"), whereby government bureaucrats regularly retired at a relatively young age and took senior positions in the enterprises that they had been guiding and regulating. Backing up this system was the long, largely uninterrupted reign of the Liberal Democratic Party, which was a conservative strongly pro-business party with close ties to Keidanren (the Federation of Japanese Businesses). Keidanren had in fact played a role in setting up the Liberal Democratic Party in 1955.

This Japanese system has evolved in major ways since the 1950s and 1960s. Foreign exchange became plentiful, international efforts to liberalize foreign trade worldwide reduced the strong protectionism inherent in this model, and the large companies became global and had retained earnings sufficient to make them less dependent on the banking system. Institutions such as the *amakudari* system came to be seen as creating corrupt conflicts of interest rather than valuable close ties between business and government, and more generally government guidance of industry played a diminishing role. It was the Japanese economic system of the 1950s and 1960s, and particularly its close ties between government and business, however, that was the Japanese system that government officials and businessmen in Korea and Taiwan in the 1960s were familiar with. In Korea, in part because the president, Park Chung Hee, had been a junior officer in the Japanese army, the Japanese experience was particularly relevant. In Taiwan this was less the case because government officials came from the Chinese mainland and had not grown up under Japanese colonial rule.

Korea's Evolving Industrial Policies

Korea's industrial and trade policies were influenced by Japan's experience, but they were not simply copies of Japan, even at the beginning of the country's rapid growth spurt. These policies evolved over time in major ways. South Korea, in fact, had a succession of very different industrial development and trade policies—no single model captures Korea's development approach over the five-decade period that began in 1960. Because the specifics of these evolving industrial policies have been written about at length in numerous books and articles, I will only underline here their key features.

Syngman Rhee, South Korea's first president after the country regained independence, was more interested in reunifying the country and keeping himself in power in politically turbulent times than in anything that could be called a coherent economic policy. Two measures pursued for other reasons, however, produced what amounted to an import-substituting industrial policy. The first measure after the end of the Korean War in 1953 was to maintain a seriously overvalued exchange rate. The second measure was to prohibit most trade with Japan. The first measure was motivated by a desire to maximize the U.S. dollars earned from support activities for the UN military forces in Korea, while the second measure reflected the president's and most of the population's strong antipathy toward their former colonial ruler. In addition, land reform had eliminated South Korea's main pre-independence export, the rice surplus that had been collected by Japanese and Korean landlords and exported to Japan prior to independence.

Thus Korea throughout the postwar years of the Rhee presidency (1953–1960) had virtually no exports.[7] Imports were paid for out of the money earned from support of the UN troops and by large-scale U.S. aid. Tight restrictions on imports and the use of foreign exchange were thus necessary, and some industries began to grow behind these high trade barriers. Other firms, such as Hyundai, grew doing construction and related work for the UN forces. There was also the need to rebuild the cities; Seoul had been burned and shelled to the ground, and most basic infrastructure was destroyed. Total industrial value added in 1961 was only US$414 million.[8] Most informed observers at the time saw the Korean economy as a basket case, likely to remain mired in poverty and dependent on large inflows of foreign aid.

Student rebellion overthrew Rhee and was followed by a brief demo-cratically elected government under Chang Myon, which was itself over-thrown by a military coup on May 16, 1961. The next several years under the general and then president Park Chung Hee saw dramatic changes in economic policy. There have been various attempts to explain what led Park to make these dramatic changes, which laid the foundation for the rapid economic development that was to follow. The policies pursued cer-tainly did not reflect the dominant international economic thinking of the time, particularly in developing countries. Even among developed country economists, the principal view then, and to a lesser degree even today, was that the key to development involved raising the rate of savings and invest-ment, and Korea in the early 1960s had a very low savings rate and relied on foreign aid to finance a large share of the investment that did occur.[9] Among developing country economists the view was that the key to indus-trialization, in addition to higher levels of investment, was to erect barriers to imported industrial products, thus creating a market for domestic in-dustrialists. This emphasis on import substituting industrialization was a widely held view, particularly in Latin America, where the dominant ex-ponent was Raul Prebisch.

Scholars have emphasized the fact that Park's power base rested on sup-port by the one strong institution then in Korean society, the Korean army, which had been turned into a modern combat army during the course of the war. Among the general population, initially at least, there was support for a time for the stability that the coup brought after years of political chaos. Land reform had also created a rural population that had a stake in continued stability. None of these groups had a vested interest in protecting domestic industries.[10] Park probably won the 1963 presidential election by a narrow margin more or less legitimately. Certainly the urban industrialists who were most in favor of protecting domestic industries were not an important part of his power base, as they were in the politics of the time in Latin America. In any case, in the economic reforms that followed in the 1960s, the domestic market for industrial products contin-ued to receive heavy protection from imports. Politics, therefore, did not constrain most of President Park's industrial development choices. The one exception was trade with Japan. Ending the prohibition on such trade was essential for almost any development strategy, and Park did end the prohibition in 1965, even though that step led to large demonstrations by students and others.

The most important reason that the Park government chose to pursue export-led industrialization was that it did not really have a choice if it wanted to have an independent economy and society that achieved sustained increases in wealth and power. Given American disapproval of the military coup, getting out from under dependence on U.S. aid must have been essential in the eyes of Park, and the only way to do that was to find alternative sources of foreign exchange to pay for essential imports. More broadly, Park himself, along with many informed Koreans, had direct knowledge of how Japan had risen from poverty to become a world power. Koreans were strongly anti-Japanese because of their colonial experience, but Koreans have also admired Japan's economic success and have learned from it, and exports of manufactures were an important part of the Japanese story. Foreign aid and foreign direct investment, in contrast, did not play a significant role in Japan.

Given the need for exports, Korea's options were limited. What few minerals Korea had were in the north under North Korean control. Agriculture as a source of exports, as already pointed out, was not possible because the redistribution of income connected with land reform had led the Koreans to consume most of their own agricultural output. What was left was manufactures, although that was also a very weak sector and clearly could not prosper and export given the policies of the 1950s. As any economist knows, export of manufactures or anything else is difficult to impossible with an overvalued exchange rate. The Chang Myon government had already begun to devalue the Korean won, and the military government continued with further devaluation.[11] For the next two decades if not longer, the Korean won was in a sense undervalued, thus giving a major boost to exports.[12] The second major change came in 1965 and was distinctly unpopular and led to major demonstrations against the government. The government, in an act involving more than a little political courage, normalized economic relations with Japan.

There were many other policy reforms in the 1960s and they have been described at length in other works. Interest rate reform (raising real interest rates to positive from negative levels to overcome financial repression) led to a large increase in bank deposits in the formal banking sector as contrasted to the informal curb market. More debatable is whether this increase played a role in the substantial rise in the overall rate of savings. What is not debatable is whether the measures used to back up devaluation with other support for exporters had the desired impact. There were direct subsidies to particular sectors, and the president himself met monthly with industrial leaders to review their export performance. The direct subsidies including such things as generous wastage allowances for those who exported. Cotton, for example, had to be imported, and thus the cotton textile industry had to have access to foreign exchange. Those that expanded exports rapidly not only got enough cotton to supply their export needs; in addition, the generous wastage of cotton allowance made it possible for them to produce substantial quantities for the protected domestic market where profits were high because of that protection.

The monthly meetings presided over by the president made it possible for manufacturers to bring their complaints about roadblocks within the government bureaucracy, and if the president agreed there was a problem, he could turn to the relevant minister sitting in the room and order him to fix it. The Korean government bureaucracy at the time and for long thereafter was riddled with all manner of regulations that could be used to block businesses for one reason or another, but these monthly meetings removed most of these blockages. Foreign direct investment, in contrast, was consistently blocked in this manner. Korea borrowed heavily from abroad, but foreign direct investment in the 1960s was small, passing US$20 million in only one year during that decade (in terms of actual arrivals of cash and equipment).

Korea began in the late 1960s to make major efforts to lure back from abroad (mainly from the U.S.) Korean scientists and engineers who had gained advanced degrees and often more than a little work experience in more sophisticated industries than existed at the time in Korea. The Korean Institute of Science and Technology was the first such effort, done in collaboration with Bechtel. The Institute had a dual purpose. It was a research institute designed to provide Korean industry with new technologies. Most of all, however, it was a vehicle, with its high salaries and well-supplied laboratories, for encouraging Korean scientists and engineers trained abroad to return home. When I first visited Korea in February 1969 as a guest of the Institute, I met with the then minister of science, who asked me if I knew how many Koreans with Ph.D.s there were who were internationally recognized in science and engineering. He said that the number was well over 1,000 but only two or three dozen were back working in Korea. He saw it as his job to get more to return. In 1971 economists were included in this effort with the formation of the Korea Development Institute, which brought 12 Koreans with economics Ph.D.s back to Korea, tripling the number then in the country. Harvard faculty played a small role in helping Korea Development Institute economists reorient themselves to the task of contributing to Korean economic policy- making rather than to Western academic debates.[13] Even more important in 1971 was the founding of the Korean Advanced Institute of Science and Technology, which now ranks among the top 100 universities in the world.[14]

In the early 1970s, Korea's and Park Chung Hee's approach to industrial policy changed significantly. In the 1960s any industrialist who wanted to export basically received the same benefits as any other exporter, or in such cases as cotton wastage allowances, any exporter in that particular industry. All benefited from the devalued exchange rate. Most benefited from their industry leaders' meetings with the president, and direct export subsidies were sufficiently pervasive so that most industrialists received some support from that source. Industrial planning for the export sector mainly involved the industrialists setting targets for themselves with the knowledge that the higher they set the target, the more likely they were to get support from the government. Beginning in the 1970s, however, Korea changed industrial policy to target specific industries and to favor particular companies.

The Korean Heavy and Chemical Industry Drive of the 1970s was the high point of government intervention in the economy. President Park established a small committee in the Blue House, led by Oh Won Chol, that was made up of government bureaucrats with technical scientific and business backgrounds, and he told them to draw up a plan to jumpstart the country's heavy industry sector—steel, machinery, and petrochemicals. The motivation for doing so at this time was apparently made up of two elements. For economic development reasons alone, the president apparently believed that it was time for Korea to move up the technology ladder and not to continue relying mainly on light manufacturers.[15] At roughly the same time the United States' (and South Korea's) involvement in the Vietnamese civil war was going badly, and President Richard Nixon had announced a new U.S. policy, the Nixon doctrine, on Guam on July 25, 1969. The United States would support its allies with a nuclear shield, materiel, and air support, but the ground troops had to be supplied by the affected countries themselves. It was up to Korea and other U.S. allies to figure out how to do this, and the Koreans and many others interpreted this new doctrine as an indication that there were clear limits on the support that would be coming from the U.S. Reinforcing this view, and hence the need for South Korea to be able to defend itself, was the continuing criticism from many in the United States of Korea's undemocratic government, although it was not until the administration of Jimmy Carter (1977–1980) that the United States actually began to withdraw some of its ground forces stationed in Korea.

Oh Won Chol studied the heavy industry development experience of other countries, particularly Japan, and he and his committee drew up a plan for what heavy industries the country should develop and the government would support. In addition to specifying particular industries, they also indicated the desired scale of the initial plants in those industries and their likely geographic location. The scale was deliberately set at a level that would produce much more than could be absorbed by the domestic market. These industries were expected to become exporters and to do so in a relatively short time, roughly five years on average. With the plan in hand, the government then went to individual companies that they thought would be capable of implementing it. If a company agreed, it got large subsidized loans for the project, it was provided with much of the required support infrastructure in government industrial parks for far less than cost, and the tax authorities, who had a large degree of discretionary authority in setting corporate taxes, would negotiate favorable tax obligations. In addition, companies were sometimes given a monopoly of a particular sector and protection of the Korean domestic market from import competition, but only for a relatively short period.

Generally when the companies were asked to participate they did so. My favorite example of how this worked in practice is based on an interview in the late 1970s with Chung Ju-yung, the founder and then head of Hyundai.[16] President Park in one of his many meetings with Mr. Chung suggested that Hyundai should take on the task of building a modern shipbuilding industry that could build supertankers to carry crude petroleum. There was logic to his being chosen because Hyundai had extensive experience in a wide variety of construction endeavors, and shipbuilding called for some of the same skills. Chung, according to his own account, said he would try, and he set out to study the experiences of other countries that had successfully developed a large-scale shipbuilding industry, such as Norway and, notably, Japan. Months later he came back to President Park and said the task was just too difficult. The president's reply, to paraphrase, was "fine—if you only want to do easy things, I understand." The clear implication was that Hyundai could continue to do "easy things," but there wouldn't be much government support coming its way. Chung Ju-yung decided he should rethink his position, and a year or so later the first Hyundai supertanker rolled into the water from the new Hyundai shipyard.

The timing of the Hyundai investment could not have been much worse. High OPEC oil prices had sharply cut the demand for supertankers, and one of the few contracts Hyundai had was canceled. No one wanted Korea's supertankers. President Park said, in effect, you have done your part, so now I will do mine, and he ordered the National Assembly to pass a law that gave favorable rates and treatment to anyone importing petroleum into Korea on Korean-made tankers—and Korea was a major petroleum importer. The result was that Chung Ju-yung initially bought his own tankers and went into the oil shipping business, the shipyard got the start it needed, and Korea became one of the major shipbuilding countries in the world. The Heavy and Chemical Industry Drive came to an end in the late 1970s, as the distortions in the economy caused by the drive became more and more apparent. President Park was assassinated shortly thereafter in 1979.

Taking the Park years as a whole, there are several generalizations one can make.

First, by any reasonable standard both the general export drive of the 1960s and the targeted heavy industry drive of the 1970s were successful. Starting in 1963, South Korean GDP grew at an average rate of 9.7 percent per year through to 1979. Possibly Korea could have done a bit better with some other strategy, given that there were real distortions, particularly in the 1970s, but it is unlikely that the GDP growth rate would have been a great deal higher. Perhaps the heavy industries were started a bit too soon, but by the 1980s and for two decades thereafter, these and closely related industries (e.g. Hyundai automobiles) have provided Korea with the bulk of its export earnings.

Second, the Heavy and Chemical Industry Drive played a major role in starting Korea down a path to an economy that came to be increasingly dominated by giant conglomerates (*chaebol*), which served the country reasonably well during this early period but came to be seen as a drag on development and an undesirable political force in later decades.

Third, economists can ask whether another approach to industrial development in Korea, namely full-scale liberalization of all markets, including imports, and letting markets determine what would happen would have done just as well or better, more or less along the lines of what later came to be called the Washington Consensus about effective development policies. It is not possible to systematically analyze this counterfactual in the Korean context, but anyone familiar with the way Korea operated in those decades should know that full liberalization of all or most markets would have been a pipe dream. Korea was riddled with regulations and a bureaucracy quite willing to use rules and regulations as weapons for whatever purpose they deemed fit, personal or otherwise, if allowed to do so. Only a government determined to cut through this maze could hope to provide a favorable climate for dynamic private entrepreneurs. The politics of getting rid of these rules and regulations in their entirety would have been a herculean task even if President Park had believed in the goal, and there is plenty of evidence that he did not.

Fourth, several otherwise excellent studies have nevertheless tried to fit this story into the neoclassical market paradigm of "getting prices right." The alternative view, stated succinctly by Alice Amsden, is that the Koreans deliberately "got the prices wrong."[17] To start, Korea clearly steadily devalued the won in an effort to keep it undervalued relative to what a free foreign exchange market would have produced;[18] and thereby provided general protection to all domestic producers. Amsden and others, however, were talking about Korea's efforts to distort relative prices of industrial products in order to favor particular industries. The first and arguably the most sophisticated attempt to test who was right about relative prices in Korea then or later was undertaken by Charles Frank, Kwang Suk Kim, and Larry Westphal, and they actually took on the difficult task of comparing individual Korean prices in the middle of the Park era (by measuring the effective rate of protection) with world prices for particular products. Their conclusion was that the numerous subsidies and barriers offset each other and that "our analysis does not prove that resource allocation . . . was relatively efficient; it merely demonstrates that the available evidence is consistent with [this] contention."[19] The problem with this argument was that their 150-sector effective protection estimates show that 44 sectors had effective rates of protection of 20 percent or more, another 24 had negative effective rates of protection of minus 20 percent or more, with the remaining 82 falling between minus and plus 20 percent.[20] If one treats negative effective rates as essentially being equivalent to world prices, as these authors do, then a great majority of

Korean product prices were not substantially different from world prices. In my view, a more plausible conclusion is that Korean prices were highly distorted to protect some industries (automobiles, machinery) while others where costs were far below world prices received little or even negative support (other than an undervalued exchange rate). Readers interested in this issue are referred to the Frank, Kim, and Westphal study. The book describes at length the myriad government interventions in product markets. Whether or not all of these interventions actually helped promote exports, then or later, is another matter that is beyond the scope of this analysis. There is no serious doubt, however, that high levels of protection in the 1960s and 1970s played a central role in the development of the heavy industries that by the 1980s dominated Korean industry and exports.

Another piece of evidence from the middle of the period this study is concerned with is for 1970 and is from the price comparisons done by Irving Kravis and his collaborators for the UN's first efforts to measure PPP. The Korean data report the number of Korean won needed to purchase in Korea what would cost one dollar in the United States.[21] The data are reported for 153 product sectors, but the nontradable sectors have been eliminated, leaving a total of 103 tradable product sectors (Figure 3.1).

The products of 73 of these sectors were priced at a level where the PPP exchange rate was below the official exchange rate, often far below. These sectors included most of the products exported by Korea at the time— sectors such as clothing, footwear, and certain food products. The sectors whose PPP exchange rate was above the official exchange rate (hence very expensive to import if imports were allowed at all) included most kinds of machinery, ships, and most motorized vehicles. The PPP exchange rate for passenger automobiles was 110 percent above the official exchange rate. These high-priced (and highly protected) sectors included most of the ones that were to form the core of the heavy and chemical industry drive of the 1970s.[22]

In summary, therefore, the evidence provides much more support for the view that Korea in the 1960s and 1970s deliberately manipulated domestic prices to support import substitution in key heavy industry sectors while the prices of light industrial products, for the most part, neither needed nor received such support, other than what almost certainly was an undervalued official exchange rate. By no logical stretch was this price

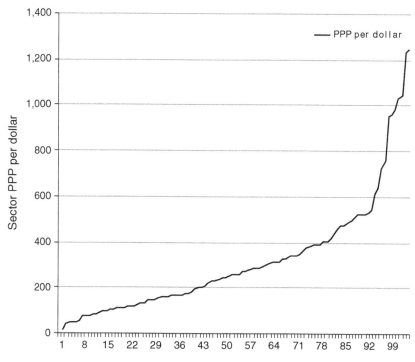

Figure 3.1. Sector PPP per dollar for Korean tradable sectors.

Note: The official exchange rate in 1970 was 361.65 won to US$1.00. The data are the PPP exchange rate for 99 industrial sectors. Thus, for example, for the ninety-ninth sector it took more than 1,200 won to purchase US$1.00 of the sector's product, while for the fortieth sector it took only 200 won. All sectors where the sector PPP exchange rate was above the official overall exchange rate were in effect highly protected, whereas those below that figure were produced at prices that required no protection (and in practice made up most of Korea's exports).

Data source: The data used to derive this figure were taken from Irving Kravis, Alan Heston, and Robert Summers, *International Comparisons of Real Product and Purchasing Power* (World Bank: Johns Hopkins Press, 1978), pp. 146–152.

structure the kind of free market pricing for traded goods that has subsequently been associated with the so-called Washington Consensus.

From the 1980s to the Present in South Korea

The years 1979–1980 marked the end of the kinds of industrial policies pursued through much of the 1970s. The Heavy and Chemical Industry Drive had effectively ended prior to President Park's assassination, largely because the economic distortions resulting from the drive were causing increasing economic problems for the economy. The year 1980 witnessed a "perfect storm" in the economic sphere in the form of a worldwide recession combined with a bad harvest in Korea and the aftermath of the Park assassination, and GDP fell by 3.7 percent. It also marked the beginning of the rule of the general and then president Chun Doo-hwan, who also came to power in a coup.

In the economic sphere Chun appointed a cabinet of technocrats, and his first chief economic adviser was one of Korea's ablest economists, Kim Jae-ik. The initial agenda focused on getting control of inflation that had averaged 14.2 percent per year from 1967 through 1978. There was also an attempt to move away from the direct support for particular industries that had characterized the Heavy and Chemical Industry Drive. The effort to control inflation was a success, and the growth rate of consumer prices from 1982 through the end of Chun's presidency in 1987 averaged 3.5 percent per year, down from 16.2 percent in the 1970s.

The effort to move away from an interventionist industrial policy was less successful. The problem initially was that during the Heavy and Chemical Industry Drive the government had made an implicit promise to help out the private conglomerates (*chaebol*) who had carried out the effort to build the heavy industries if they got into trouble. Many of these industries—such as POSCO, a state enterprise producing steel, and Samsung Electronics—had succeeded, but others had not, and the first years of the Chun regime involved its efforts to deal with them. Then, while this process was under way, virtually all of Korea's top government technocrats were assassinated in Burma by North Korean agents, and a whole new group of economic advisers had to be brought in to continue these efforts.

There were other longer-term influences, however, that also led both the Chun government and its successor to continue to intervene in the economy to support particular industries and discipline others. These influences continued even though by the latter half of the 1980s Korea was moving to greatly reduce many of its trade barriers, partly because of U.S. pressure but also because Korean firms, at least many of them, no longer needed the kind of protection offered in the 1960s and 1970s.

One such influence was that an activist industrial policy made it extremely easy to raise funds to support the presidents' political campaign needs, as well as their perceived personal needs and their friends and relatives' desires for wealth. Given the heavy involvement of the government in industry through licensing and other procedures long after tariffs had come down, a large business had to have close ties to the government to be able to get into the game, and maintaining those ties involved large financial contributions. Eventually both Chun Doo-hwan and his successor, Roh Tae-woo, were sentenced to prison for collecting hundreds of millions of dollars in this way both for their personal use and to support institutions that would, they hoped, ensure their continuing influence after they left office.

But the process of government intervention in development did not end with the two generals. The government of Kim Young-sam, which took office in early 1993, began with an effort to weed out corruption by, among other things, requiring that people put their real names down when they registered their financial assets. President Kim also presided over a major and successful effort to join the club of developed nations, the OECD, an effort that required Korea to continue to open up its markets and eliminate trade and investment barriers. Korea did eliminate many of these barriers, with the notable exception of bureaucratic barriers to foreign direct investment, but numerous rules and regulations remained that both domestic and foreign investors had to deal with in order to succeed. It was thus not difficult for one of President Kim's sons (and others) to use the power of the presidency corruptly to raise large funds, for which he was later convicted.

The other influence that kept a relatively activist industrial policy in place was that Korea's economic institutions were not capable of handling some of the transactions that a modern economy requires. This became readily apparent in the 1997–1998 financial crisis. The *chaebol* had gone on a foreign borrowing spree in the years leading up to the crisis to finance diversification into more and more fields whether or not the particular *chaebol* had much competence in those new fields. Returns to investment by the *chaebol*, partly as a result, fell steadily. The borrowing to finance these efforts was mostly short term, with the assumption that the loans from foreign banks could be rolled over year after year, as was the case with *chaebol* loans from Korean banks, from which *chaebol* also borrowed heavily. The government was generally unaware that this was going on and, due to macroeconomic mismanagement, had also allowed Korea's foreign exchange holdings to dwindle to next to nothing. When contagion from the Thai-Indonesian-Malaysian crises reached Korea, foreign banks were no longer willing to roll over the loans, there was no foreign exchange with which to repay these loans, and the entire Korean financial-*chaebol* system began to collapse.

The relevance of the financial crisis of 1997–1998 to industrial policy in Korea is that it pushed many, if not most, of the *chaebol* and all of the banks into what amounted to bankruptcy and for many appeared to be leading to liquidation—and in the case of such giants as Daewoo and 16 other major *chaebol,* it did. Korea was left with a problem of how to re-structure and make viable the remaining *chaebol* and the banking system. Bankruptcy and liquidation in advanced market economies, notably in the United States, is generally handled through the courts, although there were notable exceptions during the U.S. financial crisis of 2008–2009. For the courts to play this role, however, they need to have both the authority to oversee bankruptcy proceedings and the knowledge of how to handle them. Korean courts in 1998 and 1999, although adequate for most crimi-nal proceedings, had neither the competence nor the legal framework to handle the bankruptcy and restructuring or liquidation of large *chaebol* and banks.

The result was that the executive branch of the government had to take on the task of restructuring and liquidation. The newly elected president in 1998, Kim Dae-jung, was no friend of the *chaebol* but it became his and his staff's responsibility to carry out their liquidation and restructuring. In ad-dition to the various conditions the International Monetary Fund put on its willingness to lead a consortium to bail out Korea, the Kim Dae-jung gov-ernment itself insisted that all *chaebol* reduce their debt equity level from the 300–400 percent and higher levels of the recent past to 200 percent and to sell off many of their subsidiaries in order to focus on their core busi-nesses. State control of the banks, and the desperate financial condition of most *chaebol,* gave the government all of the power to enforce these direc-tives that it needed. The Kim Dae-jung government also became the first Korean government to actively promote foreign direct investment.

An activist industrial policy thus remained a central feature of Korean development right into the twenty-first century. Since the early 1980s, however, the government has tried to move away from direct decisions about which industries to develop and the structure of the firms doing the development. There was far less intervention at the end of the first decade of the twenty-first century than there had been earlier, but the instincts for politicians to intervene can still be seen on occasion. The Green Growth initiative of the Lee Myung-bak administration (2008–2013) can be seen in this light, as can several initiatives to improve the performance of Ko-rea's service sector. The need for intervention, however, has declined as the institutions, notably the legal system, have been strengthened to deal with complex economic issues. The tolerance of the Korean public for close relations between government and large firms has also disappeared, and the large firms in turn have seen little point in spending money on politicians who are not able to provide meaningful support.

The history of Korea's government-led development after 1961 thus went from industrial development, designed by government technocrats, that produced impressive results to an industrial policy, increasingly politicized and led by rent seeking, that over time produced increasingly undesirable economic results, ending in the financial crisis of 1997–1998. Put more succinctly, the first two decades produced, among other enterprises, POSCO, arguably one of the most efficient steel companies in the world, while the next two decades of industrial intervention produced, among other companies, the steel company Hanbo, whose bankruptcy contributed directly to the 1997–1998 crisis. As of 2011, Korea was far from being a purely market-driven economy on the model of, say, Hong Kong, but it was equally distant from the activist industrial policies of the Park era.

This overview of the Korean experience has focused on industrial policy because that was at the core of the country's development strategy. Much else was going on in the economy and the society at the same time. The Korean War, for example, had left the country with a relatively egalitarian society, in part because it made possible a thoroughgoing land reform but also because it destroyed the physical assets of virtually all urban residents. Inequality rose over time, although the data for the earlier years do not allow one to measure the level of inequality accurately.[23] Until democratic elections began in 1987, unions had little power and worker activism was suppressed. After 1987 and the advent of democratization, labor unions made up for lost time with increased militancy. Agriculture received relatively little support in the first decade under Park, other than an undervalued exchange rate, and then more support thereafter, mostly in the form of higher farm purchase prices together with some subsidies for improving access to water and upgrading the quality of rural housing (the *saemaul* movement), largely because farmers made up a large portion of the electorate in the early years. Democratization after 1987 had a major impact in all of these areas and led to the gradual increase in social welfare programs after years of neglect. All of these trends are important for understanding what has happened to the welfare of the Korean people, but the story of South Korea's rise from being a poor rural economy to a major high-income world economy is most of all a story about industrialization and exports. Managing industrial development and foreign trade well has to be at the center of any explanation of South Korea's economic success, and it is why most of the attention here has been devoted to describing what Korea actually did.

In the first two decades after independence was regained, Korea had the good fortune, at least in economic terms, of having a government that was devoted to developing the economy, and that government let technocrats unhampered by large-scale rent-seeking or by domestic political consider-ations make the key decisions. There has been much discussion in the lit-erature about just what the government and its technocrats did that worked so well, whether it was more effective coordination of investment decisions, massive export subsidies, or something else. Certainly there was coordination in the form of a serious planning effort by the government that produced five-year plans that were designed and to some degree did give direction to the industrialization effort. But this was not coordination on the model recommended over half a century ago by Rosenstein-Rodan, who suggested that one needed to develop a whole range of industries at one time, a "big push," so that one industry would generate the demand needed to sustain another industry.[24] In Korea it was intended from the start, particularly in the Heavy and Chemical Industry Drive, that the new industries would have to market a large share of their products to the out-side world through exports. More important than any specific policy in-terventions, other than the devaluation of the exchange rate, was that highly qualified technical people were given the authority to act and were supported if their ideas worked and removed if they did not. By the 1980s, however, economic power was beginning to shift away from the govern-ment and to the large firms themselves, which by then had numerous competent people of their own. And with the advent of democratization in 1987 and its further development in 1992 with the first elected nonmili-tary president since before 1961, a technocratic industrial policy led by government bureaucrats became impossible. The threat from North Korea to the very existence of a South Korean state had also waned, and that meant that industrial planners no longer faced the prospect of either suc-ceeding or watching their society disappear. By then, fortunately, the ac-tivist industrial policy planners were no longer needed, and the market, together with appropriate regulatory institutions, could become more prominent. The Blue House could get out of the industrial policy business, and politicians could concentrate on strengthening other components of Korean society. For the most part, with some exceptions, that is what has happened.

Taiwan's Variant of the Interventionist Model

Taiwan's general development approach and its industrial policies in particular had much in common with the South Korean approach, although there were important differences. This summary and appraisal of the Taiwan economic experience, therefore, will be brief. Emphasis will be on where the two economies' approaches were similar and where they differed. Where they were similar, it should be noted, it is not that Taiwan was following the Korean example—many of the critical Taiwan initiatives occurred before similar efforts were undertaken in Korea. To the degree that Taiwan's strategy reflected precedents from abroad, it was Japan that provided the model, but for the most part the similarity of the Taiwan and South Korean models reflects the fact that they faced similar challenges.

The central difference between Korea and Taiwan was that Korea, after independence was regained, was ruled by Koreans born and raised in Korea (although many had also migrated from North Korea before and during the Korean War). Taiwan, in contrast, after independence from Japan was ruled by migrants from the Chinese mainland who until their defeat in the Chinese civil war had had no experience living or working on Taiwan. Those who were native to the island had lived under a relatively benevolent Japanese rule for half a century, but these locally born Taiwanese from the 1950s through the 1980s played little role in government. The hostility between mainlanders and those born and raised on the island was further exacerbated by the often brutal way the Guomindang government reestablished Chinese control. For decades most government jobs with any significant level of responsibility and most military officers were former mainlanders. These divisions have been much less apparent since the advent of democracy on Taiwan, although they still influence attitudes in important areas, such as attitudes toward increasing ties with the Chinese mainland.

In the 1950s Taiwan, like Korea, carried out a thoroughgoing land reform. That, together with the repatriation of all Japanese after 1945 and the bombing of urban assets during World War II, meant that Taiwan, like South Korea, began development with a low level of income inequality. The 1.6 million mainlanders who moved with the Guomindang government also came, for the most part, with few assets. The 1950s was focused on establishing the Guomindang government-in-exile and in settling the influx of these new migrants. Initially there was hyperinflation imported from the mainland, but this was brought under control in the 1950s.

Throughout the 1950s Taiwan, also like Korea, had few exports (mostly sugar) and consistently ran large current account deficits that were financed mostly by U.S. foreign aid. A variety of trade barriers, including multiple and probably overvalued exchange rates, restricted imports and also made exporting of most products unprofitable. Import-substituting industrialization was thus the only viable industrial development strategy available in this context, and it also fit well with the ideology the Guomindang brought with it from the mainland as well as with the prevailing development strategy, represented by the views of Raul Prebisch.

Unlike Korea, the change in approach to industrial development did not come about because of a fundamental change in the nature of the government on Taiwan—no such change occurred. But President Chiang Kai-shek, like Park Chung-hee, was concerned with the continuing dependence on U.S. aid that gave the United States enormous leverage over Taiwan's economic policies.[25] Probably more important, although it is difficult to prove, is that Taiwan was even more vulnerable than South Korea to total collapse and the disappearance of the Guomindang government and its economic and political system. As K. T. Li (Li Kuo-t'ing), a major architect of the later reforms, when asked decades later how was it that he and his colleagues got the reform strategy right, replied, to paraphrase, "we had no choice, our very survival depended on it."[26]

The details of the reform strategy differed from the South Korean approach; President Chiang did not meet monthly with industrialists, for example, but the essence of the reform process, promoting exports, was much the same. The enabling legislation was the Nineteen-Point Program for Economic and Financial Reform signed by Chiang Kai-shek on January 8, 1960, which was negotiated by the key economic officials in the cabinet in response to a U.S. aid eight-point proposal. There was no serious effort to implement all of the 19 points, most of which had nothing to do with export promotion, however. Instead key government officials, notably K. Y. Yin (Yin Chung-long), then minister of economics, used the framework to fully implement efforts to promote the growth of manufactured exports. This included the unification and further devaluation of the exchange rate,[27] the creation of export processing zones, and low-interest export loans, among other measures. Yin himself, like many of the major architects of Taiwan's reforms, was an engineer by training. But he taught himself economics and was particularly influenced by such notable economists as S. C. Tsiang (Tsiang Sho-chieh) and T. C. Liu (Liu Ta-chung), both then with the International Monetary Fund.

As a result of these policy changes, exports in the 1960s, mostly manufactures,[28] rose rapidly at 23.5 percent per year in nominal U.S. dollar terms, rising from US$156.9 million in 1960 to US$1,049 million in 1969. The people actually doing the exporting were mostly small-scale Taiwanese businessmen, although there were also a few mainlanders, notably the handful of Shanghai industrialists who had moved to Taiwan in 1949 (even more moved to Hong Kong). As in Korea in the 1960s, there was little targeting of individual firms. Those who exported, whoever they were, had access to the various subsidies, much as in Korea at the same time.

The early 1970s in Taiwan brought a major change in industrial development policy similar to what occurred in South Korea. Efforts began to develop a heavy industry sector—steel, shipbuilding, and petrochemicals, among other sectors. The name applied to this effort was the Ten Major Development Projects, a program that also included a number of major infrastructure projects. The motivation, as in the case of Korea, was as much the changing international situation as a desire to move up to more complex industries. Taiwan lost its UN seat as the representative of all of China in 1971, and President Nixon made his famous trip to Beijing in February 1972, signing the Shanghai communiqué. The United States did not withdraw formal diplomatic recognition of the Republic of China until 1979, but from the Nixon trip forward sales of military equipment by the United States to Taiwan became a major issue in U.S.-Beijing relations. That, together with the Nixon doctrine announced on Guam, meant that Taiwan was under great pressure to provide increasingly for its own defense.

As in the case of Korea, Taiwan's heavy industry drive of the 1970s had government planners deciding which industries to target and which were going to carry out the plan. But in Taiwan there were no large firms to turn to. Smaller private firms would have to be heavily subsidized through large government-supported loans, and the money would have to go mainly to Taiwanese-owned businesses. Chiang Kai-shek's son, Chiang Ching-kuo, was by this time in charge of economic policy and was appointed premier in 1972 on his way to succeeding his father as president in 1978. Having been educated in the Soviet Union, he at first at least had some predilection to rely on state-owned enterprises to carry out the program. His two major economic ministers in the 1970s, Sun Yun-hsuan and Li Da-hai, were themselves engineers who had headed large state enterprises in the past.

Whatever the precise motivation, the first phase of the heavy industry drive was dominated by state-owned enterprises. In the petrochemical sphere the government, instead of relying on the state-owned China Petroleum Corporation, created two new state-owned enterprises, the China Petrochemical Development Corporation and Chung-tai Chemicals. In steel, the state-owned China Steel Corporation was set up in 1971, although production did not begin until 1978. In a measure similar to the practices of the Korean Heavy and Chemical Industry drive, no new private domestic steel firm was allowed to be set up between 1978 and 1983, and the existing private firms were prohibited from expanding. In shipbuilding, instead of expanding the Taiwan Shipbuilding Company, the one major existing shipbuilder and a state enterprise, the government created China Shipbuilding, which went into production in 1976. Initially it had substantial foreign investment and management involvement, but it ended up as a state enterprise. It regularly ran losses, despite government subsidies similar to those used in Korea to keep Hyundai shipbuilding alive (government contracts for ships and loans with below-market interest rates, for example).

Taiwan's industry in the 1970s, therefore, was made up of a few large state-owned import-substituting heavy industries and over 90,000 (in 1981) much smaller, mostly private manufacturing firms, many of which provided most of Taiwan's manufactured exports. The owners of the larger of these private firms were mostly Taiwan-born high school and primary school graduates raised during the Japanese colonial period. The large state-owned firms had a larger share of GDP than in most other non-Soviet-style developing economies, but the sectors accounting for the high rate of growth of GDP and exports were dominated by small firms and commanded a much larger share of GDP than the state-owned firms. These private firms, however, were not really as small as they sometimes appeared because many were organized as subcontractors to a core firm in what were called "relationship" (*guanxi*) enterprises. The core enterprises in turn were typically parts of industrial associations that handled many of their relationships with the Taiwan government. Whether this structure was more or less efficient and successful than the Korean private-*chaebol*-dominated structure remains a debatable issue to this day. Both structures, despite being very different, clearly did very well in the 1960s and 1970s.[29]

Taiwan's approach to industrial development began to change in major ways beginning in the 1980s. The country's leadership and K. T. Li in particular had begun to question the industrial development approach that relied heavily on imports of ever larger amounts of petroleum that could be cut off by foreign suppliers and whose price had soared because of actions by the OPEC cartel. There was a growing interest in focusing instead on high-technology industries that could be built on the foundation of Taiwan's human capital. First, however, Taiwan had to create the necessary human capital specific to the sector, and it began to do so in large part under the leadership of K. T. Li, who had been forced out as minister of finance in 1976 but continued as a minister without portfolio, and, more important, as chair of the Coordination Committee for the Application of Science and Technology to National Objectives. In 1978 Li organized a major conference on science and technology, supported by President Chiang and Premier Sun, that led more or less directly to the Science and Technology Development Program, which was approved by the government on May 18, 1979.

There were many dimensions to Taiwan's and K. T. Li's approach to the development of high-technology industries focusing in particular on information technology. Demand for the services of the information technology industry was created in part by computerizing government offices and activities wherever possible. The supply of skilled personnel was enhanced by government encouragement of curriculum reform in information-technology-related subjects in the universities and by setting up special training programs in high technology. New industrial research institutes were created to provide firms with technological innovations that they could then develop and commercialize. Taiwan did not totally abandon the idea of having state-owned enterprises take the lead and created United Microelectronics Corporation in 1979, with 40 percent of its capital coming from the government and the remainder from private sources. Much later, in 1987, the government set up Taiwan Semiconductor with the goal of generating the capacity to manufacture very large-scale integrated circuits. The main government efforts, however, unlike the heavy industry drive, involved creating the conditions in which private firms could thrive. The creation of the Hsinchu Science and Industrial Park in the 1980s underlined the effort to get scientists and engineers who had been trained abroad to come back to Taiwan to help develop high-technology industries. The park even included a high school that taught both the Taiwan national curriculum and a bilingual program designed for English-speaking children (mostly of Overseas Chinese) seeking an American college preparatory education.

The changes beginning in the late 1970s and carrying through the 1980s, however, involved much more than government efforts to promote high-technology industry through reliance on the private sector. The political context for economic decision-making was changing. Decisions made by technocrats largely on technical grounds were increasingly unacceptable to important groups in Taiwan society. Industrial associations with the backing of their affluent and numerous members pressed for a say in decisions that affected them. Many, given rising wages and an upward revaluation of the exchange rate, wanted to be able to invest abroad, and permission was granted. Taiwan had been the largest exporter of shoes in the world, but in the late 1980s and early 1990s the industry moved most of its manufacturing activities abroad, and Taiwan ceased to be a major exporter of shoes, although the high-value-added components of the industry (design, marketing) were retained on the island.

The environment was changing in two other ways as well. On the intellectual front, liberal economic views calling for greater reliance on market forces and less involvement of government had increasing influence, and well-publicized debates took place in the press between liberal and more interventionist economists. Influence from the United States and elsewhere reinforced these intellectual currents by pressuring the government to reduce its restrictions on trade and its many barriers to imports and subsidies of exports in particular. These pressures from the United States came in part because Taiwan's saving rate in the 1980s continued to rise while its investment rate fell, thus creating a large savings surplus, which in turn became a large current account surplus. Government intervention to restrict imports in order to preserve foreign exchange and protect local businesses no longer made much sense even without pressure from the United States. Taiwan's desire to join the General Agreement on Tariffs and Trade and then its successor, the World Trade Organization (WTO), further reinforced trade and investment liberalization. The advent of free elections later in the decade created a vigorous opposition party whose leaders no longer had to worry about being jailed for their views and actions, and this also changed the nature of government's role. By the 1990s, for example, efforts to build large polluting industries such as petrochemicals faced immediate and vigorous public opposition.

By 1983 and 1984 President Chiang Ching-guo had himself been converted to a more liberal view concerning economic policy, as had Yu Guo-hua, who was appointed premier in 1984. The average tariff rate on imports fell steadily to 6 percent by the late 1980s and 5 percent in the early 1990s, and many quantitative restrictions on imports were removed. Heavy industries such as petrochemicals continued to grow, but the new firms were private. Taiwan's industrial structure was also changing. Where earlier sales of a hundred million dollars a year were sufficient to make a firm one of Taiwan's largest in the private sector, the size of the leading firms rose steadily. By 2011 Taiwan had 40 firms among the *Forbes* list of the largest 2,000 enterprises in the world, led by Hon Hai Precision Industries (owners of the huge electronic assembly company Foxconn, with sales of US$61 billion), followed by Taiwan Semiconductor and Formosa Petrochemicals.[30]

The sector that was slowest to liberalize, in Korea as well as Taiwan, was the service sector—particularly banking, insurance, and other financial institutions. In service sectors directly related to high technology (information technology software, product design and marketing) Taiwan did very well in the 1990s and in the first decade of the twenty-first century, but not in finance. Taiwan, however, avoided the financial crisis of 1997–1998, so Taiwan's financial institutions avoided the Korean experience of government takeover and government-led restructuring.[31]

The growth rate of Taiwan's and Korea's economies by the twenty-first century, however, had slowed markedly, for reasons that I will take up in the final chapter. Here the main point is that Korea and Taiwan followed very similar industrial development paths during the first three to four decades after their turn outward in the early 1960s. There were differences (the smaller size of Taiwan's firms, Korea alone as a victim of the 1997–1998 financial crisis), but the similarities were much greater. Both Taiwan and South Korea followed three quite distinct strategies in the 1960s through the 1980s and 1990s. The first phase involved an across-the-board effort to promote manufactured exports with strong government support for whichever firms were capable of meeting ambitious export targets. The second phase, in the 1970s, shifted to government planning of heavy industry, followed by government targeting of specific firms (state-owned in the case of Taiwan, private government supported conglomerates [*chae-*

bol] in Korea) as well as specific industries. The third phase, in the 1980s and after, involved steady liberalization of foreign trade and investment, together with efforts to support high technology through the establishment of research institutes, improving education, and getting nationals trained abroad in engineering and science to return home. The governments in both Korea and Taiwan, therefore, played an active role in promoting industrialization throughout these decades, but the nature of that role changed dramatically. The large export subsidies and undervalued exchange rate of the first phase in both economies gave way to a decade of interventions targeted at specific industries, and that period in turn gave way to governments that relied mostly on market forces for directing industry but played an active role in providing industry with advanced research and highly educated technical personnel.

Hong Kong and Singapore

In discussions of economic growth in East Asia, Hong Kong and Singapore are typically lumped together with South Korea and Taiwan, the four Asian tigers or dragons. As societies, these four had much in common. The culture in all four cases was strongly influenced by modern versions of Confucian values. Three of the four spoke Chinese or a Chinese dialect as their native tongue. In the immediate aftermath of World War II, all four experienced long periods of political instability, economic instability, or outright war that undermined development efforts. I have already discussed the strains on the economy caused by the Korean War and the overthrow in 1960 and 1961 of first the Syngman Rhee government and then the Chang Myon government; and the defeat of the Guomindang on the Chinese mainland followed by the flight of 1.6 million mainlanders to Taiwan. Hong Kong also faced major disruption caused by the influx of refugees into the colony during and after 1949, together with having to adjust to the embargo placed on all trade with China. Singapore was still a colony of the United Kingdom in the 1950s, and the island was involved in the Communist insurgency in Malaya until its end in 1957. Singapore in 1962, when I first visited, was still wracked by numerous labor strikes and demonstrations, and then there was the instability involved in first joining the Malaysian Federation (1963) and then being pushed out of the Federation and becoming fully independent in 1965. In the economic sphere, in contrast, the main thing these four had in common was that all four grew rapidly after 1960.[32] The way Hong Kong and Singapore managed their economies after 1960, however, had little in common with the approaches of South Korea and Taiwan (or Japan).

Hong Kong is arguably the clearest example of a laissez-faire economy anywhere in the world in the second half of the twentieth century and continuing through the first decade plus of the twenty-first. There is no tariff on goods entering Hong Kong. Excise taxes are imposed on such goods as alcohol and tobacco, but on both imports and domestic products. The currency of the colony and after 1997 the Hong Kong Special Administrative Region has been made up of bank notes issued by three commercial banks (Hong Kong Shanghai Bank, Standard Chartered Bank, and Bank of China) and to a very limited degree the Hong Kong Monetary Authority (not founded until 1993). Hong Kong has no central bank, but the Hong Kong Monetary Authority acts as a currency board where all currency issued must be backed 1:1 with U.S. dollars. The exchange rate with the U.S. dollar was first fixed in 1967 and then, after a brief period of floating, was fixed in 1983 at HK$7.8 to the U.S. dollar, where it remained as of 2012. The currency is fully convertible. For the most part when Hong Kong prices become misaligned with world prices, it is the domestic prices, not the exchange rate, that are expected to adjust, and Hong Kong tradable goods prices (and many nontradable goods prices) have been flexible in both directions. The government has intervened when there have been speculative attacks on the fixed exchange rate, as was done during the 1997–1998 financial crisis, but such interventions are rare.

As a colony of Britain from 1841 through 1997, Hong Kong steadily built up the infrastructure required of a major international port. Most of this infrastructure was financed and managed privately. Private funding, for example, financed the building of the first cross-harbor tunnel, opened in 1972, and two subsequent tunnels in 1989 and 1997. The government initiated and built the Mass Transit Rail system, but the entity running the system, MTR Corporation Limited, was privatized in 2000. The airport at Chek Lap Kok is an exception in that it is run by the Airport Authority of Hong Kong and its US$20 billion construction cost came from public funds of one sort or another (including bonds sold to the public). The key point for understanding Hong Kong's economic growth is that most of the infrastructure needed by a modern economy was already in place in 1960 and has been steadily upgraded and expanded ever since, using private funding to a degree much greater than in other countries in East Asia or elsewhere.

The major exceptions to Hong Kong's laissez-faire approach have been the management of land sales, the construction of public housing, and in more recent years the large scale of expansion of the university system. Land in Hong Kong is owned by the government and is leased to private builders, typically for 99 years. The leases are auctioned off, and the proceeds have been a major source of revenue for the government, helping to keep other forms of taxation low. Critics have suggested that the government has tried, with some success, to keep land prices high in service to the powerful real estate companies and the many individuals who own valuable properties. Whatever the validity of this view, the government has also managed a large-scale public housing program to provide affordable housing to most of the region's population. When I lived in Hong Kong in 1961–1962, the hillsides and the areas around Kai Tak Airport were covered by shack dwellings occupied to a large degree by migrants from China fleeing the civil war and the Communist takeover. Fires and heavy rains could devastate large areas covered with these primitive dwellings. A fire in 1953, for example, left 53,000 people homeless and helped trigger the government decision to begin a large-scale public housing effort. Two decades later these shack areas had largely disappeared, having been replaced with public housing.

Government development efforts in more recent decades have focused mainly on keeping Hong Kong competitive with its rapidly developing neighbors—hence the new airport, but also a series of new universities, established to upgrade the quality of Hong Kong's human capital. The University of Hong Kong was founded in 1911, mainly to train individuals in the colony to staff the middle levels of the civil service (the highest levels were staffed by British). The Chinese University of Hong Kong came next and opened in 1963. Beginning in the early 1990s, however, tertiary education expanded rapidly with the founding of the Hong Kong University of Science and Technology in 1991 and several other universities as well as the upgrading of most of the existing schools to full university status (Lingnan, City University, and Hong Kong Polytechnic). The first fully private university, however, was not established until 2006.

The other key element of Hong Kong's economic system was the legal and court system built by the British. This system existed from the beginning of the colony but played little role in the lives of most local residents (other than criminals) until much later. For over a century it was mainly a British system. In the 1960s there were only a few hundred judges, barristers, and solicitors for a population of 4 million people. Then in 1969 Hong Kong opened its first law school, although it graduated only 50 people a year in the 1970s. By the 1980s a second law school had been established, and more lawyers were coming into Hong Kong from the United Kingdom and the United States. At the turn of the century Hong Kong had roughly 5,000 lawyers of all types.[33] Equally important, the legal system was independent of the political authority and remained so through the first years of reintegration with China. Thus the legal infrastructure required by a modern sophisticated commercial center was in place and is no doubt part of the reason why so many multinational corporate headquarters are located in Hong Kong. More generally, the nature of the Hong Kong economic system in all of its dimensions did not change significantly with the reintegration of the territory as a special administrative region of the Peoples Republic of China in 1997.

It is in this context that Hong Kong's economy first transformed itself from a center mainly for trade with China into an economy with a large manufacturing sector. The embargo on trade with China, together with China's own hostility toward any form of foreign (or Hong Kong) direct investment, meant that Hong Kong had to find new activities to employ its population. The private sector, made up in part of Shanghai cotton textile industrialists who had migrated to the colony after 1949, filled much of this employment gap. Wages in labor-intensive, low-skill industries such as garments and plastics were still low enough for companies to compete with other low-wage manufacturers, and manufacturing grew to nearly half of Hong Kong's GDP by the end of the 1970s. Small and medium enterprises dominated the sector, and they responded rapidly to market forces. To give one example, when I was living there in 1961–1962 the United States for some reason removed restrictions on the import of goldfish, and within months goldfish ponds appeared in great numbers all over the colony's New Territories.

The U.S. embargo on trade with China ended in 1971, and then China opened up to foreign direct investment after 1979. When this was combined with Hong Kong's rising per capita income (per capita GDP reached roughly $14,000 in 1980 and $28,500 in 1990),[34] low-wage, labor-intensive industries within Hong Kong were doomed. Hong Kong businesses simply moved most of their manufacturing establishments into Guangdong

Province and elsewhere. Hong Kong businesses accounted for over 60 percent of foreign direct investment in China in the 1980s and remain major investors to this day.[35] Within Hong Kong, employment in manufacturing plummeted, and by 2009 manufacturing made up only 1.8 percent of Hong Kong's GDP. Services, in contrast, accounted for 92.6 percent of GDP in that year.[36] These services included traditional sectors such as wholesale and retail trade and restaurants, but 35.8 percent of services were in finance and insurance, professional and business services, transport, storage and courier services, and other modern sectors, many of which support manufacturing in critical ways but do not involve manufacturing per se. Led by firms such as Lee and Fung, Hong Kong has become one of the principal centers for managing the complex multination supply chains that dominate much manufacturing today. A laissez-faire economic environment together with creative Hong Kong entrepreneurs thus gave Hong Kong's economy the flexibility to deal with both its rapidly rising per capita income and the external constraints of the U.S. embargo on China and China's own hostility to private investment of all kinds, and then the abrupt removal of these same barriers.

The Singapore economy prior to independence was run in much the same way as the Hong Kong system of the 1960s and earlier. Singapore was a free port like Hong Kong. It was governed by the British in much the same way—and prior to World War II even many of the British governors general moved from serving in one colony to the other. The infrastructure, built for both commercial and military purposes by the British, was the best in Southeast Asia. Taxes were low, and the University of Malaya in Singapore (now the National University of Singapore) was the highest quality education system in the region, although the number of graduates was small, and many were residents of Malaya. The legal system was also the most developed in Southeast Asia and remains so to this day, particularly in the economic sphere. The dominant companies at the time of independence were mostly British, although there were a few large Chinese enterprises.

What was acceptable for a British colony, however, was not a viable option for a newly independent country with a population many of whom had sympathized and even participated in the Communist-led insurgency. Although the far-left members of the People's Action Party, which has ruled Singapore since independence, were purged at the outset, the party was a member of the Socialist International during its first decade in power and retains strong social welfare policies to this day. The party government, for example, inaugurated a large-scale public housing program designed to accommodate the entire population and then strongly encouraged families to use their forced savings to purchase their apartments. Private home ownership thus rose from 58.8 percent in 1980 to 87.2 percent in 2010.[37] Equally important has been the Central Provident Fund, which all employees and employers must join and which requires a very high rate of savings on the part of all but low-income workers. (For workers earning S$1,500–4,500 per month in 2008, for example, the employer had to contribute to the fund an amount equivalent to 14.5 percent of the wage, and the employee contributed 20 percent if under age 50, somewhat less if older, and considerably less earning under S$1,500.) The Central Provident Fund was also used to support other policies deemed socially desirable by the government such as health care, education, and home ownership. The basic idea was that high forced savings would provide the funding required to meet the critical needs of the entire population, leaving little need for direct government subsidies to the poor.

Singapore has a vibrant private sector, but some its best known firms are state-owned enterprises, notably Singapore Airlines and Singapore Telecommunications. A controlling interest in these state enterprises is held by Temasek Holdings, the country's sovereign wealth fund, which is ultimately controlled by the Ministry of Finance. There are hundreds of other smaller state-controlled businesses of various kinds, although they play a less central role in the economy today than they did during the first decades after independence. More important than the state enterprises are the foreign direct investment enterprises. Singapore since independence has made attraction of foreign direct investment a central development goal and has become the location of choice for large numbers of multinational firms.

Industrial policy as a result has focused on providing an attractive environment for investors of all kinds but foreign firms in particular. The creation of the Jurong Industrial Park was an early initiative in this area. The steady upgrading of the Singapore education system, particularly in the technical and management sphere, has also played an important role in attracting investors. At one point Singapore even experimented with raising the minimum wage as a way of discouraging investments in industries that required large numbers of low-wage workers, workers who increasingly were not available in Singapore and thus would require import of labor from Indonesia. In contrast to Hong Kong, these various efforts to promote industry have kept the share of industry in GDP at a much higher level (26.3 percent of GDP in 2009, 19.5 percent in manufacturing alone) than in Hong Kong.[38] Singapore's economy, however, is increasingly dominated by services (69.1 percent of GDP in 2009) as are the economies of virtually all high-income countries. It would be too strong to say that Singapore confined its industrial policy to general support efforts and avoided any industrial targeting whatsoever. Government support has gone to creating particular industries, such as the airline industry and petrochemicals, but there has been nothing remotely comparable to the targeted industrial interventions of the Korean and Taiwanese heavy and chemical industry drives of the 1970s. On the other hand there has been more targeting in Singapore than in Hong Kong.

Virtually unique to Singapore has been its ability to support a range of state-owned enterprises and to regulate and support private firms without politics or rent seeking entering the picture to any significant degree. On Transparency International's ranking of countries by their degree of corruption, Singapore has consistently ranked tied for first (in 2010)[39] or only a few positions below first (fifth in 2011 and 2012) among over 150 countries. The underlying political support for keeping politics and rent seeking out of industrial development decisions derived in part from the fact that Singapore, like South Korea and Taiwan but to a lesser degree, saw itself in a relatively hostile environment, surrounded as they were by more than 200 million Malays in Malaysia and Indonesia, where anti-Chinese attitudes were common. Singapore was and is also a rich island next to a country, Indonesia, that has less than one-tenth of Singapore's per capita income even in PPP terms. What is more difficult to explain is how the People's Action Party government managed to establish an economic system that was ultimately controlled by politicians yet was run as a market-driven commercial enterprise. Once they had established such a system and it had demonstrated its economic success, moreover, it acquired steady support from the population at large that made it that much easier to continue to pursue this kind of a growth model. The People's Action Party's percentage of the vote in national parliamentary elections has yet to fall below 60 percent. The playing field for opposition parties is not an even one, but the voting itself is conducted honestly.

Unlike Hong Kong, therefore, one cannot describe the Singapore approach to management of its economy as laissez-faire. The government was involved in economic decisions in myriad ways, ranging from outright ownership of major firms to forced savings by Singaporeans and the companies that employed them. But success or failure, whether for private or state-owned firms, was and is determined by market forces, and those market forces are rarely manipulated by the government. Singapore's per capita income, as a result, has risen from US$4,700 in 1965 to US$51,600 in 2011 since independence,[40] placing the country solidly among the richest countries in the world. There have been recessions, notably in 1998–1999 and in 2009, but their causes have always been external to Singapore, and its economy has bounced back quickly.

Summing Up

Even among the most successful East Asian economies, no one strategy predominated during their high-growth decades. The largest distinction was between the economies of South Korea and Taiwan on the one hand and those of Hong Kong and Singapore on the other. The first two decades of rapid growth in South Korea and Taiwan involved a high degree of government intervention that began with general policies to promote the export of manufactures by all firms capable of doing so and then moved on in the 1970s to government targeting of specific industries and specific firms in the heavy industry sector. By the 1980s both economies began to move away from this interventionist model and toward an economy governed more by market forces. Industrial policies instead increasingly focused on efforts to upgrade the human capital needed for the development of high-technology industries. Taiwan in the early stages of these developments relied more on small-scale firms, while South Korea relied more on large conglomerates, the *chaebol*. Both South Korea and Taiwan discouraged most foreign direct investment in the earlier years and were only somewhat more welcoming in the later years.

Hong Kong and Singapore, in contrast, relied from the beginning of their high-growth period primarily on market forces to guide industrial and service sector development. Hong Kong came close to being a pure laissez-faire economy, relying mostly on the private sector even for the provision of much of its infrastructure, whereas Singapore had many state-owned enterprises and a major sovereign wealth fund. The largest difference between Hong Kong and Singapore was in the social welfare area, in that Singapore had a large forced savings program (the Central

Provident Fund) and Hong Kong did not. Unlike in South Korea and Taiwan, both Hong Kong and Singapore welcomed foreign direct investment, and much of their growth was generated by it. There was no period when Hong Kong and Singapore began to move from intervention to reliance on market forces because they relied on market forces to guide the economy throughout. Both economies actively promoted efforts to upgrade the quality of their human capital by creating new universities, among other things. For the most part, however, the role of government has been to provide security and a supportive environment for the private sector. One critical element in this supportive environment has been the development of a competent and independent judicial system. Singapore and Hong Kong have by far the strongest legal systems in East and Southeast Asia.

— 4 —

Successes and Failures
in Southeast Asia

Where the economic performance of most of Northeast Asia, plus Singapore and minus North Korea, is a story of economic success, the economic performances of the economies of Southeast Asia present a mixed picture. Five of the economies in Southeast Asia, including Singapore, have done well for significant periods, while three have done poorly for most of the second half of the twentieth century and the first decade of the twenty-first. The development strategies of the consistently worst performers will not be discussed in this chapter except in passing. The generals who rule Myanmar until recently spent much of the resources of their country on building a new capital and on rampant corruption—Myanmar is tied for 180th with Afghanistan on Transparency International's corruption perception index in 2011, ahead of only Somalia and North Korea. It is likely that Myanmar's per capita income is not much, if at all, above where it was when the generals took over the country in a coup in 1962, although there are no reliable GDP data to confirm this. Laos and Cambodia suffered for long periods from being drawn into the war in Vietnam and in recent years have had some economic growth but are also wracked by corruption and mismanagement. (Laos is ranked at 154th and Cambodia at 164th out of 182 on Transparency International's 2011 index.) They are still among the poorest countries in the world with per capita GDP roughly US$1,000 in 2011 (or less than US$3,000 in current price PPP terms).[1]

But the story in Indonesia, Malaysia, and Thailand is very different, as is the story of Vietnam, which will be discussed in the next chapter since it has the most in common with the experience of China. The Philippines has not done well by East Asian standards but is not an economic basket case either. Here I will focus mostly on Indonesia and Malaysia, partly because I know these two economies the best from having worked with the governments there at varying times, but also because they make the most interesting comparisons with the development strategies of Northeast Asia. Thailand and the Philippines will be dealt with more briefly.

The Tug-of-War over Development Strategy in Indonesia

There was no real development strategy in Indonesia during the era of rule by President Sukarno (1948–1965). He was mostly interested in his role on the international stage and in using the Indonesian military first to hold the country together and then to attempt to expand its control over neighboring territories in Borneo and New Guinea. Some of these efforts were successful (western New Guinea in 1962 became what is now the Indonesian province of Papua) and others not (the efforts to take over northern Borneo through his policy of "Konfrontasi" in 1962–1966). There are no reliable GDP figures for this period, but when I first visited in 1962 the view of economists and others at the time was that most parts of the economy were in decline (rubber yields were falling, interisland shipping was deteriorating, foreign investors had been driven out of the country, and inflation was increasing).

There is no consensus even today about the events of 1965 that brought the general and then president Suharto to power. There is no controversy, however, over the fact that the army established full dictatorial power over the country and that the largest and best organized opposition party, the Partai Komunis Indonesia, was destroyed and its members were killed, were imprisoned, or fled into exile. The immediate problem the new government faced was to bring down inflation and stabilize the balance of payments. For that purpose the government, led by President Suharto and staffed in critical positions by former and current military officers, brought in a group of Indonesian members of the Economics Department of the University of Indonesia who had been trained abroad under Ford Foundation scholarships, many at the University of California at Berkeley. Together with advisors from the International Monetary Fund and later from Harvard University, inflation was brought down and the balance of payments stabilized. For the next three-plus decades until President Suharto's fall in 1998, these economists and their protégés, together with a few other like-minded officials, dominated key economic ministries in the government, notably the Planning Commission (Bappenas) and the Ministry of Finance (Keuangan).

Economic policy in Indonesia, however, was not the sole responsibility of these two economic ministries, either in the early years of the Suharto or New Order era or later. Within the government two other elements competed for the support of the president, who had the final say in all economic matters.[2] Outside the government there were wealthy businessmen, mostly Indonesians of Chinese ethnicity, who had the ear of the president. So did the large state-owned enterprises, beginning with the state oil company, Pertamina, and other state enterprises established in the 1970s and after. Indonesia's development model during the Suharto years was a product of these competing groups. Put differently, these competing groups promoted alternative models or visions of development, and the history of Indonesian development policy during the New Order era (1966–1998) was to an important degree a history of which of these groups had the greatest influence at particular times.[3]

The economics group, sometimes referred to as the "technocrats" or the "Berkeley Mafia," was led by Professor Widjojo Nitisastro, who initially was the coordinating economics minister and head of Bappenas (Planning), working closely with the minister of finance and Ali Wardhana, a later coordinating economics minister. At any given time several other ministers or high-ranking officials were part of this economic leadership group,[4] and the titles shifted from one participant to another, but Widjojo, with or without a ministerial title, was the effective chair of the board of the group throughout. They met regularly, often late in the evening, to discuss and reach a consensus on what their position should be on one economic issue or another.

I am not aware of any publication by Widjojo or Ali Wardhana that fully articulates their development vision for Indonesia, although a collection of some of Widjojo's speeches and publications was published in 2011.[5] Over 15 years (1980–1995), however, in connection with my role as director of the Harvard Institute for International Development I had dozens of long conversations with them about their plans. While these discussions covered a wide range of topics, their primary purpose was to enable me to understand what they were trying to accomplish. I then in turn would be able to provide them with the kind of short- and long-term advisors who could assist them with the technical assistance they needed to realize their goals. As the supervisor of the Harvard advisors helping with the early drafts of reform measures of various kinds, I also observed what these economic ministers ultimately decided. What follows, therefore, is a summary version of my view of their approach to Indonesia's development.

The economics group established their reputation for a high level of economic competence by achieving macroeconomic stabilization in Indonesia's very unstable economy of the mid-1960s, and the group retained primary responsibility for macroeconomic policy narrowly defined (exchange rate policy, interest rate policy, and closely related areas) throughout most of the three-decade period. The exceptions were the run-up of foreign debt and the debt crisis of the mid 1970s and again during the financial crisis of 1997–1998 when President Suharto and certain close associates were desperately looking for a way to stop the massive devaluation of the Indonesian rupiah and, among other things, the rapid erosion of their personal fortunes.

From early on, however, the economics group was also concerned with how to get the Indonesian economy on a sustainable growth path that involved more than simply macroeconomic stabilization or the expansion of natural resource production—mostly petroleum but also rubber and other plantation crops and minerals. In concrete terms that meant industrialization, but industrialization of particular kind, labor-intensive industries that could compete in export markets, not heavy industries such as the state-owned enterprises whose financing by the government contributed to the debt crisis of the mid-1970s in Indonesia. That crisis was in a sense a blessing in disguise because it brought profligate external borrowing to support large-scale pet government projects, based on a view that oil prices would continue to rise, to a halt.[6] As I will show, this battle between alternative industrial development visions would be ongoing between the economics group and the other major parties involved in development efforts throughout the New Order era.

The emphasis on labor-intensive, export-oriented industries was no doubt in part influenced by the successes being achieved with these industries in Northeast Asia, successes that were becoming more widely known by the 1970s. But emphasis on these kinds of industries also fit an economy that had very few well-trained people capable of running more complex industries. Both as professors at the University of Indonesia and when they presided over ministries that in the 1970s had very few well-educated personnel, Professor Widjojo and Ali Wardhana, among others, clearly understood that it was unrealistic to think of creating at the start efficient heavy industries, and it was also completely unrealistic to think that their ministries or anyone else in the government could directly manage a broad-based industrial development effort in the manner of, say, Korea or Japan. In the 1980s, with large profits from the oil boom that Ali Wardhana had managed to "hide" from the more profligate ministers, the finance and planning ministries began a major effort to send hundreds of ministry personnel abroad for further training in economics and management, but that effort did not change their view that one had to rely mainly on market forces to direct the industrial development effort and for much else.[7]

For market forces to work properly in guiding industrial development, however, one needed at least two other changes. Macroeconomic stability was the first condition, and that had been achieved, lost briefly in the mid-1970s, and then restored in the late 1970s and throughout the 1980s into the early 1990s. Key to promoting manufactured exports, however, was an additional macroeconomic step: a currency that was not overvalued. But that was easier said than done in the context of the OPEC-generated oil price booms of 1973 and 1979. In 1978, however, Ali Wardhana engineered a devaluation of the rupiah, even though conventional analysis of Indonesia's balance of payments would have suggested that devaluation was unnecessary or even undesirable. For most of the next two decades the Indonesian rupiah was freely convertible, and the exchange rate was indirectly managed (through interest rate policies among other measures) in a way that kept it from becoming overvalued. Direct controls over foreign exchange were anathema to Professor Widjojo and his colleagues, not for ideological reasons but because there was little prospect that Indonesia, with limited human capital and thousands of islands, some close to Singapore, could hope to control foreign exchange flows using anything other than indirect market mechanisms. To make it even more difficult for Indonesia to consider capital controls, Singapore did not publish its trade with Indonesia, and Singapore banks held tens of billions of dollars of unreported accounts of Indonesian citizens.

The other challenge for those trying to rely on market forces to guide the economy was that Indonesian prices in the 1970s and early 1980s were highly distorted by a wide range of trade restrictions. Probably the most important barrier to a company hoping to produce and export manufactures (textiles, shoes, and the like) was the Indonesian customs service. In the first half of the New Order period it took something like 70 separate stamps or approvals to get goods through the import approval process and into the country. This was time-consuming for industries that needed to respond quickly to foreign market demand, and each step of the way typically involved side payments. Reforming a developing country's customs service is a formidable task, and efforts to do so in Indonesia made only limited progress. The solution the economics group decided on and sold to the president was the politically sensitive step of removing the customs service and replacing it with the Swiss firm SGS. The other major step to promote nontraditional manufactured exports was to design a series of deregulation packages to get rid of other kinds of trade barriers (high tariffs, quantitative restrictions on trade) piece by-piece. Simply moving to free and open trade was not an option because too many vested interests were involved in maintaining many of the restrictions. Using cost-benefit analysis, it was possible to get rid of many of the most egregious barriers by demonstrating just how high was the cost to the economy and how low the benefit. The results of these various measures were immediate. In the 1970s manufactured exports were between 1 and 2 percent of exports year after year, but in the 1980s exports of manufactures rose from 2 percent of total merchandise exports in 1980 to 35 percent in 1990 and 53 percent in 1993 before the share leveled off. Manufacturing as a share of GDP rose from 13 percent in 1980 to 21 percent in 1990 and 22 percent in 1993, and GDP growth per capita over those 13 years averaged 4.7 percent a year.[8]

This vision and development model of the economics group, however, was in regular conflict with an alternative vision and model that involved the other major players in the debates over economics, and these other players also often had the ear of President Suharto. The alternative vision focused on large-scale projects in fields such as petrochemicals, telecommunications, automobiles, and aircraft. The business friends of President Suharto included many private individuals who had made large fortunes through timber concessions, together with former military officers and other high officials. I shall label these groups the rent-seekers, even though some thought that they were promoting sustainable industrial development as well as their own bank accounts.

The saga of the petrochemical plant Chandra Asri illustrates the approach. There was some interest among the large international oil companies in building a large petrochemical plant in Indonesia, and it was reported that they could do so without protection from imports. The Indonesian businessmen, together with one of the president's sons, however, felt that the project should be built by Indonesians even though Indonesians did not have experience in the area and would require substantial protection. They would also have to borrow abroad much of the money to build the plant. Because Chandra Asri was only one of several dozen projects of this sort, most of which required substantial external financing, the economics group, through Ali Wardhana, was able to block the project for a time by arguing that this project and others like it would raise Indonesia's external debt service ratio to potentially dangerous levels. Eventually, however, the supporters of the project got around these strictures by creating a shell Hong Kong company that nominally turned the project into a 100 percent foreign invested effort, and the project was built. When it finally went into production it was completely dependent on imported feed stock, the prices for its output were depressed, and it ran up a large debt. It effectively was bankrupt, although it was not liquidated and still existed in 2012. Equally or more serious, to protect the plant and raise the price of its output, the government in the mid-1990s placed a 25 percent tariff on ethylene, thus raising the costs to all downstream users in Indonesia. Thus this large heavy industry project was in direct conflict with the goal of creating a favorable environment for more labor-intensive industrial downstream users.

This rent-seeking approach to development was a problem in the mid-1980s, but it was kept from fundamentally undermining overall industrial development, in large part because many of these large subsidized projects did not get built. As one member of the economics group used to say, the mid-1980s were a good time for policy reformers because there was enough money to fund necessary government investments but not so much money that officials and others would ignore the costs of dubious projects. All that changed in the mid-1990s as success produced hubris among the president, his family, and his business friends and an economic boom combined with massive rent seeking by this group gained momentum. As the debt piled up and the corruption became more open and on a grander scale, the groundwork was laid for the crash that was to come in 1997 and 1998, and the New Order era came to an end.

There were two other efforts to promote large-scale programs that also ultimately helped bring the Indonesian economy down but where the motive was not primarily rent-seeking. The first and best known of these programs was Indonesia's long-term effort to become a manufacturer of commercial aircraft. This venture was under the direction of B. J. Habibie, the minister of science and industry throughout much of the New Order era. (Habibie became vice president near the end of the New Order and then replaced Suharto as president for a brief period during the transition to democracy.) Habibie had been trained as an aeronautical engineer in Germany and served for a time as a vice president and researcher at Messerschmitt, the German aircraft manufacturer. He returned to Indonesia in 1974 and from the beginning focused on trying to develop a commercial aircraft industry there. While thousands of engineers were trained abroad in relevant fields and the effort produced a few airplanes, it was a very expensive failure. Very few countries have successfully developed a commercial aircraft industry, and even fewer of them are developing countries. Brazil with the Embraer aerospace company, which produces 50- to 100-seat commercial jets, is the major exception. Indonesia today buys its commercial aircraft abroad.

The other supporters of large-scale industries were people involved with state-owned enterprises that still dominate many key sectors in Indonesia such as electric power and steel. These enterprises have generally performed poorly, but privatization has not made much headway, either in the Suharto years or since democratization. One problem, both before and after democratization, has been that some of these state-owned firms have served as a ready source of financial support to powerful political figures and parties. Another problem in Indonesia is that many of the most successful private firms are owned and run by Indonesian Chinese, hence privatization is seen as turning these enterprises over to the Chinese minority. Ethnic tensions of this sort are common in many countries. It is a major reason why privatization has proceeded slowly in East Africa, for example, where the private sector is dominated by "Asians," in that case South Asians. Because the issue is more central to understanding Malaysian development policy, I shall defer further discussion of it until I take up the experience of that country.

Overall the New Order years produced an impressive economic record with per capita income averaging a rate of increase of 4.9 percent per year for 32 years (1997/1965), for a four- to fivefold rise in the average standard of living. And this increase in GDP per capita and the beginning of a major industrialization effort did not just benefit a narrow group. The various "Inpres" (Presidential Directive) initiatives and other measures transferred large sums to the rural areas to build schools and health clinics, increase rice production, and extend rural credit and facilitate rural savings among millions who prior to these initiatives had had little access to these benefits, either during the Sukarno years or under Dutch colonialism. On the other hand the excesses of the last years of President Suharto did enormous damage to the economy, and full recovery in income to the level of 1997 was not achieved until 2004, seven years later.[9]

Democratization in Indonesia formally began in 1999, first with the free election of a parliament and then with the indirect but open and competitive election of the president. Democratization has brought many positive changes in the country, most of which are outside the scope of a study devoted to understanding the country's approach to economic development. Democracy has also eliminated the worst economic excesses of the Suharto years, but corruption in government and in government involvement in the economy is rampant at all levels. (Indonesia in 2012 ranked 118 out of 174 countries on the Transparency International Corruption Perceptions Index.) The World Bank's governance indicators, which began publication in 1996, suggest that "regulatory quality" and the "rule of law" reached a low point in the year 2000 and then recovered to levels that were still well below the level in 1996 and solidly in the bottom one-third to one-half of all countries listed. "Control of corruption" troughed in the year 2000 and then rose through 2008 before falling again in 2009 and 2010, placing Indonesia in the bottom quarter of all countries on this measure.[10]

The state-owned enterprises are still very much in place and remain inefficient. Democracy has complicated the decision-making process when it comes to investment in critical infrastructure, but that was probably inevitable. Infrastructure did not do particularly well under Suharto's dictatorial powers either, although electric power, a critical sector, grew twice as fast during 1990–1997 as from 2000 to 2010, despite huge fuel subsidies that in part helped the power sector in the latter period. Under President Dr. H. Susilo Bambang Yudhyono political stability appears to be solidly based, and growth has resumed at a rate only a little below that of the Suharto years. Per capita GDP since 2004, when recovery of per capita income to precrisis levels was achieved, was 4.7 percent per year, and total GDP growth was 5.8 percent per year, as contrasted to 4.9 percent per capita and 6.8 percent for total GDP in the last 17 years of the Suharto era. Indonesian growth in recent years, however, has been buoyed by high natural resource prices that have fueled a steady expansion in the service sector as well as the resource sector. Industry in contrast has averaged a growth rate of 4.4 percent since 2004, far below the 8.0 percent industrial growth rate in 1980–1997.

There is also nothing in recent years that can be called a coherent development strategy, however. The different components of the economy that were in place when the Suharto era ended, with the notable exception of many of the more egregious projects of the Suharto family, are still in place today and are moving ahead on similar tracks. There has been effective macroeconomic management, but there is no reforming vision comparable to the effort to promote export-oriented industries fostered under the leadership of Professor Widjojo, Ali Wardhana, and the many other ministers of the economics group. The relatively high growth rate during the Yudhyono presidency has been maintained mostly by high natural resource prices and thus is probably not sustainable if natural resource prices fall. High natural resource prices have also led to a large revaluation of the rupiah, which has effectively slowed the growth of manufactured exports and of Indonesian manufacturing more generally.

Malaysian Development Strategy and the Ethnic Divide

The Malaysian development experience is of particular relevance to this analysis because for a sustained period in the 1980s and 1990s Malaysia explicitly attempted to adopt the interventionist Korean (and Japanese and Taiwan) industrial development model of the 1970s. Malaysia, however, attempted to introduce this model into a very different economic and political context from what had existed in Northeast Asia earlier.[11]

Prior to independence in 1957 Malaya, under British colonial rule (it became Malaysia in 1963 with the addition of Sabah and Sarawak),[12] had achieved a degree of prosperity by developing natural resource-based products, notably rubber and tin. Unlike Northeast Asia, which had few natural resources, Malaysia was well endowed with a tropical climate suitable for rubber trees and later for palm oil and other tropical crops. In addition to being rich in tin, it was well endowed with tropical hardwood forests and today is also a major producer of oil and gas. The economy was open, and trade barriers were modest. Most large firms were foreign owned, and after independence was achieved in 1957 there was a limited effort to develop import-substituting industries. Most urban businesses, other than the largest (which were foreign owned), were owned and operated by Malaysian Chinese, who at the time made up one-third of the population. Malays made up just over half of the population (later with the creation of Malaysia and the addition of other indigenous groups in Sabah and Sarawak under the term Bumiputera [Sons of the Soil] the share rose to above 60 percent). Malays were mostly farmers or members of the civil service or the army. In part because the Communist insurgency in Malaya had been led by ethnic Chinese, the British at the time of independence reserved government service and the army mainly for Malays or Bumiputera. There were virtually no Bumiputera businessmen. A study of Bumiputera entrepreneurs done at the time had to include individuals who owned their taxis in order to get the number of Bumiputera entrepreneurs up to something like 50, a minuscule number. Indians, the other substantial minority at roughly 10 percent at the time of independence, were mainly laborers on the rubber plantations, railroad workers, and policemen. In short, there was a clear identification between occupation and ethnicity.

Affirmative action policies were designed in the 1960s to promote more Malay participation outside agriculture, but for the most part the private sector of the economy was left relatively free of government regulation. The key economic ministry, the Ministry of Finance, was led by the head of the Malaysian Chinese Association, a partner in the governing alliance, which was led by the United Malay National Organization. The finance minister, Tan Siew Sin, saw an important part of his role as protecting the Chinese community from being pressured to pay taxes to support various investment initiatives that benefited mostly Malays.[13]

This picture changed dramatically on the night of May 13, 1969, when, following elections in which opposition parties (the ones dominated by non-Malay minorities) gained substantially, there were large-scale riots in which hundreds, mostly Malaysian Chinese, were killed. The country that summer was paralyzed, with the streets emptying as soon as it got dark, and there was recognition among virtually all Malaysians that something had to be done to deal with the deep ethnic divisions that the riots had revealed. What was eventually done in response to this situation has fundamentally shaped Malaysian development policy ever since.

The problem was that no one had a clear idea what needed to be done. The leader of the Harvard team of advisors in the Economic Planning Unit, together with two other advisors, met for long hours over lunch during the summer of 1969 at the leader's home, thrashing out what needed to be done. Eventually a paper was produced that formed the starting point for an initial discussion at Fraser's Hill, in the Malaysian highlands, among the leading civil servants of the government about what to do to restore stability and development in the country.[14] The difference between what was written in this paper and what eventually became the New Economic Policy of the Malaysian government is instructive as to what the

Malay leadership saw as what needed to be done. The three Harvard advisors involved saw the problem as being one of Malay poverty. Most Malays made up a majority of the poor in the country and few Malays had the education and skills needed to participate actively in the Malaysian business world. Thus the advisors' paper stressed the importance of more education for the Malays and vigorous enforcement of affirmative action programs to get them experience in various occupations where they were not represented. Since Malays dominated the politics, one did not have to be sensitive about using formal quotas. The key, in our mind, however, was raising the Malays up to be able to compete without killing the "goose that laid the golden eggs," Malaysia's dynamic private sector. The paper also recommended direct efforts to improve the quite unequal income distribution, including a discussion of the need for land reform that would eliminate the large-scale tenancy that prevailed among Malay farmers.

What actually eventually emerged from the many discussions the Malay leaders had among themselves was quite different. There was plenty of affirmative action, but redistribution through land reform never saw the light of day; most of the landlords were Malays. There were quotas everywhere, most notably in the universities, in addition to the civil service and army quotas inherited from the British. But the policy that got the most attention and arguably has had the largest impact on economic performance was the requirement, to be implemented over time, that Malays reach an ownership share in the economy closer to their share in the population. That target was to be achieved by requiring that any expansion by a domestic firm had to include measures to ensure that 30 percent of the endeavor would be owned by Bumiputera. Manufacturing firms that primarily exported their products were excluded because most of them were foreign direct investment enterprises that could easily move elsewhere. The goal of the Malay leadership, therefore, was not so much to reduce income inequality as to erase the identification of race with occupation that had prevailed in Malaysia up to that time. As this is being written (2012), most of the New Economic Policy system introduced in 1969, notably the ownership share, are still in place, although there have been some modifications over the years. To a large degree the identification between race and occupation has been erased, although it remains controversial as to how much of this can be explained by the New Economic Policy system, as contrasted to general efforts to raise education levels and the like.[15] Poverty has been reduced in a major way both among Malays and other groups, but again much of this reduction can be explained by the overall increase in per capita income that resulted from sustained economic growth. Inequality in Malaysia remains at very high levels, with a Gini coefficient of around 0.48.

I place so much emphasis on what happened in 1969 because it has shaped what has happened in economic policies ever since. Much of the industrial development of the 1970s was carried out by foreign investors, mainly Americans and Japanese, who saw Malaysia as a country with relatively good infrastructure and stable market-oriented policies that actively promoted foreign direct investment. Affirmative action was not a problem, because these firms were exempt at the executive level, and at the worker level it turned out that young Bumiputera were perfectly well suited to the requirements of labor-intensive industry. Private domestic firms continued to be mostly Chinese owned, but now they had to think about how the ownership requirement would affect them if they expanded. Thus from the outset, the New Economic Policy, together with other policies designed to promote foreign direct investment, created an industrial structure where most of the internationally competitive industrial firms were foreign owned, while domestically owned, mostly Chinese firms had great difficulty moving up from import substitution to international competitiveness. A part, probably a large part, of the reason for this difficulty was the drag of the ownership policies. Manufactures were a steadily increasing share of Malaysian merchandise exports, rising to 19 percent of the total in 1980 (and to 49 percent by 1989 and 80 percent in 1999 before declining to 54 percent in 2009), but few domestically owned firms were involved.

Beginning in the 1980s, however, the government became much more actively involved in promoting economic policies, including industrial policies. An early indication of this change was the "dawn raid" on the London Stock Exchange, when Malaysian government interests gained majority control of Guthries, a major foreign-owned plantation firm. Of more relevance to this discussion is that in the early 1980s the Malaysian government began to take an active role in the promotion of particular industries, mainly in the heavy industry sector. The leader of this effort was Mahathir Mohamad, who became prime minister in 1981 after having served as deputy prime minister, in which office he had begun to think about and push for a more activist industrial policy.

Mahathir was directly influenced by the Japanese and Korean industrial policy experience. He said so explicitly, and a Japanese businessman was one of his closest advisors. Unlike that of Indonesia, Malaysia's program to develop heavy industries in the 1980s was not a rent-seeking effort. The prime minister felt it was time for Malaysia to develop its own heavy industries and that the government needed to play a major role if that were to happen. Having "one's own" heavy industries in the Malaysian context meant more than that these firms would not be foreign owned; from the government's point of view it meant that Bumiputera had to play a major role in developing and running them. Given that there were virtually no Bumiputera with industrial entrepreneurial experience of any kind, the initial solution was for these enterprises to be state owned, much like the already established oil monopoly, Petronas, and some of the utilities.

The industries chosen for this program had the automobile company Proton in the lead, together with a new steel company, Perwaja Steel, several cement plants, and a number of machinery firms, many of them related to the automobile sector under the Heavy Industries Corporation of Malaysia Berhad, founded in 1980. The government poured large sums into these industries in the early 1980s, initially using the expanded earnings from petroleum created by the second oil price increase generated by OPEC in 1979, but then oil prices came down and the government fiscal deficit ballooned, at one point to over 17 percent of GDP. Malaysia throughout most of its independent history has effectively maintained macroeconomic stability, so this level of deficit led to action by then minister of finance Daim Zainuddin in the mid-1980s to bring the deficit down, in part by cutting back on the Heavy Industries Corporation of Malaysia Berhad investments.

With the exception of the cement plants, none of these heavy industries performed well during the first decade, and the decision was made to privatize them, but it was a privatization with a difference. The ownership shares were to go mainly to Bumiputera, including the unit trusts (mutual funds) set up to manage Bumiputera shares in the private sector.[16] Later the government, through government-controlled banks, would lend large sums to individual Bumiputera entrepreneurs in an explicit effort to create Bumiputera "billionaires" and additional large-scale Bumiputera businesses, although most of these were in sectors such as finance and real estate. The failures of some of these highly leveraged businesses outside the heavy industry sphere contributed to Malaysia becoming one of the victims of the 1997–1998 financial crisis.

There is no question that Prime Minister Mahathir was sincere in pushing for Malaysian heavy industries because he thought it would be a good thing for Malaysia, not because he thought it would benefit him and his family personally. During his time as prime minister he actually spent over a week at a Hyundai automobile plant in Korea to try to learn what could be done to improve the performance of Proton. He could also talk in a systematic and interesting way about a wide variety of high-technology products, as I learned from personal experience. This fascination with high technology led him in later years to promote the high-technology corridor in Malaysia, another state-led industrial development effort.

None of these efforts has yet to produce successful internationally competitive industries on the model of South Korea in the 1970s and 1980s. The cement firms were not a problem but cement involves simple technology and has built-in domestic protection because of the costs of transporting low-price bulk goods. Perwaja steel went from one crisis to the next. The key to success, however, was Proton and its related machinery industries, and Proton has never been internationally competitive. Thanks to protection from imports, Proton has dominated the local market, and unlike so many other automobile companies in developing countries, it was much more than a complete-knockdown-kit operation. But Proton products priced at cost were never internationally competitive, despite three decades trying. By the first decade of the twenty-first century, the world automobile industry itself had been transformed such that a true Malaysian automobile was no longer possible. The automobile sector worldwide had entered into the world of supply chains where parts are made and imported from all over the world, depending on where they can be made best and at lowest cost. Mahathir's successors (he stepped down as prime minister in October 2003) no longer believed in or supported the creation of a Malaysian automobile.

Malaysia's effort to take the lead in information and other high-technology areas has not fared well in the twenty-first century either, although there are high-technology firms in Penang's Bayan Lepas Free Industrial Zone and a few elsewhere. These industries depend critically on highly skilled manpower in engineering and the sciences, and Malaysia's universities do not produce it in large enough numbers, in part because many of the ablest Malaysians in these fields go abroad to study and then do not return home. Their decision not to do so is in part because of the barriers many feel they face if they are not Bumiputera. Malaysian immigration restrictions also place obstacles in the path of domestic firms working in the high-technology field. Silicon Valley would not be the catalyst for new high-technology ideas that it is if the United States had immigration laws similar to those in Malaysia.

While Malaysia's efforts to create its own heavy and high-technology industries have not borne much fruit, the country's economic performance overall has been well above the average of developing countries around the world. Per capita GDP has grown on average at 3.8 per year over a half century, resulting in a sixfold increase in average real per capita GDP, and total GDP has risen at 5.4 percent annually.[17] But if one breaks down the growth, industry from the beginning of the NEP in 1970 to 2000 grew at 8.1 percent per year, while services grew at 7.6 percent annually. After 2000 and through 2010, however, industry slowed dramatically to 2.9 percent per year while services grew at 6.6 percent. As in Indonesia, natural resource rents, averaging 14.6 percent of GDP in 2000–2010, as contrasted to 6 percent in 1970–1972, generated much of the demand that kept services growing fairly rapidly. In fact resource rents have been a large share of GDP ever since the mid-1970s.[18]

Malaysia has some high-technology research, although this is in part due to investments by foreign high-technology firms such as Intel. These large expenditures on heavy industry and high technology may have contained large elements of waste, but Malaysia's natural resource wealth provided the government with more funds than those of many other developing countries, and these funds were not, for the most part, frittered away on sending large parts of the nation's wealth to Swiss banks or on large unsustainable subsidies for the population at large, except for the notable exception of subsidized shares going to Bumiputera. But there is little doubt that the country could have grown faster and would have a higher per capita income today if it had made full use of its domestic human and entrepreneurial resources. The counterargument, and it is a legitimate one, is that the policies pursued may have avoided a political upheaval that would have done more damage to economic development than the New Economic Policy system.

Thailand and the Philippines

Thailand has some features in common with Malaysia, with two central differences. The common features are that Thailand began its development in the second half of the twentieth century, relying heavily on natural resource exports such as rice and hardwoods such as teak. Thailand remains a major exporter of rice to this day, but its hardwood forests have largely been cut down, and Thailand instituted a ban on commercial logging of teak in 1989, in part to preserve what forest remained as protection against major increases in flooding in Northern Thailand caused by deforestation, protection that proved far from adequate in the massive floods of 2012. Manufactures replaced natural resource products as the main source of exports by the 1990s, and a large portion of these manufactures came from foreign-owned firms, with Japanese firms accounting for the largest share, followed by the United States and in recent years the four Asian tigers. The overall economic performance of Thailand has been similar to that of Malaysia and Indonesia, with per capita GDP rising eightfold at 4.4 percent annually for the half century beginning in 1960, increasing from a very low level in 1960 to over $7,600 per capita in PPP terms (in 2005 prices) in 2011. This growth rate was well below that of the four tigers during their peak growth periods but well above that of most other developing countries.

Thailand has never had a leader who focused on industrial policy in the manner of Park Chung Hee or Mahathir Mohamad. Macroeconomic policy under the alternating civilian- and military-led governments was generally in the hands of technocrats and was conservatively managed. Bloodless coups were the main way governments changed. This political process began to change in more recent years as elections played an increasing role in choosing government leaders, but nondemocratic methods of changing the government continue to be used. The domestic economy, outside agriculture and the foreign direct investment firms, was dominated by ethnic Chinese in Bangkok, together with military and other politically connected figures. Corruption was and is widespread, with Thailand ranked 88th on Transparency International's 2012 Corruption Perception Index, about halfway between Malaysia (60) and Indonesia (100).

Partial democratization has been accompanied by, if anything, lower economic performance, although the one may or may not have caused the other. There was essentially no growth in per capita income between 1996 and 2002 other than the recovery from the deep trough Thailand dug itself into in 1997–1998. Since 2002, when the per capita income of 1996 was recovered, per capita GDP growth has averaged 3.6 percent per year. The reasons for the earlier slowdown are readily apparent. In 1997 Thailand was the lead country in starting the Asian and global financial crisis of 1997–1998. Thailand had a bubble economy based on heavy borrowing abroad by investors without hedging for foreign exchange risk. The government attempted to maintain an overvalued exchange rate because devaluation would, and soon did, lead to widespread bankruptcies in major sectors of the economy, including among the politically well connected. Thailand lacked sufficient foreign exchange reserves to sustain the overvalued exchange rate, the resulting devaluation was precipitous, and the economy was driven into a severe recession. This process was repeated in Malaysia, Indonesia, and Korea. In short, Thailand by the late 1990s no longer had a conservative macroeconomic policy, and it paid a substantial price as a result.

The longer term problem that accounts for the economic slowdown in the second half of the first decade of the twenty-first century is that Thailand's political stability has also been undermined. Ever since the end of World War II, Thailand has been ruled by a constitutional and highly popular monarch, but King Bumibol Adulyadej turned 85 in 2012, so there was uncertainty connected with the succession to a much less popular crown prince. More important, however, was that there was a deep division in the country. Unlike Malaysia and Indonesia, this division was not on ethnic or religious grounds. Thailand had a substantial ethnic Chinese minority (10–12 percent of the population), and as already pointed out, that minority dominated much of the business sector, particularly in Bangkok. In the late 1940s and 1950s that minority was seen by many as an alien group, and Thailand passed a number of laws designed to restrict it in various ways.[19] Several decades later, however, most ethnic Chinese in Thailand, unlike in Malaysia or Indonesia, had fully integrated into Thai society and were accepted as such.

The deep division in Thai society lay elsewhere. It was in the divide between the more prosperous urban population of Bangkok and the much less prosperous population in the rest of the country, particularly in the rural areas. The form this division took at the start of the twenty-first century was an election of the populist prime minister Thaksin Shinawatra, who, although personally wealthy, built his base on the disaffected majority, the "red shirts," as they were sometimes called because of the shirts they wore during demonstrations designed to paralyze Bangkok. The Bangkok elite in turn used nondemocratic methods to depose Shinawatra and replace him with one of their own. The result was off-and-on instability, which discouraged investors, particularly foreign investors, and together which natural disasters such as the floods of 2011 slowed growth.

There is a division in Philippine society that has some features in common with Thailand's, although this division's origins are different. As in Thailand there is a Chinese minority in the Philippines, although formally ethnic Chinese constitute only 1 percent of the population. Chinese in the Philippines, however, have intermarried with Filipino groups for generations and are fully integrated into Philippine society (President Corazon Aquino is an example). The division in the Philippines is more between a large poor majority who vote for well-known populist figures (and some of whom supported a Communist-led rebellion in earlier years) and an oligarchy dating to Spanish colonial rule who have controlled the government and much of the economy for most of the time since the Philippines gained independence from the United States in 1945. For twenty-one of those years (1965–1986), Ferdinand Marcos served as president of the republic.

For the four decades that began with independence and ended with the fall of President Marcos, the Philippines followed a fairly conventional import-substituting policy. Manufacturing was a quarter of GDP, but manufacturing exports did not pass 25 percent of total merchandise exports until after Marcos's fall. Corruption and crime were a serious problem before Marcos became president, and corruption accelerated during his long authoritarian rule. During his rule GDP per capita grew at less than 1 percent per year, and at the end of that rule the Philippines had a large international debt, its banks were loaded up with nonperforming loans and had to be recapitalized, and GDP per capita had fallen, in 1985, by nearly one-fifth from its high point in 1982. Transparency International was not yet publishing indexes of corruption during the Marcos years, but in 2011 the Philippines ranked way down at number 129, although it rose significantly to 105 in 2012, and there is little doubt that corruption was more pervasive during the Marcos years.

There is little point in this study of East Asian growth of dwelling on the Marcos years. There was no coherent effort to develop the economy at that time; rent seeking was the norm. This did not make the Philippines unique among developing countries—in fact extractive governments and elites are a major reason for poor economic performance around the world as Acemoglu and Robinson argue[20]—but it also means that there is little to learn from its experience of that time that is not patently obvious. Suharto and his family may have generated as many rents for themselves as did the Marcos family, but Suharto presided over a government that had a coherent development policy, and for long periods that policy was carried out with positive results. Nothing comparable happened under President Marcos.

With the overthrow of Marcos, the Philippines returned to the politics of the pre-Marcos era in many respects, but economic policies did change. The first years under President Aquino were difficult ones, and per capita GDP stopped falling, but it did not rise much either. Since that time, despite the continuing threat of a coup and the political instability surrounding the removal, using the legal system, of the one elected populist president, GDP growth per capita has accelerated. From the time President Aquino left office in 1992 until the eve of the global recession that began in 2008, per capita GDP grew at 2.3 percent per year, well below what was achieved in Malaysia, Indonesia, and Thailand but above average in worldwide developing country terms. Manufacturing grew along with the rest of the economy, but more important, the Philippines opened to the outside world, and manufactures by the twenty-first century dominated Philippine exports, although services such as international call centers also made a contribution. In addition, a substantial portion of the country's labor force worked abroad, sending back large remittances that contributed in a major way to the country's foreign exchange earnings. There is much more to the Philippine development story of recent years than this, but treating that story in depth is not essential for the basic argument of this book.[21]

Summing Up the Southeast Asian Experience

The economic growth and industrial development experience of Southeast Asia has been different in important ways from that of Northeast Asia. Like early development in Northeast Asia, the most successful economic and industrial performances in Southeast Asia were generated by policies that promoted the rapid development of internationally competitive labor-intensive industries. This was clearly the case in Indonesia but was also true of Malaysia, Thailand, and even the Philippines (but only during the last two decades in the Philippines). Malaysia and Thailand have also made some progress in moving up to more sophisticated industries, many of them foreign owned, but government initiatives have had little to do with these developments. The major government initiatives to promote heavy industries in Indonesia and Malaysia were largely failures. The failures in Indonesia were first of all due to using these industries to promote opportunities for rents, but even in Indonesia part of the problem was that the country did not yet have an adequate foundation for such industries. This was clearly the case with the effort to develop commercial aircraft but is also part of the explanation for other high-cost producers who required protection from imports. Indonesia's human capital had advanced beyond its abysmal level at the time of independence but was far short of what heavy and high-technology industries require. In Malaysia, rent seeking was not a major goal of industrial policy, except in the sense that politics dictated that government initiatives be mainly oriented toward supporting Bumiputera interests, and Bumiputera as a group were the least well equipped in the engineering and other skills needed by a sector as complex as automobile manufacture. The problems with Malaysia's high-technology corridor can also be partly attributed to the weaknesses in the education system at the tertiary level and the fact that so many Malaysians who have studied abroad have stayed abroad.[22]

In Korea and Taiwan it is likely that the poor performance of heavy industry initiatives would have led quickly to the abandonment of the program, largely because neither economy could afford massive failures either in economic or political terms. The contrast with Indonesia and Malaysia in this respect is not just that they were not subject to being taken over by a hostile power. It was also the fact that both countries had relatively rich natural resources, and oil revenues in particular could be used to subsidize these large-scale heavy industry projects. As pointed out earlier, econometric and other studies have shown that being rich in natural resources on average leads to lower economic growth performance. Indonesia and Malaysia are concrete examples of why this is often the case, even though both countries managed their oil wealth better than the majority of developing countries with rich mineral resources.

The other part of the Southeast Asian story is that politics remains a problem whereas in Northeast Asia (leaving aside North Korea) for the most part that is not the case. The extreme case is the closing of society and repression in Myanmar from 1962 through 2010 and in earlier times the impact of war in Indo-China and the repression and massive corruption in the Marcos Philippines. But even the more successful economies of Southeast Asia have had periods when political instability has slowed growth for a time. That was certainly the case with the downfall of President Suharto and the years of the difficult transition to democracy that followed. It is also true, in Thailand and the Philippines, with their deep divisions in society between the more prosperous groups and the large, much poorer populations who support populist leaders. In Malaysia, and to a lesser degree elsewhere in Southeast Asia, the division between the large Chinese minority and the Bumiputera majority has made it impossible to carry out development policies where qualifications and merit are the sole basis for success. There are also divisions in the societies of South Korea (between the residents of the Kyongsang and Cholla provinces for example) and Taiwan (between mainlanders and Taiwanese), and these divisions have a major influence in elections, but they have had a limited impact on most economic policies.

The comparisons in this study are between the economies of Northeast and Southeast Asia, and in that context Northeast Asia has fared better than Southeast Asia. But if one compares much of Southeast Asia with developing countries in general, it has performed, at least in large part, far above the average. I have stressed the problems some of these economies have encountered, but overall Southeast Asia has been an integral part of the great structural transformation in income, poverty reduction, industrial development, and urbanization that has taken place throughout Northeast and Southeast Asia.

—5—

From Command to Market Economy in China and Vietnam

The accelerated transformation of the economies of Northeast Asia together, with the less dramatic but still large transformation of four economies in Southeast Asia, was a historic event, one of the most significant achievements of the second half of the twentieth century. It involved a fivefold-to-ninefold increase in the average per capita income of economies supporting 537 million people (2009), many more than live in the United States and Canada, and similar to the total population of the 27 countries of the European Union (501 million in 2010). In terms of the welfare of the world's population, the fifteenfold increase in the per capita income of China's 1.3 billion people during the last two decades of the twentieth century and the first decade of the twenty-first (2010/1978) is of even greater significance. Because of China's rise, roughly half of the people of the world now live in economies where the average income of the population is substantially closer to that of the high-income countries than it is to the low-income countries, which prior to World War II included all of the countries of Asia except for Japan.[1]

The question to be addressed first here is whether China has achieved this transformation following a path very similar to that of the other successful developers in East Asia or whether there are fundamental differences. I will also ask a similar question about Vietnam, since its experience in many ways parallels that of China, although in some respects it fits better with the Southeast Asian experience.

China (and Vietnam) started their economic boom from a very different point from the other economies in East Asia. Both were command economies patterned on the Soviet system. Market forces played only a minor role, mainly in the retail sales of secondary consumer goods. All industrial inputs

122

and most outputs were allocated by administrative means through government channels or through informal arrangements between individual state-owned enterprises. Major consumer goods such as grain were allocated using ration coupons. Who got what was decided by thousands of central planners in the State Planning Commission. The financial system, with a monobank that included both central bank and commercial bank functions, was structured for the primary purpose of monitoring and enforcing the central plan. The plan targets had the force of law, but since there were so many targets it was impossible to construct a consistent set, so enterprise managers had to use their own judgment as to which targets mattered more than others.

This system makes most sense in a wartime economy, and the original model the Soviet Union learned from was Germany in World War I. In wartime, military procurement planners do not decide how many tanks or fighter planes they need and then raise the price of those items and hope that private entrepreneurs respond. They order the enterprises, whether private or public, to restructure so that they can provide whatever the military requires. These orders are backed up by law, patriotism, and social pressure on the unpatriotic.

In a very real sense, China, the Soviet Union, and Vietnam were all wartime economies when this system was first adopted. The Soviet Union in the 1930s and 1940s faced the threat and then the reality of German invasion. China fought the United States in Korea from 1950 through 1953 and then faced an embargo on trade with most market economies after 1953 until it was removed in the late 1960s. Vietnam, of course, was involved in an all-out war on its own territory off and on from the time of regaining its independence from France (formally recognized internationally in 1954) and 1975 and then also faced an embargo against trade with most market economies until the early 1990s. Equally or more important than the requirements of war was the development model that China, like the Soviet Union, believed in: one that minimized dependence on foreign trade (they followed a closed economy development strategy); so it was important they develop their own heavy industry or investment goods sector (steel, machinery, etc.) as quickly as possible. Because China's industry in 1949–1950 focused on labor-intensive consumer goods industries, mostly textiles, and included little heavy industry, radically changing the structure of industry to favor machinery and steel would have been difficult using market methods. The conversion to a centrally planned command economy thus made some sense.

It is also useful to remember that the Soviet command economy in the 1950s was not the stagnating, inefficient entity it appeared to be in the 1980s. In the 1950s the Soviet Union was transforming itself into a military superpower, and its economy was one of the most rapidly growing in the world. It was not just China that attempted to adopt the Soviet model; Indian economic policy was also heavily influenced by it. China and particularly Mao Zedong, however, were never fully satisfied with the Soviet model. It was too centralized for Mao's taste, so he attempted to accelerate development by relying on his political mobilization skills, and the disastrous Great Leap Forward was the result. The collapse of the Chinese economy in 1959–1961 and the accompanying famine with its 30 million deaths, however, did not lead anyone in the Chinese leadership to reject the centrally planned command model of development. The Chinese leadership, when it was acting coherently and not in the grip of the Cultural Revolution (1966–1976), tried to improve efficiency with various forms of decentralization, none of which involved significant reliance on market forces. In Vietnam, after the war ended in 1975 and the country was reunified, the leadership attempted to impose the Soviet-type model of the north on the market economy of the south, with poor economic results for both the north and south. When I first visited Hanoi in January 1989, there were very few shops, and the shelves in them were mostly empty. We were told that only a year earlier one could see many suffering from severe malnutrition on the streets of the city.

The motivation for a change in the approach to development in China in 1978 was very different from what motivated the leaders of South Korea and Taiwan in the early 1960s. The Chinese motivation was also very different from what occurred a decade later in eastern Europe. To begin with, unlike eastern Europe, where local Communist Parties were removed from control of governments, in China after Mao Zedong passed from the scene in 1976 and most of those who shared his political views at the time were removed from office, the Chinese Communist Party remained intact and in control. Unlike the leaders in South Korea and Taiwan, those who returned to power in China were not faced with the danger of the collapse of their political and economic system. China was faced with a possible invasion from the Soviet Union, but that had little to do with the desire for a change in the economic system. Many in the Chinese leadership were also not necessarily that dissatisfied with the centrally planned command system itself. Chen Yun, the second most powerful nonmilitary leader after 1978 and an economic specialist, wanted to retain the main features of the command economy well into the 1980s. What the leaders were dissatisfied with was the performance of the economy over the previous two decades. Officially the real growth rate from 1957 through 1978 is to this day reported as being 5.4 percent per year or 3.4 percent per capita per year,[2] hardly a weak performance justifying abandonment of the entire economic system. In reality, the growth rate with price distortions removed was much lower, at 3.9 percent or 2.0 percent per capita, and the actual improvement in the living standards of the population grew substantially more slowly than that or hardly at all.[3] Most of the increase in GDP went to an increase in the rate of investment, much of which involved producing obsolete machines to produce more obsolete machines. Because China was closed off and had closed itself off from many of the advances in world technology, both in the civilian and military spheres, it was falling further behind potential rivals even in the military sphere.

There were two positive elements in the Chinese economy on the eve of reform in 1978. There was little inflation, and China had already reoriented its international trade from the planned economies of the Soviet Comecon trading system. Chinese trade mostly involved the sale of manufactures, agricultural products, and natural resource products to market economies. Vietnam, in contrast, on the eve of reform (the key Vietnamese political leadership changes were in 1986, but the economic reforms themselves really began in 1989) had a very high level of inflation, over 60 percent per year in 1989 and 1990,[4] and its foreign trade had almost entirely been with the Soviet Bloc and had been subsidized by the Soviet Union. The subsidies ended, Comecon disappeared in 1991, and with the freeing of eastern Europe from Soviet Control Vietnam faced a potentially very serious economic crisis. Whereas the embargo by Western economies toward China had been lifted in 1971, the embargo in Vietnam was still very much in force.

The First Phase of China's Economic Reforms

Given the situation in China in the late 1970s, it is not surprising that the leadership did not immediately set out to create a radically different economy. The history of these reforms has been written about in hundreds of articles and books, so this chapter will only briefly describe these reforms' key features and how they fit into the broader East Asian and general experience of the transition from socialism around the world.[5]

China did not start out from the beginning to create a market economy or to copy its East Asian neighbors. The turn outward of the economy actually began in 1977, when enterprises were told they were free to purchase needed technology from abroad after decades in which reliance on foreign technology was a guarantee that one would be vigorously criticized or worse by the radical left. The only problem was that to import large amounts of equipment from abroad one needed the foreign exchange to pay for it, and Chinese exports provided only US$7.6 billion in 1977, as contrasted to the US$600 billion in imports that one Hong Kong firm estimated Chinese enterprises had signed letters of intent to purchase. Initially China had hopes that the discovery of large reserves of offshore oil would provide at least some of the needed foreign exchange, but initial exploratory efforts proved disappointing. China thus faced a choice not unlike that of South Korea in the early 1960s. China did not have sufficient natural resources or a large agricultural surplus to pay for the imports needed to fuel rapid economic development.

That left manufactures as a source of exports, and only China's light industrial products, notably textiles, were internationally competitive. So China set out, ultimately with great success, to promote the export of labor-intensive consumer manufactures. In 1978 China's exports of manufactures were US$3.6 billion. Only six years later in 1984, exports of industrial products had risen to US$14.2 billion, or 54 percent of total exports of US$26.1 billion. Compared with China's industrial exports of 2010 of US$1,496.2 billion (or 95 percent of total exports of US$1,577.9 billion) these figures from the early 1980s appear small.[6] But by raising exports more than threefold in only six years, China had the foreign exchange it needed for critical imports.

There were two major reasons why China could achieve rapid growth in manufactured exports despite decades of trying to minimize dependence on foreign trade. One was the fact that China already had some experience with exporting to market economies, as mentioned earlier, albeit mainly through the planned economy approach of the Guangzhou Trade Fair. The other was that Hong Kong could and did step in with the missing knowledge of Western markets, with their emphasis on quality and style. By 1984 Hong Kong took 27.5 percent of total Chinese exports, retaining a little over half and reexporting the rest, and these figures do not include the involvement of Hong Kong firms in export from China that did not go through Hong Kong for reexport. By 1989, 48 percent of Chinese exports went to or through Hong Kong.[7]

The other major reform of the immediate post-1978 period was the elimination of collective agriculture (the Rural People's Communes and their brigade and team subsidiaries) and the return to an agricultural system based mainly on household production.[8] This was more a bottom-up than a top-down process, although both were involved. It began with decisions to allow the poorest agricultural regions to return to household farming, since this had helped China recover from the 1959–1961 famine, although support for this earlier effort was one of the major charges leveled during the Cultural Revolution by the leftists against Deng Xiaoping. The popularity of the measure among farmers (although not so much among political cadres, who feared being labeled rightists and purged) led to the rapid spread of the transfer of land use rights to households. When some officials balked at what was happening, Deng quietly used his power to let the process continue, and by 1984 the household system, called the "household responsibility system," was in place throughout the country. Farmers still did not own their land, and land ownership rules were still being worked out more than a quarter of a century later, but the basic incentive system in agriculture was radically changed.

What happened throughout the country as a result of this transformation of the rural scene surprised most people, including me. I had been forecasting in print since 1981 that China's GDP growth rate was likely to rise to 6–8 percent per year, as a result of reforms, from the much lower rate of the prereform period, but I thought most of this growth would be generated by industry, not agriculture.[9] It was clear that there were incentive problems in Chinese agriculture, and these manifested themselves most dramatically in 1958–1959 during the first phase of the commune system, when centralization of farm management to a unit with over 5,000 families contributed in a major way to the resulting crop failures and famine. But the worst incentive problems had been dealt with by returning the basic agricultural production unit to the production team, a unit of around 20 families. Thus few anticipated that a return to household agriculture would lead to a 52.5 percent jump in agricultural output (a real rate of growth in agriculture of 7 percent a year in both value-added and gross value terms over the 1979–1984 period). Rural net income actually increased much more than this (by 149.5 percent or 16.5 percent per year) because prices paid to farmers rose substantially and far more rapidly than the rise in prices paid by rural residents. Farmers were to some degree also allowed to switch to production of more lucrative crops, although much land still was required to be planted in grain crops.

The increase in agricultural output between 1978 and 1984 involved much more than just an improvement in household production incentives. Farm purchase prices, as already mentioned, rose (the big jump was in 1979, when the agricultural purchase price rose by 22.1 percent).[10] There were major increases in the production and use of chemical fertilizer, from 8.84 million tons in 1978 (roughly 74 kilograms per hectare) to 17.4 million tons in 1984 (roughly 145 kilograms per hectare). Rural use of electric power also rose from 25.3 billion kilowatt hours in 1978 to 46.4 billion kilowatt hours in 1984.[11] The amount of land irrigated, however, did not rise at all during this period, if the data are accurate. Efforts to measure the different contributions to agricultural growth in this period estimate that TFP accounted for roughly half of the rise while capital, labor, and increased intermediate inputs accounted for the rest.[12] The rise in TFP is presumably caused by improved incentives, better management practices, and perhaps some improvements in plant varieties used and other technological innovations, although there is no completely reliable way of measuring the specific contributions of each of these elements.

In many ways the most important contributions of the opening of the economy to foreign trade, together with the return to household agriculture, was that these reforms were dramatically successful, resulting in immediate improvements in the standard of living of the population and the productivity of industry and agriculture. This success gave enormous credibility to the reformers and laid the groundwork for extending the radical reform process into areas that were more controversial within the Chinese Communist Party.[13] The first major move into the urban industrial sphere (other than the increasing use of imported inputs and sale of manufactured exports) began in October 1984. The 1984 reform document began the process that was to end the era of the centrally planned command economy and replace it with market forces. The first step was to free up the prices of industrial inputs, but to do so with a dual-price system where existing state-owned enterprises could continue to receive inputs at the old state-set (and low) prices while everyone else would buy their inputs on the market at market prices.[14] This dual-price system would lead to a number of major problems, but it solved an important and more immediate political problem by ensuring that no powerful group had to suffer because of the reforms, what has been called "reform without losers."[15]

The freeing up of industrial inputs and many other products was designed in part to be included in a package of reforms that would improve the performance of China's state-owned enterprises. At the time there were no truly private enterprises, although there were many rural and ur-ban "collective" enterprises that in 1984 accounted for 30 percent of the gross value of industrial output. The dual-price reform had limited impact on the state-owned enterprises. They increased their growth rate slightly from the first six years of reform (7.0 percent per year from the end of 1978 through 1984) to the next five years after the price reforms were intro-duced (9.3 percent per year from the end of 1984 through 1989), and as long as they could access inputs at state prices, most ran a profit. The con-trast was with collective industrial enterprises that were relabeled town-ship and village enterprises (*xiangzhen qiye*). These grew in 1984 alone by 34.9 percent and after 1984 at a rate of 22.3 percent a year through 1989, as contrasted to a substantial but much slower rate of 12.3 percent from the end of 1978 through 1983.[16]

The boom in township and village enterprises has long puzzled many economists and others because it appears to contradict the view that well-established property rights are essential for the kind of growth that oc-curred in these enterprises in the 1980s and 1990s. Formally they were collectively owned, with close ties to the local governments where they were situated, but in practice they behaved much like private enterprises, despite having weak formal property rights, and much later most of them were privatized.[17] My own view is that local townships and even villages had substantial implicit rights over their property, as long as local govern-ment leaders and enterprise leaders were working on the same broad wavelength in a mutually beneficial relationship. Higher levels of govern-ment did not normally attempt to take ownership of these enterprises away from the locality, except when a major initiative of the central government (the building of the Three Gorges Dam for example) was involved.[18] Later in the 1990s and particularly after 2000, the interests of local governments and the local populations they governed often diverged, although mostly over agricultural land ownership rights rather than enterprise ownership. The result was land disputes, land transfers involving local government abuses of the previous "owners," and considerable popular resistance. As contrasted to going to the courts, popular resistance became the preferred mechanism of many in enforcing their property rights, but that was long after the 1980s.

During this second phase of reform (1985–1988) GDP growth acceler-ated from the high 9.2 percent annual rate of 1979–1984 to an extraordi-nary 11.3 percent annual rate in 1985–1988. By 1988 and 1989, however, some of the side effects of these reforms and the high growth rate were beginning to be felt and to raise political issues, both in the general population and among the leadership. Most apparent to the general population was that inflation accelerated. Consumer prices rose at a rate of 7.7 percent a year in 1985–1988 and then jumped to 18.4 percent per year in 1988–1989. These rates were not particularly high in comparison to what occurred in the early decades of growth elsewhere in East Asia. South Korean urban consumer prices during the high-growth period between 1967 and the end of the Park Chung Hee era in 1980 averaged 15.5 percent a year.[19] But Chinese prices had not risen that rapidly since the famine year of 1961. The average rate of consumer price increase in the first phase of reform through 1984 averaged only 3.1 percent per year, and the rate prior to that in the 1960s and 1970s was effectively 0 percent per year. (Prices were fixed by the government, and inflationary pressures, when they existed, manifested themselves in other ways.) In 1989 many in the general population and in the Communist Party leadership still remembered the hyperinflation of the 1940s that had done so much to undermine Guomindang Party rule and bring about the victory of the Communist forces in 1949.[20]

The other side effect that had a negative political impact was rising corruption fueled in part by the dual-price system. Anyone with the right political connections could use them to obtain goods at the low state-set price and then could turn around and sell them on the market at a much higher price and pocket the difference. No one knows how much money was made by individuals in this way, but dual pricing and other areas of state control (the issuing of licenses for new companies and projects for example) provided ample opportunity for rent seeking by officials, some of it perfectly legal. Financial rent seeking or corruption of this kind was either unknown or well hidden in the prereform period, although many other kinds of abuse of power were rampant. The market reforms got the blame for this "new" phenomenon, although it would be more accurate to say that it was the continuing interference of the state in the operation of the market that created these rent-seeking opportunities.

Rising prices and increasing financial corruption probably did not cause the student political movement of the first half of 1989 but contributed to a general sense among many, including the students, that reforms were a source of problems as well as successes. The decision to crush the student movement on June 4, 1989, was driven mainly by a fear on the part of an elderly leadership that the Communist Party was losing control of the country,[21] but the resulting change in leadership also brought to power many who opposed one or another major aspect of the economic reforms. The inflation rate was brought down to 3.3 percent in 1990 and 1991, and efforts to introduce new economic reforms ground to a halt. Two of the most influential reform think tanks were either disbanded or absorbed into long-established and more conservative government bureaucracies. The booming township and village enterprises came under attack from those close to the large state enterprises, in part on the grounds that they were getting special privileges that made it difficult for the state enterprises to compete. These criticisms of the township and village enterprises, however, began to fade when the leadership realized that most of the increase in nonagricultural employment had come from them, not from the state sector. There were also political attacks on the special economic zones, notably Shenzhen, for fostering undesirable political and social activities. The GDP growth rate in 1989 and 1990 fell to 4.1 percent per year.

It is an interesting question what would have happened if this conservative reaction to the reforms of the 1980s had been sustained. A return to the system before 1978 was not very likely, and certainly not in agriculture or in the opening of the economy to foreign trade. But a reimposition of tighter central planning was a real possibility in the urban industrial sphere, an economic system where the market was clearly subordinate to the planners. Such a system might have produced economic growth rapid enough to keep the people in general and those influential in the Party satisfied for a time, say a growth rate of 6 percent per year.

Deng Xiaoping's Tour of the South and the Economic Reforms of the 1990s

But what might have been with a conservative government in power did not happen, because Deng Xiaoping took it on himself to reverse the conservative slowdown of reform in 1992. In his eighty-eighth year of life Deng made a tour of southern China, visiting and praising some of the reform icons of the 1980s, including Shenzhen. As with his support for then premier Zhao Ziyang in the early 1980s, he clearly sided with efforts to fundamentally transform the nature of the economic system against those, notably Chen Yun, who basically wanted to use the market mainly as a way of ameliorating many of the inefficiencies of the command economy while retaining the core features of central planning. As one Chinese friend of mine said at the time, "the good news is that Deng has reversed the conservative reaction and made it possible again to pursue vigorous reform. The bad news is that we had to wait for Deng to act before we could go ahead."

It was not that Deng himself had a clear vision of what needed to be done in the economic sphere.[22] Deng was a brilliant strategist in military and geopolitical affairs. In the three meetings with Deng in which I was a participant, he could talk at length and in detail on the strategic consequences of everything from the possible breakup of Pakistan to the military gains and weaknesses of China's punitive invasion of Vietnam in 1979.[23] When it came to economic issues connected with U.S.-China economic relations, however, he generally turned to his aides to provide comment. What Deng did know is that, like some of the nineteenth-century Chinese reformers, he wanted China to be wealthy and powerful, and he was prepared to back anyone who could produce that result. In the 1980s it was Zhao Ziyang, and in the 1990s it became Jiang Zemin and Zhu Rongji.

By 1993 the economic boom had begun again with a vengeance. In 1993 and 1994 GDP growth averaged 13.5 percent a year, but inflation also accelerated to 19.3 percent a year. China's banking system had been changed from a Soviet-style monobank system where the functions of the commercial banks and the central bank were combined in one institution. The main role of this kind of bank is to monitor and enforce the central plan, and it is the central planners who are responsible for controlling the money supply and inflation. China in the 1980s had separated out the central bank as an institution and created four large commercial banks so that on paper the banking system was similar to that found in most market economies. In reality, the commercial banks continued to behave like branches of the old monobank in that they largely lent to whomever the local political leadership told them to.[24] The result was that when the government relaxed controls on lending and investments by the state enterprises, their investment boomed, bank lending expanded rapidly to accommodate the boom, the central bank accommodated the commercial banks by allowing the money supply to expand (M2 grew by an average of 36 percent per year in 1993 and 1994), and inflation took off. The inflation was curtailed by putting a powerful and decisive figure in charge of the central bank, then deputy premier Zhu Rongji, who imposed quotas on lending by the banks and lowered the growth rate of the money supply.

Ending inflation, however, did not fundamentally change the behavior of the commercial banks or of the state enterprises that were their major clients. Politically driven lending by the mid-1990s had led to a steady accumulation of nonperforming assets on the banks' books—by some outside estimates as much as 40 percent of total bank assets. Even the official figures indicated that a quarter of bank assets were nonperforming.[25] Some suggested that this was likely to lead to a major financial crisis and economic collapse, but that was never in the cards. The banks' liabilities were all owed to domestic depositors and were denominated in renminbi, and that meant that the government could always refinance the banks if necessary by printing money. Allowing the banks to fail and having depositors lose their savings would have been political suicide for the leadership, so it was not going to happen. Over time the government refinanced the banks by various means, bringing their nonperforming assets down to a sustainable level (2 or 3 percent), although the four asset management corporations formed to take over the bad assets would at some point also have to be refinanced or liquidated and their losses absorbed by the government.

The real challenge, however, was to change bank behavior so that banks made loans mainly on commercial criteria, but that was difficult to do unless one also changed the behavior of the state-owned enterprises that were doing most of the borrowing. Between them the state-owned enterprises and state-owned banks had considerable political influence, and they continued to invest and expand, often for the sake of expansion whether or not the investment was likely to be profitable. Senior government officials could and did order them to change their behavior, and efforts were made to separate bank lending from local political pressures, but none of these efforts worked well in the 1990s.[26] Many state-owned enterprises by this time were losing money as the dual-price system disappeared and market prices gradually revealed the losses of those that up to that point had depended on subsidized prices for profitability. In 1996, for example, state-owned enterprises in 22 of 38 industrial sectors were running losses overall. Petroleum, tobacco processing, and electric power, all state monopolies, accounted for virtually all of the net profits in industry as a whole.[27] The loss-making enterprises, however, continued to borrow to cover their losses, even though there was little prospect of being able to repay the loans.

It was in this context that the government, led by Zhu Rongji with the support of President Jiang Zemin and others, outmaneuvered the state-owned enterprises and brought about what arguably was one of the two most important economic reforms of the late 1990s. The vehicle was China's efforts to join the WTO. China had been attempting to join the WTO for many years. A major sticking point was that China wanted to be treated as a developing country, which would allow it to retain a number of trade and investment restrictions, whereas the United States and Europe insisted that China join only after accepting the full panoply of free trade rules that governed trade between the high-income members of the WTO. The debate made little progress because China was unwilling to give up many of its controls over trade and investment and the West was unwilling to treat China as a developing country, largely because China was already one of the largest trading nations in the world, with exports by the end of the decade approaching US$200 billion and doubling every four to five years throughout the 1990s.

In April 1999 Premier Zhu Rongji made an official trip to the United States and met with President Bill Clinton and Treasury Secretary Robert Rubin in the White House. At that meeting Zhu in effect offered that China would accept most of the terms for entry into the WTO that the United States was insisting on, a major change in the Chinese negotiating position. Because of political concerns associated with the opposition of many in Congress to any trade deal with China, however, Clinton and Rubin did not take China up on its offer. When Zhu left Washington and went on to his next major event, a speech to a large business group in Denver, he outlined what he had offered to Clinton. The U.S. business community then began to make calls to the White House that, to paraphrase, argued that the U.S. administration was crazy not to accept this offer, it was better than anything the business community could have hoped for. By the time Zhu got to Boston and then to Canada, the U.S. administration had changed its position and agreed to negotiate, largely on the basis of the Zhu proposal. A year and half later, after negotiations, mainly with the United States and the European Union, had concluded, the WTO membership in November 2001 unanimously voted to approve China's entry into that body.

Why did the senior leadership take this dramatic step at this time? It was certainly not popular at home with many powerful interests, notably those with ties to the state-owned enterprises. Membership in the WTO did make it easier to deal with foreign complaints about China's trade practices, particularly the ones that were driven more by politics in the complaining country than any real trade violation. These complaints could be turned over to a WTO body that would decide them on their technical merits, not politics. But China by the late 1990s did not really need this change in order to promote its exports. China had what were then called "most favored nation" agreements with most of its trading partners that effectively guaranteed that its exports would receive the same treatment as most other countries' exports. The most likely answer to this question is that China saw membership in the WTO as a way to bring pressure for reform on the state-owned enterprises and on China's economic system more generally. Well before China had joined the WTO, one government statement after another warned Chinese enterprises and organizations that the WTO was coming and most of the protection they enjoyed from foreign competition was going to disappear. By signing a treaty with the world economic system, China was tying its own hands when it came to protecting its industries and financial institutions. Enterprises could lobby, but the government would be powerless to act. There were ways around some of the WTO rules to be sure, but these were difficult to carry out in practice.

Perhaps the most dramatic reform, which began before Zhu Rongji's 1999 trip but was accelerated by anticipated WTO membership, was the decision to force the state-owned enterprises to jettison their large numbers of surplus workers. During this period 30 million or more regular employees of the state enterprises were let go. Some were retired, others were transferred to lower paying jobs outside the enterprise, and some of the rest received compensation or welfare payments if the enterprise could afford it. Many could not. Loss-making enterprises were either closed down or merged with more successful enterprises. The political risk connected with laying off 30 million workers was substantial but the government succeeded in reversing the steady trend that saw state enterprise losses balloon as state-set prices and subsidies were replaced by market prices and no subsidies. Many of the state enterprises had effective monopolies in their domestic market (the state oil companies among others) so the rising profits after the year 2000 indicate more than improvements in efficiency, but there was no question that state enterprises overall were performing much better than they had been.[28]

Accelerating Foreign Direct Investment

The other major change in the 1990s was not the result of a particular dramatic policy initiative similar to Zhu Rongji's WTO initiative. It was more that policies that had gradually been put in place beginning in the early

1980s began to bear large-scale payoffs in the 1990s. China had rejected foreign direct investment outright prior to 1978, but it was accepted in principle with the opening of the economy to the outside world after 1978.

Acceptance in principle did not lead to much foreign direct investment in practice. The total amount of foreign direct investment actually utilized from 1979 through 1989 was only US$17.2 billion or US$1.6 billion per year. Furthermore, most of this investment came from Hong Kong and went mostly to Guangdong Province next door. In 1986, for example, Hong Kong and Macao accounted for US$1.32 billion of a total of actually utilized foreign direct investment of US$2.24 billion, and US$863 million of this amount was used in Guangdong Province.[29] The largest European investors in contrast, France, Germany, and Italy, taken together only invested US$100 million while Japanese firms invested US$263 million and U.S. firms (mainly oil companies) invested US$326 million.

The reason for this low level of investment and the dominance of Hong Kong firms was that China had provided none of the supporting rules and institutions required by the large multinational companies of the West and Japan. The large multinationals were used to signing contracts negotiated by lawyers and backed in part by the legal system and laws of the country receiving the investment. But China had abolished the legal profession during the Cultural Revolution and was only beginning to rebuild it in the 1980s. The laws governing foreign investment were themselves opaque, where they existed at all. In effect each investor had to negotiate the rules governing its operations, typically with local officials. Enforcement of the rules depended on personal relationships between investors and officials or local partners. In this context, it was Hong Kong businessmen (and a few other overseas Chinese, mainly in Southeast Asia) who knew how to build the ties needed if their investments were to be secure. The average size of an investment in 1986 was only US$2 million.

By the 1990s, in contrast, tax laws and some other rules governing foreign direct investment were in place, and Deng Xiaoping's southern tour made clear that the reform agenda was back on track. Foreign direct investment soared. By the end of the 1990s it was averaging over US$40 billion per year (see Table 5.1), and it rose steadily thereafter, breaking the US$100 billion level in 2010. Hong Kong still accounted for half of all foreign direct investment, but Japan, Europe taken as a whole, and the United States accounted for another US$12 billion or 14 percent (in 2009). There was also nearly US$14 billion from the Cayman and British Virgin Islands, but some of this may have been Chinese domestic investment round-tripped through these tax havens in order to take advantage of the special tax rates given to foreign as contrasted to domestic investments.[30] China did not begin to eliminate these tax breaks for foreigners until 2007 and later.

What was important about the boom in foreign direct investment, however, was not its aggregate size. China's total investment was nearly US$400 billion in 1999 (converted to dollars at the official exchange rate at the time) and US$2.83 trillion in 2010. Thus foreign direct investment never amounted to more than 10 percent of total gross investment in China, and by 2010 it had fallen to under 4 percent of the total. But foreign investment brought much more than money. It brought ready access to foreign markets, and a large and rising share of China's manufactured exports came from foreign direct investment companies in China. Foreign direct investment from Japan and the West often brought with it the best technology and knowledge of how to produce high-quality products that could compete with the best in the world. Anyone who remembers the blurry images of Chinese color TV sets in the 1970s and 1980s and the domestic automobiles the Shanghai sedan and the Hongqi (Red Flag) limousine will appreciate how far the quality and technology of Chinese manufactured products have come over the past two or three decades. Not all of this increase in quality and technological sophistication can be attributed to foreign direct investment, but much of it can. Most of the rest, outside of the

Table 5.1. Foreign direct investment (FDI) in China (annual rate actually utilized).

Period	Rate of FDI ($US billion)
1979–1982	0.44
1983–1988	2.01
1989–1991	3.75
1992–1995	27.45
1996–1999	43.19
2000–2006	53.97
2007–2011	95.79

Data sources: National Statistical Office, *Xin Zhongguo 60 nian* [60 Years of New China] (Beijing: Statistics Press, 2009), p. 662; and National Statistical Office, *Zhongguo tongji zhaiyao 2012* [China Statistical Abstract 2012] (Beijing: Statistics Press, 2012), p. 70.

military sphere, came from other kinds of connections between foreign and domestic firms.

At the turn to the twenty-first century China's economy looked in many ways much like the economies of its East Asian neighbors two to three decades earlier. In per capita income terms China in 2000 was at roughly the same place as South Korea in 1972 or Taiwan in 1970.[31] The share of industry in GDP (45.9 percent in 2000) was even higher than in South Korea and Taiwan in the late 1980s (43.2 percent in Korea and 44.4 percent in Taiwan in 1988), when South Korea's and Taiwan's industrial share in GDP actually peaked and began to decline as the share of the service sector rose. China's exports in 2000 amounted to 20.8 percent of GDP, and manufactures made up the great majority of those exports.[32] South Korea's exports as a share of GDP passed the 20 percent level in 1973, peaking much later at 41.5 percent of GDP in 1987.[33] Taiwan's exports were already over 30 percent of GDP in 1970 and rose to over 50 percent by the late 1980s.[34] These exports in all three economies were made up mainly of manufactures of consumer products. The absolute size of China's trade in 2000 was much larger than that of South Korea and Taiwan in these earlier years, of course, but the three economies' reliance on export demand was similar. In the case of both Taiwan and South Korea, this dependence on exports rose steadily for another decade and a half before peaking. China's exports reached 32 percent of GDP in 2008 but then fell to 24.1 percent in 2009 in the face of declining world demand due to the world recession. Exports in dollar terms recovered in 2010 to the level of 2008, but whether China's export share in GDP will resume its upward rise in the future remains to be seen and will be discussed further in the next chapter.

Vietnam's Reforms and the Chinese Model

Vietnam's economic reforms are important in their own right, given that Vietnam is the thirteenth largest country in the world in terms of population and has proved to be able to "punch above its weight" in both economic and geopolitical terms. In the context of this study, however, Vietnam's recent experience is also a test of whether the Chinese reform experience was unique to China or was equally valid elsewhere.

Vietnam began its reforms later and from a different point from China. Prior to 1986 Vietnam was still trying to implement a Soviet-type system—specifically, it was trying to impose that system on the market economy of the southern part of the country after reunification was achieved in 1975. There were some of what the Vietnamese call "fence-breaking" reforms in the early 1980s, but for the most part these were the kind of reforms designed to make the command economy work better, not to replace it with market forces. Officially the Vietnamese economy grew throughout the 1980s, but the actual performance was poor enough, particularly in agriculture, that the country experienced serious famine and malnutrition in the winter of 1987–1988.[35] Furthermore, much of the growth actually achieved depended on large subsidies from the Soviet Union. Vietnam's imports from 1985 through 1987 rose from US$1,590 million to US$2,191 million, but the deficit with the Comecon countries (in effect an explicit or implicit subsidy for the Vietnamese economy) rose from US$721 million in 1985 to US$1,276 million in 1987.[36]

The leader of the post-1975 effort to impose collective agriculture and central planning on the southern part of the country, Party Secretary General Le Duan, died in July 1986, but by then many in the Party realized that the efforts of the past decade had gone badly and needed to change. At the Sixth Party Congress in December 1986 they elected the reformer Nguyen Van Linh as general secretary. What really accelerated the need for radical change, however, was the collapse of Soviet control of eastern Europe in 1989 combined with the Soviet Union's own worsening economic conditions and its eventual breakup in 1991. The willingness to continue economic subsidies to Vietnam ended by 1989, even before the breakup of the Soviet Union. As the data on Vietnam's trade in 1988 make clear (Table 5.2), the end of subsidies meant that Vietnam had to find an alternative way of paying for 62 percent of its imports. The alternative, cutting back imports of this magnitude, would have thrown the country into a deep recession.

For those familiar with the Vietnam of the twenty-first century, it would be hard to recognize the country in 1989. When I led a small delegation to Vietnam in January 1989 to explore whether the Harvard Institute for International Development could help in making the transition to a more market-oriented economy, there were very few shops of any kind in Hanoi, and the shelves on most of them were empty. The situation in the Mekong delta was marginally better, largely because it was possible to smuggle in goods such as Johnny Walker Scotch, Kodachrome Film, and motorbikes through Cambodia. The leadership, however, was clearly ready for fundamental change and had begun to take steps in that direction. Our host at

Table 5.2. Vietnam's foreign trade, 1986–1990 (in millions of U.S. dollars).

Period	Total exports	Total imports	Exports to convertible area
1986	789.1	2,155.1	350.1
1987	854.2	2,455.1	366.3
1988	1,038.4	2,756.7	447.7
1989	1,946.1	2,565.8	1,138.2
1990	2,404.1	2,752.4	1,352.2

Data source: General Statistical Office, *Economy and Trade of Vietnam, 1986–1991* (Hanoi, 1992).

Note: Vietnam's trade in these years was expressed in both rubles and dollars, which formally were treated as equal.

the time, Foreign Minister Nguyen Co Thach, had just been reading Samuelson's textbook *Economics* in an effort to learn about how market economies worked. By my next visit a year later the streets of Hanoi were full of shops, and the goods were flowing out the front door onto the street. Televisions sets, beer, and numerous other consumer products from all over Asia were there for purchase if one had the money.

What had happened was that Vietnam had freed up virtually all prices and removed most restrictions on imports, and if there were still some restrictions, no one seemed to be enforcing them. When Vietnam began its transition to a market economy, however, it had two major problems that were absent in the Chinese case (although they were also present in the Soviet and eastern European transitions). The first problem was the one already mentioned: the huge foreign trade deficit. The second was that the country was suffering from a very high rate of inflation.

The solution to the end of Soviet subsidies and the financing of the trade deficit was partly the result of the reform effort and partly due to luck. As for the lucky part, Vietnam in a joint venture with the Soviet Vietsovpetro had been drilling for oil off the coast of Vung Tau in the southern part of Vietnam, and the wells began producing in 1989, providing Vietnam with several hundred million dollars of foreign exchange. As for the reform part, the end of the effort to collectivize agriculture in the south, together with the freeing up of prices of farm products, led to a boom in rice production, the elimination of any need for rice imports, and the renewal of Vietnam's traditional role as a rice exporter. Oil and rice exports (and the

end of rice imports) together filled roughly two-thirds of the foreign exchange gap in 1989 and 1990. Foreign aid from the West, Japan, or the
World Bank, it should be noted, did not play any role. Vietnam was still
subject to a total embargo with most Western countries plus Japan, and
the World Bank as a result was also not allowed to lend to the country.[37]

In freeing up prices and opening to foreign trade, Vietnam did not follow the Chinese dual-price approach of the second half of the 1980s. With
the exception of a handful of energy-related products, all prices were freed
up, and all purchasers had to pay the market price. Vietnam, however, had
a major inflation problem that predated the liberalization of prices. Inflation in 1986–1988 and before was running at over 400 percent per year
(roughly 14 percent per month). With price reform and the big increase of
goods on the market in 1989–1991, the rate of inflation had come down
but was still running at 60 percent a year on average.[38] Rates of this magnitude were not consistent with a program designed to increase the rate of
growth of GDP and exports. By 1992, however, the inflation rate of consumer retail prices had fallen to 17.5 percent, and it fell further to 5.2 percent in 1993. It stayed down for the rest of the 1990s and well into the following decade.

The causes of inflation in Vietnam were similar in important respects to
the causes in China, only more so. Poorly performing state enterprises—
most of the Vietnamese state enterprises in these early reform years—lost
their captive markets at home and abroad and borrowed heavily from the
state banking system to cover their losses. The central bank, as in China,
accommodated them by allowing the money supply to rise rapidly. Solving
the inflation problem, therefore, involved sharp cutbacks in the subsidies,
the closing of the worst performing firms, and cutting back on the excess
employment in the firms remaining. Visiting factories at the time, one often saw many of the workers no longer on the production line and instead
in classrooms learning new skills. There was no talk of privatizing enterprises in the early 1990s, however, or much later as well. Vietnam, like
China, was still ruled by a Communist Party that saw state ownership as
essential in key areas of the economy.

In some respects the Vietnamese reforms of 1989 and the years immediately thereafter fit the "big bang" model for reforming a socialist system
minus privatization. Prices, including the exchange rate, were freed up
quickly, inflation was brought under control by sharp cutbacks in subsidies within less than four years, and the Soviet Comecon system of planned

foreign trade was abolished and Vietnam's foreign trade system integrated with the international system, at least that part of the international system that was not enforcing an embargo on Vietnamese trade. Working with the Vietnamese government on reform issues at the time, I thought their willingness to rein in the state enterprise expenditures as vigorously as they did indicated a willingness to move rapidly and firmly on state enterprise reform more generally. That did not turn out to be the case. Once inflation was under control, the state enterprises once again were given a central role in the government's development efforts, a role that they still had as of 2012. It is also possible that the rise of foreign aid after diplomatic normalization with the United States in 1994 actually slowed down the reform process by making substantial amounts of foreign exchange available without taking further steps to reform the state enterprises.

Vietnam also moved dramatically to end collectivization of agriculture in the north and to end efforts to implement it in the south. The 1988 land law effectively returned ownership of arable land to the household, although there were debates at the time as to just who would get the land—specifically whether there would be some further redistribution to reward those who had fought for the revolution. In addition, the farmers got only land use rights, not outright ownership, and these rights were to expire after 20 years. Rice land, in most cases, continued to have an obligation to grow rice. The return to family-owned farms led to an immediate jump in rice output that restored Vietnam's role as a rice exporter after years of importing rice. Agricultural reform combined with price reform led to a boom in higher valued agricultural crops such as coffee, fruits, rubber, and farmed fish, all of which, together with rice exports, made major contributions to solving the country's balance-of-payments problems as well as raising the incomes of farmers.

Even before inflation was under full control, the performance of the Vietnamese economy and the development model it pursued looked more and more like the Chinese model. The GDP growth rate in 1989 was only 4.7 percent, or 3 percent per capita, but the average per capita growth rate throughout the 1990s was 5.9 percent per year. Exports grew slowly in the early 1990s, but with the ending of the U.S. embargo in early 1994 (and many other countries ended it earlier), Vietnamese exports took off. From 1994 through the year 2000 exports grew at 25 percent per year, passing US$14 billion in 2000. The content of Vietnam's exports was both similar and different from that of China's during the first decade of reform.

Consumer manufactures, notably shoes, accounted for one-third of Vietnam's exports during the 1990s, but minerals, mostly petroleum, accounted for more than a quarter of the total, with agricultural and aquatic products (rice, coffee, shrimp. etc.) making up much of the rest—not the case in China. Manufactured exports in China, in contrast, accounted for two-thirds of exports in the latter half of the 1980s. Vietnam, partly because it was in the tropics and partly because its per capita income was lower than that of China, had larger surpluses of agricultural products that could be sold abroad.

By the end of the first decade of the twenty-first century, Vietnam's economic model looked much the same as it did in the late 1990s. From the end of the 1990s, GDP continued to grow through 2007 at an average rate of 7.6 percent a year, actually accelerating to over 8 percent a year in 2005–2007. Exports in nominal terms also continued to grow rapidly at 19.7 percent a year from the beginning of 2000 through 2007, but the structure of exports did not change much from the 1990s. The dominant exports continued to be shoes, textiles, and garments, with some increase in the assembly of electronic products, all mostly produced by foreign direct investment firms, plus petroleum, coffee, rice, and other agricultural and fishery products. In China in the 1990s exports came increasingly from heavy industry products such as machinery and transport equipment, but in Vietnam heavy industries, other than petroleum, continued to produce at high cost behind high protective barriers, including favored access to land and credit and favored interpretations or noninterpretations of law.

The major policy change in the first part of the post-2000 decade was the passage of laws (the Enterprise Laws of 2000 and 2005) that legitimized domestic private business, providing security for Vietnamese investors in that sector comparable to what foreign investors in Vietnam already received. Prior to these laws, private industry above household size was virtually nonexistent, although there were a few private industrial firms, disguised under other ownership categories. After the passage of the Enterprise Laws, the private sector boomed. Private industry in 2006–2010 grew at an average annual rate of 21.6 percent per year, even faster than the 16.6 percent annual growth rate of foreign direct investment industry. Both sectors slowed down at the height of the global financial crisis in 2009 but then bounced back in 2010.

State-owned industry did not fare anywhere near as well, growing at an average annual rate of 8.7 percent in 2006–2010. A number of the major state industrial enterprises began to spread out into businesses unrelated to their main activity, notably into real estate speculation. Vinashin, the state shipbuilding company, was the most notorious, raising roughly US$1 billion from foreign sources in 2007 and then investing the money in speculative activities, most of which had little to do with building ships and which performed badly, effectively forcing the government to bail out the company. But Vinashin was not alone. As in China in the 1980s and 1990s, there was a close relationship between the large state enterprises, the state banks, and the leadership of the Communist Party. Many of these state enterprises borrowed heavily from the state banks and then used the money on real estate projects and other speculative activity unrelated to their core businesses. The large increases in the money supply that resulted from this profligate borrowing began to show up in consumer prices. Whereas the average rate of increase in the consumer price index starting in 2001 and carrying through 2007 was 5.6 percent per year, in 2008 the rate jumped to 23 percent, fell to 6.9 percent during the global financial crisis in 2009, and then rose to 9.2 percent in 2010 and 18.6 percent in 2011 and back to 9.2 percent in 2012. The nominal exchange rate rose much more slowly than inflation, resulting in an overvalued exchange rate and a sharp fall in Vietnam's foreign exchange reserves in 2011.

Vietnam in the latter half of the first 12 years of the twenty-first century had more in common with China in the early 1990s than with China in the latter half of that decade. As this chapter is being written, there is no evidence that anyone comparable to Zhu Rongji is going to take command in Vietnam, rein in bank lending, and force the state industrial enterprises to face international competition. Vietnam's GDP growth rate has fallen from 8 percent per year in 2005–2007 to 5.9 percent per year in 2008–2012, a respectable rate by global developing country standards but far below China's rate during the same years. The global financial crisis is partly to blame for this slowdown, but stalled economic reforms are clearly also part of the story.

By 2010, both Vietnam and China's economies had moved a long way from the prereform period, and in key structural ways their economies had much in common with those of South Korea and Taiwan in the 1970s and 1980s. But it would be a mistake to describe what happened in China or Vietnam as a decision by the Chinese and Vietnamese leadership to abandon the Soviet model of growth and switch to the model of South Korea or Japan.

To begin with China: as Deng Xiaoping said, China's reforms were like a person crossing a river feeling for the stones. China had no clear model that it followed from the outset. Instead it faced a series of problems and tried to solve them one by one. The first problem was the need to take full advantage of the superior technologies available abroad instead of trying to reinvent the wheel within in China. That step required foreign exchange, and after decades of neglecting foreign trade China didn't have much foreign exchange—hence the decision to accelerate the growth of exports. Since China couldn't afford to squeeze food consumption further and the country was not rich in natural resources (and offshore oil finds initially were disappointing), exporting manufactures was the only alternative.

In these early years of reform, China also faced a severe poverty problem, mainly in the countryside, and the solution chosen to achieve a sharp reduction in poverty was to abandon the commune experiment and return to household farming. The immediate result was a large jump in farm output, but after 1984 China reverted to much slower agricultural growth and a rapidly declining share of agriculture in GDP. Better incentives could remove many of the inefficiencies of the commune system, but they could not overcome the fact that China had very little arable land per capita (0.6 hectares per rural family or 0.15 hectares per rural person),[39] and the yields on that land were often already comparable to the highest yields elsewhere in the world.

The next problem was how to accelerate the growth of industry so that China did not continue to fall further behind its neighbors both in per capita income and in industrial technology terms. The initial focus was on trying to make the state-owned enterprises perform better, and a wide variety of measures were tried, none of which was particularly successful. But one of the measures tried, making industrial inputs available on the market at market prices, had a surprising side effect. The townships and villages outside the large cities experienced a boom, as local manufacturers and entrepreneurs could now get the inputs they needed, and township and village enterprises boomed and carried the entire economy with them.

The tragedy of June 4, 1989, temporarily derailed this step-by-step movement across the river and threatened a return to a more state-directed economy, but Deng Xiaoping reversed that retreat with his southern tour in 1992. It is hard to imagine the success achieved by China's reforms in the absence of Deng Xiaoping. Given the politics and ideologically driven programs of the prereform era, China could have gone down a very different path of state-controlled and state-directed slower growth possibly for decades before running into the massive inefficiencies of such an approach as the economy became more and more complex. But Deng Xiaoping was there and he did endorse continued reform, and so the step-by-step approach resumed.

In the 1990s the drag of the weak performance of the state-owned enterprises was causing a variety of connected problems that threatened overall economic performance. The close relationship between the state industrial enterprises and the state banks was leading the banks down a path to insolvency as nonperforming loans piled up. The ease with which state enterprises could get state bank loans also led to accelerating inflation that was a threat to political stability. So China's leaders took the dramatic but highly practical step of forcing the state enterprises to reform or go out of business. They did this by joining the WTO and making it difficult for the state to continue to give the kind of support to state enterprises that had been the norm in the past. In this respect, China was quite different from South Korea, Taiwan, and Japan. China has steadily moved toward a trading system that is open on both the import and the export side, with the notable exception in recent years of the undervalued exchange rate. And China has promoted foreign direct investment. Japan, South Korea prior to 1998, and Taiwan, in contrast, tightly restricted foreign direct investment and during the first decades of their high growth implemented high tariff and nontariff barriers to imports.

Thus China ended up in a place similar, although far from identical, to that of its East Asian neighbors. China had no doubt learned from their experience but had got to where it was in 2000 by its own path and in its own way. This way has sometimes been described as a gradual approach to development in contrast to the "big bang" radical transformations instituted in eastern Europe and many of the states of the former Soviet Union. Some of China's reforms were certainly gradual. It took two decades before China faced up to the need to do something dramatic and effective vis-à-vis the state-owned enterprises. On the other hand the rural reforms were carried out over a period of only a few years, and the opening of the economy to foreign trade occurred quickly as well. Where all that was involved was getting rid of an institution that did not work well (the rural communes for example) one could move quickly. Where new institutions and attitudes had to be created, moving quickly was never possible. Moving quickly was also not possible because China's goal was a very general one, to become wealthy and powerful, but the country had been struggling with how to do that since the nineteenth century. Implementing such a general goal involved far more difficult choices than reform in Poland and elsewhere in eastern and central Europe in the early 1990s, where the goal of many of the countries was to join the European Union and become as much like the existing EU countries as fast as possible.

The Vietnam economic reform story from 1989 on has much in common with the Chinese story and hence with the experiences of South Korea and Taiwan, and Vietnam went down a similar route for many of the same reasons that China, South Korea, and Taiwan did. Some years ago a senior member of Vietnam's Politburo whom I had gotten to know criticized an essay I had written in which I suggested that Vietnam's economic reform path was patterned on that of China.[40] As he rightly pointed out and this chapter has attempted to show, the economic reform process in Vietnam as well as China was driven by the economic and political context in which reform decisions were made. The leaders of Vietnam certainly knew about and learned from the reform experiences of China that preceded their reform effort. As one senior Vietnamese official said to me after one of my many lectures there on China's reforms, "we are always interested in hearing what China's is doing because we know that we will soon be facing many of the same problems they are dealing with."

When it came to the decision to open up the economy to trade with market economies, for example, Vietnam's initial problem was that they had to deal with a loss of Soviet subsidies and Comecon markets together with high inflation, problems that China did not have in the late 1970s. The beginning of production of the Bac Ho (White Tiger) oil field solved part of the first problem, and the 1988 land law that involved the abandonment of collectivization of agriculture also helped solve the balance-of-payments deficit. Thus Vietnam was able to meet its foreign exchange needs initially with exports of petroleum and a restoration of its traditional rice-exporting status. China, in contrast, given the limited success of its oil exploration efforts, had little choice other than to promote the rapid expansion of labor-intensive manufactured exports where it already had experience. The partial shift in emphasis to manufactured exports came about later in Vietnam, in part because of the embargo that was still in place in the early 1990s and in part because by the mid-1990s Hong Kong, Korean, and Taiwanese manufacturers of shoes and textiles were looking for production platforms that would diversify their businesses so as to escape from overdependence on China.

When it came to the speed of reform, both China and Vietnam moved quickly to abandon collectivization, although the approach of China was bottom up and took several years, while that of Vietnam was more top down and was completed more quickly, in part because collectivization had never taken hold in the Vietnamese south, whereas all of China had been collectivized for over two decades. Vietnam's decision to deal decisively at the outset with closing inefficient state-owned enterprises was driven mainly by the need to rein in rapid inflation, and the effort slowed as soon as inflation was under control. The fact that state enterprises in Vietnam were a smaller share of the economy may have made it politically easier for the leadership to avoid halfway reform measures like China's dual-price system in the latter half of the 1980s. China's initial efforts to reform state owned enterprises were quite modest throughout the 1980s, and reform was further set back after June 4, 1989. What changed in 1992 was Deng Xiaoping's personal decision to use his status and power to force the restoration of the reform effort, followed by Zhu Rongji's determined leadership to force state enterprises to become internationally competitive in the late 1990s. There has been no comparable political effort in Vietnam vis-à-vis state-owned enterprises, and they continue to operate as import-substituting firms behind government protective barriers. The failure to further reform Vietnam's state-owned enterprises is probably one of the reasons why China's GDP growth rate has averaged over 9 percent per year while that of Vietnam has risen at 7 percent a year during the 23-year reform period and less than 6 percent per year during the most recent five years ending in 2012.

The decisions made by China and Vietnam, therefore, reflected their specific contexts, but the many similarities in their reforms derived in part, though only in part, from the fact that both were moving away from similar failed Soviet-style command economies. The fact that China started a full decade ahead of Vietnam also meant that Vietnam had a model to learn from and follow where appropriate. In addition, these two economies both ended up with development strategies that in key respects looked much like those pursued by Japan, South Korea, and Taiwan. The decision to turn outward with respect to reliance on foreign trade and the export of manufactures was common to all of these economies. In all five economies the government played an active role in directing economic activity, especially during the first decades of reform and rapid growth. All of these economies had major government programs to promote heavy industries. Japan and to a large degree South Korea relied on private firms to carry out these plans whereas China, Vietnam, and Taiwan (in the early phase of the program) relied more on state-owned enterprises, but the direction came from government. Japan, South Korea, and Taiwan used higher tariffs, quantitative restrictions, and undervalued exchange rates to limit imports that would compete with domestic producers, whereas China mainly used an undervalued exchange rate; but that difference reflected the terms China had to accept to become a member of the WTO, whereas Japan and South Korea were already members and started their reforms in an era when the United States was much more tolerant of developing country trade restrictions. Vietnam has not deliberately tried to keep its exchange rate undervalued, and that may reflect in part its greater reliance on the export of natural resource commodities as opposed to manufactures.

Overall, the fact that all of these economies relied on active government intervention to promote industrialization and economic growth probably reflects, in part, the fact that all had large, well-organized bureaucracies staffed with relatively well-educated personnel who had the capacity to make government intervention in the economy work with a reasonable level of efficiency. It is not entirely clear where this organizational capacity came from. In China it was probably a combination of centuries of experience with the bureaucratic rule of the Confucian governmental system, the Communist Party's own experience over two decades of managing a complex war and revolution against both the Japanese and the Guomindang, and an increasingly well-educated population. In Vietnam, French colonial rule eliminated any substantial personal experience among the Vietnamese with managing a bureaucracy, but they had 30 years of successfully managing a revolutionary war involving the mobilization and supply of millions of troops, the constant need to repair infrastructure destroyed by bombing, and much else. And the fact that they managed this against the French, the Americans, and the South Vietnamese Government created considerable organizational capacity. No such government capacity existed in most of Southeast Asia outside Vietnam.

The major differences between the development strategies of these economies, as contrasted to their similarities, include the fact that China and Vietnam welcomed large-scale foreign direct investment while Japan,

South Korea, and Taiwan did not. All of these economies at the beginning of the second decade of the twenty-first century, however, are part of the complex multicountry supply chains that characterize most manufacturing in the region today. One suspects that the hostility to foreign direct investment in the three earlier developers was more a product of politics and culture than anything else. Japanese business practices and business-government relations have never been accommodating to the inclusion of outsiders. In South Korea, in addition to strong nationalist feelings, there was the fear that opening up to foreign direct investment would lead to renewed Japanese control of Korean businesses. China's leaders, in contrast, seemed to worry little about their ability to control the activities of foreign investors. Somewhat like Koreans, many Vietnamese worry about the ability to control Chinese foreign direct investment in their country but not investment from elsewhere. In fact, involving foreign investment in offshore oil exploration is seen by the Vietnamese as a way to protect themselves against what they perceive as Chinese encroachment.

In broad terms, the factor endowment of these five economies is similar, so it is not surprising that their development strategies have been similar. All had limited endowments of arable land relative to the size of their population, and all, except Vietnam, were in the temperate zone. None had plentiful nonagricultural natural resources relative to the size of its population. All had a Confucian heritage that generated a strong desire for education, backed up by a premodern base of education that was readily expanded into a modern mass education program, resulting in increasingly well-educated labor forces. All five started with governments led by individuals mostly talented at making war and revolution but then made the transition to leaders devoted to modernizing their economies. The main difference in the timing of the rapid growth period of each country had to do with when the emphasis on war and revolution gave way to the emphasis on development. It happened first in Japan with defeat in World War II, moved on to Taiwan and South Korea in the early 1960s, where survival depended on successful economic development, and then to China in the late 1970s and Vietnam in the late 1980s, when revolutionary leaders gave way to leaders who wanted to make their countries wealthy and powerful. These leaders not only wanted to implement development programs that would achieve these goals but also led governments that had the capacity to carry out interventionist policies without excessive political and rent-seeking distortions.

Finally there is the question of whether or how the nature of the political systems in Northeast and Southeast Asia shaped the development strategies pursued, and what the experience of those East Asian economies that have achieved high-income status implies for China and Vietnam. Full treatment of this subject would require a separate book, but a few generalizations are possible from the analysis in this and previous chapters. All of the rapidly growing economies of Northeast and Southeast Asia began with authoritarian political systems, with the possible exceptions of Singapore and Malaysia, where votes were honestly counted in elections and there were opposition candidates, although the playing field was not an even one. Some of these authoritarian governments managed highly effective development policies while others oversaw economic disasters. In the case of South Korea and Taiwan, external threats to the very existence of their economic and political systems kept governments focused on following economic policies that worked and dropping those that did not. Potential external threats of a somewhat different kind also played a role in Singapore.

External threats, however, had little to do with why the governments of China and Vietnam were able to stay focused on effective development policies. The key change in both China and Vietnam was the transition from a generation of leaders mostly skilled at making revolution and fighting wars to leaders who were mainly concerned with making their countries wealthy and powerful. In Vietnam's case, the end of subsidies from its powerful ally the Soviet Union was a further impetus. The changeover from a revolutionary leader to the next generation is also part of the explanation for Indonesia's relative success, but authoritarian rule under President Suharto had a mixed development record. It was effective during periods such as the late 1960s and the 1980s when major economic crises in the immediate past kept the ablest technocrats in control, but poor policies led to crises in the mid-1970s and the 1990s, when prior success bred hubris on the part of senior politicians. In the Philippines, authoritarian rule by President Marcos was an unmitigated disaster.

Did the transition to democracy in several of these countries change policies, were the changes positive or negative for economic growth, and are there any implications for China and Vietnam in the experience of the countries that made this transition? In South Korea and Taiwan, democracy coincided with a shift away from a high level of government intervention in the economy to greater reliance on market forces, but that transition began before the change in the political systems and reflected more the requirements of increasingly sophisticated and open economies. The slowdown in growth in South Korea and Taiwan, as will be seen in Chapter 6, had nothing to do with the transition to democracy.

The transition to democracy in Indonesia has been accompanied by fairly high GDP growth, but that is mostly due to high international prices for natural resource exports, not a coherent and effective government development strategy. The transition back to democracy in the Philippines has led to improvements over the Marcos years, but not dramatic improvements. In Malaysia, democracy—arguably in place since independence— has brought political stability to the country that has helped growth, but stability was bought in part with policies strongly favoring one ethnic group that have inhibited economic growth. If there are any lessons for China and Vietnam's approach to development in this recent political history, it is not clear what they are. The one certainty is that China and Vietnam will have to find more and more ways to accommodate the demands of an increasingly prosperous and well-educated population, but how this will impact their development strategies remains to be seen.

Next I shall explore whether the similarities in economic structure and reform strategies continued in East Asia as the high-growth spurt in some of the economies reached its end. For the countries of Southeast Asia, including Vietnam but excluding Singapore, this end-of-high-growth story is some way off, but in Northeast Asia it has already arrived. In China, however, high growth has been sustained in an economy with an increasingly unusual economic structure.

—6—

The End of High Growth Rates

We have seen an economic transformation whose speed is unprecedented in world history. In half a century, 1.97 billion people in East and Southeast Asia, or 26 percent of the world's population, have experienced anywhere from a sixfold to a fourteenfold increase in income.[1] The total GDP of these countries in 2010 was US$14.65 trillion in the prices of that year (US$10.5 trillion in 2000 prices) or roughly the same as that of the United States (in PPP terms the GDP of these countries taken together was nearly $18 trillion). Excluding Japan, the total GDP of the other high-performing East and Southeast Asian economies was only US$262 billion in the years before their economic boom began. Per capita income in U.S. dollars was around $200 in China, Vietnam and Indonesia; around $400 in Thailand and $1,000 in Malaysia, South Korea, and Taiwan; and just under $3,000 in the comparatively rich port cities of Hong Kong and Singapore.

Various writers have attempted to project East Asia's economic performance into the future. As with so many of these exercises, forecasting the future is done by projecting forward the recent past, and when this is done the results can be astonishing. Thus Japan's GDP, in the view of some analysts four decades ago, would match that of the United States by the year 2000 and then presumably keep on growing rapidly from there.[2] It seemed possible and for some frightening when the projections were made, but it did not happen. In 2010 Japan's per capita GDP had almost caught up with that of the United States, but total GDP was 34.1 percent of that of the United States, as contrasted with 30.6 percent in 1973, the year when Japan's superhigh growth rates came to an end.[3] As this book is being written, there are numerous people doing similar projections for China. At current rates of growth, China's total GDP could pass that of the United

States by the year 2020, if not before. Even if China's growth rate slows down, its total GDP is almost certain to match that of the United States, given that China's population is more than four times larger. But if one projects China's GDP forward at 9 percent a year for one and two decades, one gets a GDP of roughly $19 trillion in 2020 and an extraordinary $45 trillion in 2030, as contrasted to the United States' total GDP in 2011 of $15.1 trillion. By 2030 China's GDP per capita would be roughly three-quarters that of the United States. The implications of such a massive increase in GDP in the short period of two decades, for everything from global warming to the price of petroleum, would be dramatic. There is no point in speculating about these implications, however, because GDP growth of this magnitude is not likely to happen—at least not within the short time frame of two decades.

For GDP growth rates of 8 to 10 percent a year are catch-up growth rates, and there is now considerable evidence that rates of this magnitude are not sustainable once a country has begun to catch up with the high-income countries of the world. Among the economies this study is most concerned with, GDP growth rates fell significantly when they reached around $13,000 per capita in 2000 PPP dollars. This was the case in Japan, South Korea, Taiwan, and Singapore. Hong Kong similarly slowed down at around $12,000 per capita.[4] It turns out that almost all of the economies that have achieved high-income status have slowed down at a similar point, although many never grew as fast as those in East Asia. The pattern is presented in Figure 6.1. The exceptions to this pattern among high-income countries more generally, such as Norway, a small country that benefited from the discovery of a major oil field in its offshore economic zone, have little relevance to East Asia or most other high-income countries.[5]

A brief review of when and in what manner growth decelerated in the high-income East Asian economies is instructive. In Japan the deceleration was abrupt. Japan's GDP growth roared through the 1960s and was slower but still rapid in the early 1970s but then fell sharply in 1974, right after the first increase in oil prices engineered by OPEC in 1973. Through 1990 Japan continued to enjoy fairly high GDP growth rates but ones only half the level or less of the 1950s and 1960s. Japan's growth then decelerated even more after the bursting of its enormous stock market and real estate bubbles in 1991, and for the next two decades Japan managed GDP growth of only 1 percent per year. The virtual stagnation after 1991 reflected weaknesses in the Japanese economy that were exposed when the bubbles burst,

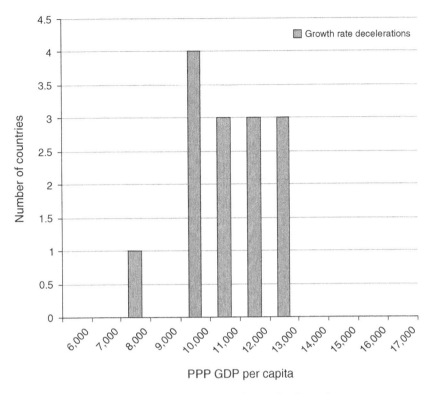

Figure 6.1. Per capita income at which growth rate decelerated.

Note: This is a sample of sustained decelerations for 14 economies that reached a per capita GDP of over $10,000 (in 2000 PPP prices). Only European economies that could plausibly be described as still being developing economies with per capita GDP under $4,000 (in 2000 prices) in the early 1960s were included (Greece, Portugal, and Spain).

Data source: Barry Eichengreen, Dwight H. Perkins, and Kwanho Shin, *From Miracle to Maturity: The Growth of the Korean Economy* (Cambridge, Mass.: Harvard Asia Center, distributed by Harvard University Press, 2012), pp. 34–35.

and there is a large literature debating just why Japan's economy has performed so poorly for two decades. No attempt will be made to review that literature here. At the center of most explanations, however, is the weakness of the Japanese financial system, and that weakness was in turn, to an important degree, a direct result of the same government-led industrial policies that have often been given credit for the boom of the earlier years. The earlier GDP growth deceleration in 1974, however, cannot be explained by the problems of the financial sector or by policy mistakes made by Japanese government economists. It also cannot be explained by the rise in oil prices in 1973 and 1978. Those prices had come down by the mid-1980s. Something more fundamental was going on.

The slowdown in South Korea was similar to the Japanese slowdown in 1974 in the sense that it happened abruptly as the result of a major external economic shock. In Korea's case, it was the financial crisis of 1997–1998 that led to a sharp recession in 1998, caused by failures in Korean macroeconomic policy and the profligate short-term borrowing abroad in the 1990s by the Korean *chaebol*. When similar unwise and unhedged borrowing had brought down the economies of first Thailand and then Indonesia and Malaysia, the contagion spread to Korea when foreign lenders called their loans and Korea lacked the foreign exchange to cover them. Ultimately the IMF had to come to the rescue.

The crisis in Korea, however, was soon over, and the recovery was rapid, with very high GDP growth rates in 1999 and 2000. But then the growth slowed throughout the next decade, to a rate below 5 percent per year through 2007, at which point it fell further as a result of the global recession of 2008–2009; it then recovered in 2010 with a growth rate of 6.3 percent, slowing in 2011 to 3.6 percent. Because the governments in office between 1998 and 2007 were left of center and promoted various social welfare policies (although more were promoted than actually implemented), many in Korea attributed the slowdown to these policies. Lee Myung-bak, who was elected president in 2007 and took office in 2008, ran on a platform that called for a return to a sustained growth rate of 7 percent a year. The global recession certainly made that goal unobtainable during his term, but the contention here, and in a more in-depth study of Korean growth,[6] is that no such goal was realistic, for reasons more fundamental than the two externally generated economic crises. A more realistic appraisal is that the relatively high growth of the 1990s was sustained by a *chaebol* investment boom that was out of control and that the deceleration in growth that occurred after 1998 was due to more fundamental causes that could not be altered by achievable changes in government policies.

The experience of Taiwan, particularly in the political sphere, had important elements in common with Korea, although Taiwan was not much affected by the late 1990s global financial crisis. Taiwan's GDP growth rate did not come down suddenly, as in the case of Japan and South Korea. It instead came down gradually from an average of 7 percent in 1990–1995 to 5.6 percent in 1996–2000 and to 4.2 percent in 2001–2007, at which point the global recession lowered the rate further (it averaged an annual rate of 2.9 percent over 2008–2012). Ma Ying-jeou ran successfully for president on a platform of raising the growth rate but was sworn into office in 2008, when any hope of accelerated growth was blocked by the world economic crisis. But was there any reason to think that a sustainable GDP growth rate greater than 4 or 5 percent a year was realistic? The contention here is that it was not.

As for the experience of Hong Kong and Singapore, they started their post–World War II economic booms from a higher per capita income than either Korea or Taiwan and so would be expected to reach their deceleration point at an earlier date. For Hong Kong, that was the case. The last true boom years in Hong Kong were the 1980s, ending after 1988, when the GDP growth rate averaged 7.8 percent per year. In the nine years that followed prior to the financial crisis (1989–1997), Hong Kong GDP growth averaged only 3.9 percent a year. No external economic events or Hong Kong policies can plausibly explain why growth was so much slower in this latter period, unless the prospect of restoration of Chinese sovereignty over Hong Kong somehow caused the slowdown. The growth rate from 1998 through 2012 was no higher, averaging 3.4 percent a year.

The Singapore experience was somewhat different. As late as the 1990–1997 period Singapore's growth rate averaged 8.6 percent a year, before dropping to an average of 5.4 percent per year in the following years prior to the global recession (1998–2007) and 4.3 percent a year during the recession and its aftermath (2008–2012). Singapore is the one case where an initial albeit short-lived slowdown in the mid-1980s was followed by renewed high growth for a substantial period.

As for the other economies that have been the focus of these lectures, leaving aside China for the moment, none of them, unlike Japan, Korea, and Taiwan, has yet caught up to the point where it no longer enjoys the benefits of being a follower country that can proceed along a path pioneered by others. Malaysia would be the one exception in that its PPP GDP per capita was over $10,000 in 2010 and thus close to where growth begins to slow down. The per capita GDPs of Thailand, Vietnam, and the Philippines, not to mention Cambodia, Laos and Myanmar, were much lower, with all but Thailand being under, often well under, $5,000 per capita. Malaysian GDP grew at near-double-digit rates (9.3 percent per year) in 1988–1997 and then fell to 5.5 percent a year in 2000–2008 and fell further during the global recession. Malaysia may fit the more general picture of a deceleration because of catching up. However, its GDP growth rate from the 1960s through the 1980s was well below the rate of 1988–1997 at 6.7 percent per year, so the 5.5 percent per capita rate after 1999 could be seen as a return to Malaysia's long-term trend growth rate. Malaysian growth rates are also still subject to major fluctuations driven by the volatility of natural resource prices. More work needs to be done and perhaps more time has to pass before we can judge whether Malaysia, given the right policies, could still achieve near double-digit growth rates.

If one cannot really explain the deceleration in growth in the highest performing economies in East Asia by external shocks and internal policy errors, what then is the explanation? What were the more "fundamental reasons" for deceleration? Some of the underlying reasons for deceleration are measurable. In a book on Korean growth,[7] my co-authors and I ran a regression on the deceleration in growth of all of the economies used in constructing a figure similar to Figure 6.1. The dependent variable was the growth deceleration, and the three explanatory variables that were statistically significant in the estimated equation were the PPP per capita income of the country or the ratio of that income to the income of the frontier economy; the dependency ratio; and the share of manufacturing employment in total employment. The per capita income and ratio to the income of the frontier country (these were alternative specifications in two separate equations) represents the well-known (convergence) result that growth rates slow down as per capita incomes rise. The only difference in this equation is that the growth deceleration is sudden, in contrast to the gradual deceleration in the typical income convergence equations. The dependency ratio measures the share of people in the workforce in relation to the total work force and captures the importance of a low dependency ratio in maintaining a high rate of savings and investment. As the ratio rises, as it has in most maturing economies, savings and investment falls. It is also likely that this variable also captures the impact of the end of migration from low-productivity traditional occupations (mainly agriculture) to higher productivity modern and largely urban occupations that was occurring with the rise in the dependency ratio. Finally, most countries experiencing rapid growth also experience a rise in the share of manufacturing employment in total employment. This rising share, however, comes to an end at levels of income not much above $10,000 and then begins to fall, and employment in services and the share of services output in GDP rises.

Productivity growth in services is typically slower than in manufacturing, and the shift to services thus lowers the growth rate.

These measurable variables, however, explain only a part of why growth decelerates. The more important part is impossible to measure. When countries begin to catch up to those ahead of them in terms of per capita income, they no longer can simply follow the growth strategies of the leaders, making small adjustments for local conditions. They also cannot simply import technology, make a few small modifications in that technology, and then count on low labor costs to outcompete the higher income countries that pioneered the technology. Countries must build their own research and development programs, and research is an uncertain process, with more failures than successes. It can also take a long time from discovery to implementation, something a true follower country does not need to worry about but a country near the frontier does have to think about. The surprising thing about the East Asian experience is that this impact of catching up occurs at per capita incomes well below, roughly one-third of, those of the highest income countries. When incomes reach that point, continued high growth depends on investing in research and development and building effective R&D institutions. That in fact has been the case in all of the most rapidly growing East Asian economies.

When Will China's Growth Rate Decelerate?

Five and possibly six of the economies of East and Southeast Asia have made the transition from follower status to producing, at least in part, on the frontier and have experienced a marked slowdown in their growth rates. The total population of these countries was 240 million in 2010 if Malaysia is included. Of far greater global significance is the question of when the 1.3 billion people of China are going to experience a growth slowdown. The foregoing analysis gives us a basis for trying to answer this question.

The first step in this analysis is to make a judgment as to the level of PPP GDP in China. The problem is that China's PPP has not yet been measured systematically using appropriate data. The World Bank and the Asian Development Bank together made a systematic estimate of China's PPP GDP but used only urban prices in the calculations, and that procedure probably understates true PPP GDP per capita.[8] The current World Bank estimate of China's PPP GDP for 2010 (in 2005 prices) is $9.114 trillion or

$6,800 per capita. The Penn World Tables (version 6.3) give PPP GDP per capita estimates for 2007 in 2005 prices of $7,853–8,554, which would be $10,370–11,290 in 2010. If the World Bank figure is an underestimate and the Penn World Tables are a slight overestimate, then the "true" figure in 2010 in 2005 prices might be around $9,000. For lack of a better alternative, I shall work with that figure, with occasional reference to the World Bank figure.

If China's GDP growth rate is going to slow down at roughly the same stage as in countries that have already achieved high-income status, that slowdown is going to occur within the coming decade and possibly as soon as 2012–2015. The growth rate in 2012 was already below 8 percent, and the Chinese leadership in that year began to prepare the country for a slowdown by lowering its own planned future growth rates, albeit very modestly. If China's GDP per capita continues to grow at 9 percent per year, PPP GDP per capita is likely to slow down no later than 2017, when PPP GDP per capita passes $16,000 in 2005 prices (or 2020 if the World Bank figure is right). The deceleration could come much sooner, since China will have passed the $10,000 figure per capita in 2012 (by 2015 using the World Bank's figure). If the growth rate slows below 9 percent a year, say to 6 percent per year, it will take longer for a major deceleration to occur if China follows the patterns of most other countries, but China at that rate would reach $13,000 per capita within five years after 2011.

Going behind these simple correlations, China on the supply side faces major challenges. The data in Table 2.4 indicated that more than one-third of China's high growth rate through 2005 was accounted for by the rise in TFP at 3.8 percent a year. The only year when TFP was higher was in the early 1990s, when Deng Xiaoping through his trip to the south was able to reverse the cautious economic policies then in place in the aftermath of June 4, 1989. In the forecast we made in that earlier work, we showed that to maintain a rate of growth of 9 percent a year, China would have to accelerate its TFP growth to nearly 5 percent a year or more after 2015. Except for brief periods, China has never achieved TFP growth of that magnitude.

Furthermore, much of the high productivity growth of the previous three decades was achieved by dismantling the inefficient institutions of the centrally planned command economy and opening up the economy to rapidly expanding international trade and foreign direct investment. Growth in the 1980s was first generated by opening up to foreign trade and then was followed by an agricultural boom through 1985 that was generated by the abandonment of the rural communes in favor of a return to household agriculture. The decision in 1984 to make industrial inputs available at market prices did not do much to improve the performance of large state-owned enterprises but made possible the boom in township and village enterprises that sustained high industrial and GDP growth through the mid-1990s. By then the institutions supporting foreign direct investment, such as the tax system, were in place, and foreign direct investment accelerated to over $50 billion and then $100 billion a year, bringing in better technology, better management practices, and higher quality products. At the same time China bit the bullet of state enterprise reform and laid off tens of millions of redundant state enterprise workers. In addition, joining the WTO shortly thereafter put large competitive pressures on all sectors that until then had enjoyed some degree of protection of their domestic markets. All of these moves contributed in a major way to the growth of TFP, although it is difficult to specify precisely by how much.

Contrast those productivity-generating moves of the past with the forces likely to be the main source of productivity growth in the future. There is little left to dismantle of the old command economy system. China is a market economy, except for a few niches such as the lack of established markets for rural land and the continued political involvement in credit allocation. Solving the rural land problem is socially important but will have a modest impact on agricultural productivity, and getting politics out of credit allocation is extremely difficult to do, given the nature of the Chinese political system. Most Chinese productivity growth going forward is likely to come from research and development expenditures. Finding the money to expand these expenditures will not be difficult, but one must also develop the creative engineers and scientists, and that in turn requires both strong educational institutions and first-rate research institutions. China is making clear progress on these fronts, but it is a slow process. Furthermore, research and development is by its nature uncertain, with mistakes and dead ends an inherent part of the process. No high-income country comes anywhere close to achieving TFP growth of 4 percent a year or more on a sustained basis through research and development.

China, however, does have a considerable way to go before it has an efficient market economy and an efficient financial system, and there will be productivity gains from reforms in these areas if done properly. For a fully functioning market system where most decisions are decentralized to the firm level, one must have well-established rules for settling disputes over large matters and small, and that in turn requires an efficient and fair legal system that is independent of political manipulation. China is making progress in this direction as well, but it has a very long way to go before its legal system is even up to the not very high standards of its East Asian neighbors. Progress in this area is a matter of decades, even generations. A truly strong legal system and a financial system free of political manipulation will probably not be possible until there is some kind of fundamental political reform that gets the government and the Communist Party out of the business of making microeconomic and legal decisions.

There is also a question going forward of just what kind of a market-oriented economic system China will push for in the decades ahead. Will it be something like Japan in 2010, despite the obvious problems that Japan faces with an aging population (China's population is also going to be aging rapidly), a high debt-to-GDP ratio, a weak financial system, and slow growth? Or will China's system look more like that of the United States, for all of its problems at the time this is being written, or perhaps Germany, with its strong social welfare safety net and strong export performance? These kinds of choices will have a large influence on China's future TFP.[9]

These supply-side considerations thus suggest that China will have difficulty maintaining TFP growth at the levels of the past. We also know with virtual certainty that the growth rate of the labor supply will slow and then begin to decline since most of those who will enter the labor force over the next 20 years have already been born. The beginning in the decline of the numbers in the workforce will start within a few years, and work hours per laborer are likely to decline. There will be continued improvement in the quality of this labor through rises in the average level of education of the workforce, but that too will slow down because education is now almost universal through lower middle school and is rapidly approaching universal attendance at upper middle school. Most of the increase in the average level of formal education of the workforce thus must come from expansion of university-level education, and that is typically a much slower process than the movement toward universality at the primary and secondary levels. Education, of course, does not end when formal schooling ends. People learn on the job and through reading and access to the internet. A free and open society also creates more opportunities to learn from others at home and abroad than a less free and open society. China in 2012 was far more open in this respect than prior to 1978 but well short of what is possible in most of the highest income countries. Estimating how fast China will progress along the road to greater freedom and openness is well beyond the scope of this book and the capacity of its author.

Thus, slowing labor force growth and slowing TFP growth leaves only a rising rate of investment or gross capital formation as a way of maintaining a GDP growth rate at the level attained during the first decade of the twenty-first century. But a rising investment rate will only raise growth if that rising rate is not offset by a declining return on that investment. China's investment rate has risen substantially since the year 2000, but the output produced per unit of investment has been falling (the incremental capital output ratio has been rising). The issue of the current and likely future productivity of capital, however, is best left to the discussion of the demand side of China's future economic prospects, which I take up next.

China's Growing Demand-Side Challenge to High Growth

Keynes demonstrated in the 1930s that one could not ignore aggregate demand in the economy of a wealthy nation if one wanted to understand its current economic situation, let alone its future prospects. The lack of sufficient aggregate demand led to the Great Depression of the 1930s and was central to the major global recession of 2008–2009. However, in analyzing the prospects for growth of low-income countries, it is common practice to ignore the demand side of the problem. Unemployment and underutilized resources in low-income countries are usually structural problems resulting from the lack of sufficient capital to fully use these resources. If the government attempts to pump up demand by increasing expenditures while holding revenues constant, the result is usually inflation, not real GDP growth. China was like other low-income countries in this sense well into the 1990s. That has not been the case since the late 1990s, however. Maintaining aggregate demand at a level that fully utilizes China's labor force and its industrial capacity has become an increasing challenge.

The changing structure of Chinese GDP on the demand side is presented in Figure 6.2. The first thing to note in this figure is that household consumption as a share of GDP was low relative to that of most other

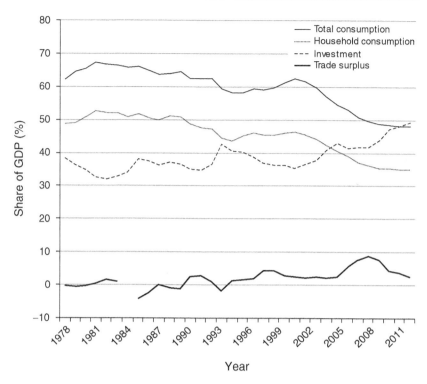

Figure 6.2. China's GDP shares: the expenditure side (percent).

Data source: National Statistical Office, *Zhongguo tongji zhaiyao 2012* [China statistical abstract 2012] (Beijing: Statistics Press, 2012), p. 36.

countries when the reform period began in 1978 and that share has fallen steadily over the ensuing three decades, reaching the unusually low figure of 34.9 percent in 2010 and 2011.[10] In the more typical economy this figure would be 60 percent of GDP, and in the United States it is 70 percent. To maintain the full utilization of China's production capacity, therefore, demand for 66 percent of GDP had to be found elsewhere. One possibility was government consumption (the military, social welfare expenditures, government employee salaries, maintenance, etc.), but that has fluctuated between 13 and 15 percent of GDP throughout the three-plus decades of reform, with no apparent trend, despite the large increases in social welfare expenditures under the Hu Jintao/Wen Jiabao government beginning after 2003 (the figure was 13.3 percent of GDP in 2011).[11] Much is also made of China's dependence on exports, but what matters for domestic demand are net exports. Net exports peaked at a high 8.8 percent of GDP in 2007 but fell to 3.7 percent of GDP in 2010 and to 2.6 percent in 2011, a still substantial figure in dollar terms but not one capable of filling much of the gap between domestic consumption (household and government) and China's total GDP production capacity. This has left investment as the only remaining component that could fill that gap.

Investment in China in fact was already at a high level at the start of the reform period and rose dramatically in the first decade of the twenty-first century to 49.2 percent of GDP in 2011. How can such a high level of investment be profitable? In most middle- and high-income countries investment is driven by increases in consumer demand. An increase in consumption requires an increase in production capacity, and investment is made to provide that capacity.[12] Real consumption (household and government) in China during the most recent decade (2001–2010) grew at 9.5 percent per year, and GDP during the same period grew at 10.7 percent per year.[13] New investment was thus needed to provide the capacity to produce this increase in consumption goods and services. But the amount of investment needed to produce the increase in consumption was perhaps 14 percent of GDP in 2000, falling to around 11 percent in 2010.[14] Put differently, the other countries in East Asia that grew at rates of GDP growth of 8–10 percent per year for two decades or more did so with investment rates that were typically around 30 percent of GDP, sometimes rising into the mid-30s. Hong Kong and Taiwan through much of their high-growth periods had gross capital formation rates below 30 percent. Only Singapore, and then only for five years in the early 1980s, had rates over 40 percent. How then did China manage to utilize nearly 50 percent of GDP, or an average of 42.3 percent of GDP, during the 2001–2010 decade?

The answer is that China has had an enormous housing and office building program combined with an infrastructure construction program on an unprecedented scale. In the six years 2005–2010, China completed construction of 7,584 million square meters of urban housing, or enough to house 76 million families at 100 square meters per family of three (comfortable by Chinese urban standards). In addition, during the same period urban construction enterprises completed another 5,136 million square meters of offices and other similar buildings. In 1978 the average Chinese urban family of three had 20 square meters of living space; by 1990 this had doubled to 41 square meters, and by 2006 it had doubled again to 81 square meters.[15] The housing construction since 2006 through 2010 added another 19 square meters per urban family, although demolition of existing older apartments would reduce the net increase figure by an unknown amount. Rural families had more space than urban families, but most rural housing construction is done locally and does not end up in the national housing construction statistics. The gross value of all construction activity and completed buildings in 2010 was 9,520.6 billion and 5,298.1 billion renminbi, respectively. The larger of the two figures was equivalent to 23.9 percent of total GDP.[16] Housing construction alone was probably equivalent to roughly 15 percent of GDP.

In addition to housing and office buildings, there was a massive development of transport infrastructure. In 1987 there were no high-speed, multilane, limited-access highways in China, and in 1997 their length was still less than 5,000 kilometers. By 2010 there were 74,000 kilometers of high-speed highways, roughly the same total length as the entire U.S. interstate system. After 1997 China added on average 5,000 kilometers of new high-speed highways each year, 9,000 kilometers in 2010 alone. When I first visited Beijing in 1974 the airport terminal was a tiny building with a few rooms, and flights were few in number. By the time of the Olympics China had built its second enormous airport terminal to complement one built earlier, and flight delays were routine because the traffic was so heavy. Furthermore, every provincial capital had an airport far larger and more modern than either the 1970s Capitol Airport in Beijing or Hongqiao Airport in Shanghai, and the government announced in 2010 that it was going to build and expand new airports and terminals in another 43 cities.

Beijing for decades had only one subway line, built as much as an air raid shelter as a form of public transport. As of 2011 it had 14 operating lines 336 kilometers in total length, most built in the previous decade. Shanghai's subway lines were a bit longer, and even Guangzhou had seven lines making up almost 200 kilometers in length. Most of these lines were built during the first decade of the twenty-first century. High-speed long-distance rail lines were another focus of large-scale investment. The annual investment in high-speed rail lines came to more than 800 billion renminbi in 2010. The process slowed some in 2011, as a result of corruption in the Railway Ministry and questionable construction and operating practices that led to many delays and one major accident, but the process continues. Shanghai and Tianjin were also spending hundreds of billions of renminbi on modernizing port facilities, and Shanghai is moving its port out of the central city to the coast.

There were East Asian precedents for a building and infrastructure construction program of the kind China began after 1997. In Japan during 1944–1945 and the Republic of Korea in 1950–1953, heavy bombing and other wartime destruction had burnt most Japanese cities to the ground and left few buildings standing in Seoul and other cities in Korea. Infrastructure in the form of rail lines, electric power, and much else was destroyed. There was thus a clear need for a large-scale construction effort in Japan and Korea that lasted for two decades or more. The transfer of large numbers of people from rural farms to the cities, especially in Korea, also required large-scale construction and hence abnormally high rates of investment. In the summer of 1972, when my family lived near the northern banks of the Han River in Seoul, most of the land on the south side of the river was empty. Four decades later Seoul extends with high-rise buildings for many miles south of the Han River. In 1972 Korea had one high-speed highway, from Seoul to Pusan, and the other roads were mostly unpaved and rock-strewn once one drove more than a few kilometers outside the major cities. A decade later Korea had a high-speed, limited-access highway system much like China's today, and feeder roads were all paved.[17] Taiwan, in comparison, did not experience such heavy wartime destruction, and the investment rate there fell below 30 percent in the mid-1980s as the need for more infrastructure and housing declined earlier than in the case of Korea. Japan's gross capital formation rate stayed at or slightly above 30 percent after growth slowed in 1974 but fell below 30 percent in 1980 and for the most part stayed below 30 percent thereafter. Korea kept investment high in the 1990s, but as already pointed out the 1990s were a period when investment was artificially boosted due to excessive and poorly thought-out *chaebol* investment. Korea's investment rate after 1998 was 29 percent of GDP—nowhere near the 37 percent average rate of the eight years before the 1997–1998 crisis.

China's investment boom in recent years was not made necessary by wartime destruction. China's lack of urban housing and transport infrastructure was instead a product of the Soviet-style development strategy that China pursued prior to 1978. The basic approach of the Soviet Union toward transport was to use and overuse existing infrastructure until it began to break down, at which point the minimum necessary investment to keep it functioning was made. Housing or the neglect thereof fit the Soviet approach of neglecting all consumer goods and favoring steel, heavy machinery, and weapons. In China's case the prohibition against most migration from rural areas to the cities also limited the need for more urban housing until that restriction was lifted, mostly after 1990. Thus China had a large unmet housing and infrastructure demand. In the mid-1970s, when I first traveled in China, the trunk roads between major cities were paved but were only two lanes wide, and most feeder roads were not even paved. Railroad passenger travel in "soft class" was comparatively luxurious for the few who could afford it, but the railroad freight system was operating at overfull capacity.

China's massive investment program of the past one to two decades thus met very real needs. Going forward, however, there is a serious question whether a continuing effort of this magnitude is justified. During the past two decades (1991–2010) China has seen a net increase in urban housing of over 18 billion square meters, and the net increase in the rural areas has been a little below 10 billion square meters. Given the large-scale demolition of older housing, the gross figure would be much larger. The gross figure for housing construction over the past two decades in the United States, which has one-quarter of China's population but is much richer (and it has the largest housing area per capita in the world) was around 5 billion square meters. Japan during the years of rapid housing construction from 1958 through 1983 experienced a net increase in housing of perhaps 1.5 billion square meters for a population of 120 million.[18] It would appear, therefore, that China's housing boom has succeeded in meeting most of the needs of the urban population, except for the "floating population" of country-to-city migrants who are still registered as living in the country and the many hundreds of millions more who will move to the cities over the coming two decades. Meeting the housing needs of the migrants could involve the construction of another 8 billion square meters of mostly public housing over the next two decades.[19] Higher income families will want to move to larger and better quality apartments, and older buildings will continue to be demolished, but will this be sufficient to justify new housing construction each year of well over 1 billion square meters?

Similar statements can be made about the need for continuing transport infrastructure investment. The high-speed, limited-access highway system can be expanded further, but much of that expansion is scheduled for more lightly populated areas such as western China. The requirements in the most populated areas will mostly involve maintenance of what has already been built plus limited expansion in select areas. As the United States learned as its interstate highway system was nearing completion, citizens don't want to see new highways constantly expanding through established residential areas. China's high-speed rail system is far from completed as of 2012, but it is a system that will benefit most of the same people who fly from city to city. There is thus a limit to the demand for high-cost high-speed rail in China. Another area where there is clearly a need for large-scale construction investment is for the transport of water from the south into the low-rainfall areas of northern China. The water table on the North China Plain is falling rapidly, and the government has announced a program of investment in water conservancy of 4 trillion renminbi over the next decade, or 400 billion renminbi per year.

There will thus be a continued need for public investment in both housing and infrastructure over the coming decades, but the magnitude of this investment is not likely to justify a gross investment rate approaching 50 percent of GDP, with roughly 24 percent of that 50 percent appearing to have been devoted to the various kinds of construction investment just described. The new water conservancy initiative, for example, amounts to only 1 percent of GDP and much less than that a decade in the future. Housing construction alone in 2011 completed 1.9 billion square meters or enough to house more than 50 million people at a cost of over 5 percent of GDP in that year. If housing fell to a still considerable but more sustainable 1 billion square meters per year, the share of housing investment in GDP would fall to 2.8 percent of GDP.

It is not that China cannot come up with large-scale construction projects to fill the gap in demand. Keynes argued that building pyramids was better than doing nothing if a country was trying to avoid a depression. But Keynes's statement was a policy prescription designed to deal with a temporary situation. If China attempts to keep this state-led investment effort at anything close to the current level for a sustained period of a decade or longer, three things are likely to happen. One, as already discussed, is that this investment will go to lower and lower priority projects with lower rates of return and hence the GDP growth rate will also decline. Second, there is a serious question whether a state-led investment program of this magnitude can be continued indefinitely while still keeping corruption within reasonable bounds. In addition, the current method for financing much of this investment has created other distortions that are politically as well as economically problematic. The stimulus efforts of 2008–2009 were turned to a substantial degree over to local governments that borrowed heavily to finance these efforts and now have a debt of well over 10 trillion renminbi.[20] The major source for paying back these loans is land sales, since local taxing power is severely limited. Thus there is pressure to force farmers to sell their land at prices far below its market value, and that has been a major source of discontent in the countryside.

The third thing that is not only likely but certain to happen is that the recurrent costs needed to maintain all of this new housing and infrastructure will rise rapidly once these facilities begin to age. If the quality of all of this construction has been low this rapid rise in recurrent costs will come sooner than if the quality has been high, but either way it will be a major expenditure item to be covered both by the government and home owners. Where expenditures to replace worn-out or obsolete machinery with new machinery typically involve major upgrades in the quality of capital and hence an increase in its productivity, maintaining housing, roads, railroads, and irrigation canals typically does not involve a rise in productivity. A rising share of recurrent or maintenance costs in GDP, therefore, is also a reason to expect a fall in China's GDP growth rate. Alternatively, if the government and population ignore these recurrent costs, the productivity of the existing housing and infrastructure stock will fall, as is currently happening in the United States.

There are solutions to some of these specific problems, such as the current way local government expenditures are financed, but the point here is that China is not likely to be able to continue productively investing 50 percent of its GDP. The achievements of the past decade of high investment are considerable, but continued investment at this level is likely to create increasing problems and produce less valuable results. A 50 percent investment rate will not itself be enough to sustain a growth rate of 9 percent or more.

The obvious solution to this structural problem is to change the structure by increasing the share of household consumption and the Chinese government has been talking about the need to increase domestic consumption for years. It is easier said than done, however. There are three principal reasons why household consumption is such a low share of GDP in China. The first is that household consumption started the reform period in 1978 at a low level because of two decades of Soviet-style growth that involved making machines to make more machines without much concern for expanding consumer goods. Incomes were held down by the state to match the level of consumer goods that was available. The second reason is that during the reforms China took a number of steps that encouraged a high level of savings by households. These steps involved the one-child-family policy, which led to a sharp fall in the dependency ratio, the weakening or outright abandonment of the limited social safety net that had existed with the commune system in the rural areas and state enterprise employment in the urban areas, and the privatization of urban housing whereas before urban housing had been provided by the state and rent was nominal. The third and probably most important reason is that the growth rate of incomes has until recently lagged behind the growth rate of GDP. This lagging but still rapid increase in incomes was not driven by state wage policies for the most part. Wages by the year 2000 were mostly driven by market forces. Wage growth slower than GDP growth was a normal reflection of a "labor surplus" economy, such that a large reserve of rural unskilled labor was available for the factories and service businesses of urban China at wages that only had to match the average income from farming. Since agricultural income grew considerably more slowly than GDP, the wages for unskilled labor in the cities also grew more slowly than GDP. Chinese wage data, though reported in a way that limit their usefulness for the purposes of this analysis, are presented in Figure 6.3.

As the data in Figure 6.3 indicate, real wages in urban collective enterprises, which had a higher share of unskilled workers than the state-owned sector, followed the trend in rural incomes through about 2001, at which point collective enterprise incomes began to rise faster than average real rural income per capita (the gap between rural incomes and state enterprise wages began opening earlier, around 1998).[21] By the period 2005–2010, average real wages in the urban collective sector were rising at a rate of 13.8 percent a year, or well above the rate of growth of GDP and even faster than the real wage increase in the state sector of 12.8 percent per year. The market forces driving these rapid real wage increases partly reflect the increase in the skill level of the work force in these sectors but also result from the fact that there is no longer a large reserve of underemployed labor in the countryside. Most of the members of the labor force registered as being located in the countryside who are under the age of 40 are now actually working mainly in urban areas and have left agriculture entirely. Farming is mostly done by their aging parents.

If these wage trends continue or if wages begin to grow even faster in relation to GDP than was the case through 2012, then consumption as a share of GDP will begin to rise toward a more normal level. If China's efforts to establish an adequate social safety net for all of its population in the form of a national pension system and affordable health insurance, the rate of

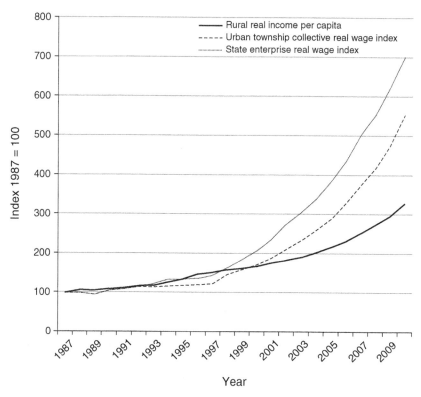

Figure 6.3. Real wage and rural income indices.

Data sources: National Statistical Office, *Zhonguo tongji zhaiyao, 2011,* [China Statistical Abstract 2011] (Beijing: Statistics Press, 2011), p. 48; National Statistical Yearbook 2010, p. 132; National Statistical Office, *Xin Zhongguo 60 nian* [60 Years of New China] (Beijing: Statistics Press, 2009), p. 610; and National Statistical Office, *China Statistical Yearbook 1997* (Beijing: Statistics Press, 1997), p. 123. There are minor differences between the indexes in these different sources, but they are too small to affect the trends described in Figure 6.3.

household savings may also come down, and the consumption share will rise that much faster. The process will be slow, however. If wages grow 3 percent a year faster than GDP and household consumption rises at a similar rate, it will take a decade for Chinese household consumption to rise to 45 percent of GDP and two decades to rise to over 60 percent. There is no guarantee that this will happen, as the data on China's successful neighbors indicates (Figure 6.4). Japan, South Korea, and Taiwan all experienced a decline in the share of household consumption in GDP during their high-growth periods, but only in Taiwan did that share rise back to 60 percent of GDP.

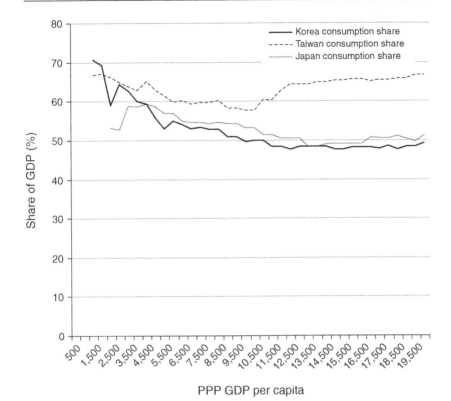

Figure 6.4. Consumption share of GDP in high-income East Asian economies.

Data source: These data were derived from Alan Heston, Robert Summers, and Betina Aten, *Penn World Tables 6.3 and 7.1* (Philadelphia: Center for International Comparisons of Production Income and Prices, University of Pennsylvania, August 2009 and July 2012), and are the share of household consumption in PPP GDP. The per capita GDP figures on the x axis are a rough approximation of the GDP per capita level for the various share levels of household consumption.

Deceleration

China, therefore, is not likely to be an exception to the fact that all countries as they approach high-income status begin to experience a deceleration in their rate of GDP growth. In all high-income countries the ability to learn from and avoid the mistakes of others ahead of them gradually disappears, and growth is increasingly driven by reliance on one's own research and development efforts. That has been the case in the high-income economies of

East Asia and is rapidly becoming the case in China. Migration of labor from low-productivity occupations, mainly in the countryside, to higher productivity jobs in the urban areas also comes to an end, and that is in the process of happening in China as this study is being written. Thus the easier sources of high TFP growth in China are disappearing. They have long since largely disappeared in Japan, South Korea, Taiwan, Hong Kong, and Singapore.

China has managed to sustain a high GDP growth rate despite the steadily declining share of consumption in GDP, consumption that drives growth in most countries. It has done so with a massive housing and infrastructure development program that made up for decades of neglect of these two important sectors, but a massive catch-up effort in them is no longer needed or possibly even desirable. In addition, as this new housing and infrastructure ages, recurrent costs will rise simply to maintain the quality of that housing and infrastructure at its current level.

Thus China's GDP growth rate will come down from the nearly double-digit rates of the past three decades, although no precise date can be given until it actually happens. A deceleration in the growth rate, however, does not mean that China's catching up with the per capita incomes of the high-income countries will come to an end. A slower growth rate could well mean a growth rate of 5 percent a year or even a bit more for some time into the future; it does not mean stagnation or even growth rates at North American and Western European levels of the twentieth century. Japan did well for a time but then let real estate and stock market bubbles get out of hand, followed by little effort to reform in ways that would lead to the rapid recovery of growth. The financial system that worked well for so many years during the high-growth period has served Japan poorly in more recent times. What China's actual growth rate will be and what the growth rate of other high income East Asian economies will be will depend on how well each of them manages growth once the double-digit boom comes to an end.

Notes

Acknowledgments

Index

Notes

Introduction

1. These opening remarks focus on the last 50 years because that is the time period that covers all of the examples of accelerated economic and industrial growth of the economies of East and Southeast Asia except for Japan (which began its growth spurt around 1900). It was also 50 years ago that I first lived and traveled in the region, and thus it reflects the period when I have observed the many changes firsthand. Thanks to a grant from the Ford Foundation, I was able to spend a year doing research in Hong Kong beginning in 1961 with a month in Japan and Taiwan and concluding at the end of 1962 with two months traveling to Vietnam, Cambodia, Indonesia, Thailand, and India. The next chapter will go back many years earlier than this past half century, but the purpose of reviewing this earlier economic history is to better understand what made possible the accelerated growth of this most recent half century.

2. Sung Hwan Ban, Pal Yong Moon, and Dwight H. Perkins, *Rural Development: Studies in the Modernization of the Republic of Korea 1945–1975* (Cambridge, Mass.: distributed by Harvard University Press, 1980), p. 313.

3. There has actually been some economic growth in several of the countries, such as Cambodia and Laos. Mongolia has also begun to make substantial progress, notably in mining, and the political changes in Myanmar open up the possibility that that country will also begin to develop more rapidly. It remains to be seen as this is being written, however, whether or not this growth will be sustained or, in the case of Myanmar, whether the recent changes will in fact be sufficient to trigger accelerated growth. Given the limited amount of work on these economies and my limited familiarity with their performance, they will not play a large role in the chapters that follow.

4. We do not have careful estimates of PPP GDP for China's regions. This figure was derived by assuming that the ratio of PPP GDP per capita to the exchange rate GDP per capita calculation was similar but somewhat less than the nationwide ratio of the Penn World Tables PPP per capita to the GDP per capita

derived using the official exchange rate (which in 2007 was about half of the PPP rate).

5. See Fulbright Economic Teaching Program and Rajawali Institute Faculty, "Choosing Success, The Lessons of East and Southeast Asia and Vietnam's Future," Occasional Paper of the Rajawali Institute for Asia, Harvard University, January 2008.

6. These figures for the bottom 20 percent of the income distribution are crude estimates because the data for the beginning of the reform period were not reported in a way that allows for a precise measurement and, in the case of urban income, the analyst must estimate the large share of income that came in the form of the many urban subsidies, notably housing. The estimates for Gansu and Guizhou do not have these particular problems. The bottom 20 percent data are for 1978 through 2009 while the provincial data are for 1978 through 2008. National Statistical Office, *China Statistical Yearbook, 2010* (Beijing: Statistics Press, 2010), pp. 363; National Statistical Office, *Xin Zhongguo 60 nian* (Beijing: Statistics Press, 2009), pp. 627, 734, and 742; and National Statistical Office, *Statistical Yearbook of China 1990* (Beijing; Statistics Press, 1990).

1. The Historical Foundations of East Asian Development

1. Among the early efforts are Zhang Zhongli (Chang Chung-li) for China, *Income of the Chinese Gentry* (Seattle: University of Washington Press, 1962), and for Japan E. Sydney Crawcour, "The Tokugawa Heritage," in William W. Lockwood, ed., *The State and Economic Enterprise in Japan* (Princeton: Princeton University Press, 1965), pp. 17–44. Historical GDP estimates for Southeast Asia are for the most part more recent—see, for example, Raja Nazrin for Malaysia, "Essays on Economic Growth in Malaysia in the Twentieth Century" (Ph.D. diss., Harvard University, 2000). The Asian Historical Statistics Project of Hitotsubashi University has attempted estimates for Vietnam, Cambodia, and Laos as well as Korea, Japan, and China.

2. Beginning in 2011 there were significant changes in the way Myanmar (the name was changed from Burma by the military government in 1989) was governed. While the military remained in ultimate control, competitive elections were introduced, and numerous other political and economic reforms were begun.

3. China, of course, has Tibetans and Uighurs who have individuals/groups who are pushing for independence, but the combined populations of these two groups is only about 2 percent of the total population. This applies even if all other Hui (Muslims) are added to the total, although when territorial coverage is taken into account, it is larger than their population share. Minorities of all kinds in China makes up just over 8 percent of the total population.

4. Keith Hart, *The Political Economy of West African Agriculture* (Cambridge: Cambridge University Press, 1982). For studies that bring out more of the complexities in the African experience see Basil Davidson, *Africa in History, Themes and Outlines* (London: Macmillan, 1968) and Roland Oliver, *The African Experience*, 2nd ed. (Boulder: Westview Press, 2000).

5. These brief sentences, of course, oversimplify many subtle differences between different parts of Sub-Saharan Africa. Liberia and notably Ethiopia were self-governing. The French tried to create an integrated West Africa but obviously failed in part because of the ambitions of African political leaders, in the run-up to independence. It is not that Africa would have had large unified states in the absence of colonial rule. The differences in languages and the narrow control of many precolonial rulers/leaders would have ensured that modern states in Sub-Saharan Africa would have been small for the most part. There are some similarities between the experience of East Africa, notably Kenya, and that of Malaya. But there was nothing comparable to the cultural and political unity of the Vietnamese, Burmese, and Thai, let alone the Chinese, Koreans, and Japanese. And where there were similarities in the situation in Africa and Southeast Asia prior to European colonization, the European colonization, at least in the Philippines and what became Indonesia, lasted much longer (over three centuries) than that in most of Africa.

6. Malaysia, of course, has a large Chinese and smaller Indian minority, but Malays are an absolute majority even if one recognizes that many groups in northern Borneo (e.g. Dayaks) who are considered to be Bumiputera ("sons of the soil") do not share a Malay cultural heritage. There are also substantial minorities in Myanmar, but again the Burmese have a clear majority. In the Philippines there are the Moslems in the south, but these are a tiny minority of a population that is primarily Catholic Christians.

7. The main exception in Sub-Saharan Africa would be the Portuguese colonies in West Africa that got started in the 1600s.

8. There have been a number of econometric studies using cross-country regressions that have shown that ethnic diversity or "fractionalization," as it is sometimes called, is negatively related to economic growth. See, for example, Alberto Alesina, Arnaud Devleeschauwer, William Easterly, Sergio Kulat, and Romain Wacziarg, "Fractionalization," *Journal of Economic Growth* 8 (2003), pp. 155–194. See also the earlier work of William Easterly and R. Levine, "Africa's Growth Tragedy: Policies and Ethnic Divisions," *Quarterly Journal of Economics* 111, no. 4 (1997), pp. 1203–1250.

9. Earlier studies of Japan suggested that modern economic growth began shortly after the fall of Tokugawa and the beginning of the Meiji Restoration, but subsequent work demonstrated that much of the estimated growth during the first decades after the Restoration was built on data that underestimated

Japanese GDP in the latter part of the nineteenth century. When corrections for data bias were made, most of the estimated growth in this period disappeared.

10. I estimated that the population fell by 75 million during the Taiping Rebellion period; Dwight H. Perkins, *Agricultural Development in China 1368–1968* (Chicago: Aldine, 1969). Peter Schran, "China's Demographic Evolution 1850–1953 Reconsidered," *China Quarterly* 75 (October 1978), pp. 639–646, has argued that the fall in population was less than this but still larger than the 25 million deaths that is the widely cited estimate of deaths caused directly by the rebellion itself (including increased disease as well as civilian and military casualties).

11. Wang Yeh-chien, *Land Taxation in Imperial China, 1750–1911* (Cambridge, Mass.: Harvard University Press, 1974) estimates that taxes of the imperial government during the Qing Dynasty amounted to only about 2 percent of GDP. For the impact of this on Qing Dynasty policy see Dwight H. Perkins, "Government as an Obstacle to Industrialization: The Case of Nineteenth Century China," *Journal of Economic History* 27, no. 4 (1967), pp. 478–492.

12. This is the estimate of Thomas G. Rawski, *Economic Growth in Prewar China* (Berkeley: University of California Press, 1989).

13. The classic work on the Tongzhi Restoration is Mary C. Wright, *The Last Stand of Chinese Conservatism: The T'ung-chih Restoration 1862–1874* (Stanford: Stanford University Press, 1957).

14. See Benjamin Schwartz, *In Search of Wealth and Power: Yen Fu and the West* (Cambridge, Mass.: Harvard University Press, 1964).

15. To say that the major benefits went to Japan, however, does not mean that Korea did not gain experiences with modern economic institutions that contributed to economic development of the country after independence. See, for example, Carter Eckert, *Offspring of Empire: The Koch'ang Kims and the Colonial Origins of Korean Capitalism 1876–1945* (Seattle: University of Washington Press, 1991).

16. The first systematic efforts to estimate GDP growth during the Japanese colonial period in Korea were by Suh Sang-Chul, *Growth and Structural Change in the Korean Economy, 1910–1940* (Cambridge: Council on East Asian Studies, Harvard University, 1976). More recently the Asian Historical Statistics Project of Hitotsubashi University has estimated GDP on both the expenditure and production side in current and constant 1934–1936 prices. One gets slightly different average rates of growth depending on the series chosen and the assumptions made to make the pre- and post-1915 data compatible, but the average annual rate of GDP growth over the 27 years (1938/1911) was 3.5 percent, or around 2 percent per capita, since population was growing at 1.4 percent per year (www.ier.hit-u.ac.jp).

17. British colonial Hong Kong might be seen as an exception to this statement, but we do not have GDP figures for this period for Hong Kong and so cannot readily measure whether rapid economic growth had already begun.

18. Robert Barro in one of his cross-country econometric exercises designed to explain growth found that that inequality was related to slower growth in all low-income countries, although the effect diminishes as income rises and may even become positive at very high incomes. Robert J. Barro, "Inequality and Growth Revisited," ADB Working Paper Series on Regional Economic Integration (Manila, Asian Development Bank, 2008).

19. Ronald Dore, *Education in Tokugawa Japan* (Berkeley: University of California Press, 1965).

20. In this discussion (and in the discussion of Indonesian education under the Dutch) I have benefited immensely from in-depth discussions with my colleague the Chinese literature scholar Wilt Idema.

21. The best quantitative estimate of the number is in Zhang Zhongli, *Income of the Chinese Gentry*.

22. Evelyn Rawski, *Education and Popular Literacy in Ch'ing China* (Ann Arbor: University of Michigan Press, 1979), p. 23.

23. Wilt Idema, "Review of Evelyn Sakakida Rawski, *Education and Popular Literacy in Ch'ing China*," *T'oung Pao* 66 (1980), p. 322.

24. John Lossing Buck, *Land Utilization in China* (Nanjing: University of Nanjing Press, 1937).

25. Idema, "Review," p. 322. This estimate is of the number of urban residents who received some schooling in the late nineteenth century.

26. These figures are all taken from Leo Orleans, *Professional Manpower and Education in Communist China* (Washington, D.C.: National Science Foundation, 1961), pp. 68–69 and 126.

27. National Statistical Office, *China Statistical Yearbook 2010* (Beijing: China Statistics Press, 2010), p. 756.

28. See, for example, Isabel Bird Bishop, *Korea and Her Neighbors: A Narrative of Travel with an Account of the Vicissitudes and Present Position of the Country* (originally published 1898; republished London: Routledge, 2002).

29. Lauriston Sharp, "Colonial Regimes in Southeast Asia," *Far Eastern Survey* 15, no. 4, February 26, 1946, p. 49.

30. These data are from Buro Pusat Statistik, *Statistik Indonesia 1988* (Jakarta: Buro Pusat Statistik, 1988), pp. 118–138.

31. Times Higher Education, *The World University Rankings (2010–2011)*, www.timeshighereducation.co.uk/world-university-rankings.

32. Jiaotong University, Academic Rankings of World Universities 2010, www.shanghairanking.com/index.html.

33. QS World University Rankings 2010, www.topuniversities.com/university
-rankings/world.

34. National Center for Education Statistics, U.S. Department of Education Institute of Education Sciences, http://nces.ed.gov.

35. For a more in-depth discussion of education in Malaysia see Donald R. Snod-
grass, "Education in Korea and Malaysia," in Henry Rowen, ed., *Behind East
Asian Growth: The Political and Social Foundations of Prosperity* (London:
Routledge, 1998).

36. These estimates were derived from school enrollment data in State Statistical
Bureau, *Statistical Yearbook of China 1981* (Beijing: Statistics Press, 1981),
p. 451, and data from the 1953 and 1964 censuses reported in Nai-Ruenn
Chen, *Chinese Economic Statistics: A Handbook for Mainland China* (Chicago: Aldine, 1967), p. 135. The percentage enrollment figures are rough
estimates because the age data in the censuses was not grouped by primary
and secondary school age groups, so the size of the populations in those
two groups had to be estimated from these data. There is also the fact that
primary and secondary students varied in age even within a single grade
level.

37. For a similar view by a longtime scholar of Southeast Asia, see Anne Booth,
"Education and economic development in Southeast Asia," in K. S. Jomo, ed.,
From Southeast Asian Paper Tigers? Miracle to Debacle and Beyond (London:
Routledge, 2003), pp. 173–195.

38. A case can be made that most local people in regions such as Malaya had little
incentive to do what many poor Chinese immigrants were willing to do in
hopes of returning to China rich. Most Chinese immigrants did not become
rich, and many died trying, especially in the early years. The story of the founding of Kuala Lumpur is one where 87 Chinese came to the area to develop a
tin mine and all but 17 died of malaria.

39. It is not possible to find evidence of how hard individuals work, but it is possible to find which countries have workers that put in the longest working hours.
Among OECD countries, Koreans worked more hours per year (2,193 hours in
2010) than any other country, with the exception of Mexico (2,250 hours in
2010). The only other OECD country in East Asia was Japan, which worked
substantially fewer hours in 2010 (1,733); in Japan's case the number of hours
worked has been declining steadily for decades, but I am not aware of a source
with data from the 1960s and 1970s that would be most relevant for comparisons with other East Asian countries. OECD StatExtracts, "Average Annual
Hours Worked Per Worker," stats.oecd.org/Index.aspx?DatasetCode=anhrs.

40. This saying basically implies that poor individuals work hard and become
successful but then spoil their children, who stop working hard and spend all
of the wealth, leaving the next generation poor again.

2. Understanding East Asian Growth

1. For a broad survey of the large number of these econometric efforts to explain growth, see Steven N. Durlauf, Paul A. Johnson, and Jonathan R. W. Temple, "Growth Econometrics," chap. 8 in Philippe Aghion and Steven Durlauf, eds., *Handbook of Economic Growth 1A* (Amsterdam: North-Holland, 2005), pp. 555–650.

2. The statistical reason is that many of the variables are endogenous (they contribute to the rate of GDP growth and their magnitude itself is strongly influenced by GDP growth, directly or indirectly).

3. Ross Levine and David Renelt, "A Sensitivity Analysis of Cross-Country Growth Regressions," *American Economic Review* 82, no. 84, September 1992, pp. 942–963.

4. Xavier Sala-i-Martin, "I Just Ran Two Million Regressions," *American Economic Review* 87, no. 2, May 1997, pp. 178–183.

5. The earliest work that dealt with this issue that I am aware of was in a study by Alan Gelb that led to his edited volume *Oil Windfalls: Blessing or Curse,* World Bank Publication (Oxford: Oxford University Press, 1988). For a survey of the literature on this subject from the mid-1980s to the present see Jeffrey Frankel, *The Natural Resources Curse: A Survey,* Faculty Research Working Paper Series (Cambridge: Harvard Kennedy School, 2010), 45 pp.

6. Alberto Alesina, Sule Ozler, Nouriel Roubini, and Phillip Lee Swagel, "Political Instability and Economic Growth," *Journal of Economic Growth* 1, no. 2 (1996), pp. 189–211.

7. Hong Kong has had large infrastructure investment, but much of it has been privately financed.

8. Stanley Fischer, "The Role of Macroeconomic Factors in Growth," *Journal of Monetary Economics* 32 (1993), pp. 485–512.

9. The institutions that made up the index used for this variable included (1) the perceived efficiency of the government bureaucracy, (2) the extent of government corruption, (3) efficacy of the rule of law, (4) the presence or absence of expropriation risk, and (5) the perceived risk of repudiation of contracts by government.

10. Dwight H. Perkins, "Corporate Governance, Industrial Policy, and the Rule of Law," in Shahid Yusuf, M. Anjum Altaf, and Kaoru Nabeshima, eds., *Global Change and East Asia Policy Initiatives* (Washington, D.C.: World Bank, 2004) pp. 293–336.

11. Daron Acemoglu, Simon Johnson, and James A. Robinson, "The Colonial Origins of Comparative Development: An Empirical Investigation," *American Economic Review* 91, no. 5 (December 2001), pp. 1369–1401.

12. Daron Acemoglu and James A. Robinson, *Why Nations Fail: The Origins of Power, Prosperity, and Poverty* (New York: Crown Business, 2012).

13. This book is also not the place to do full justice to work by Acemoglu and Robinson. I largely agree with their view of how European economic history fits into their framework of extractive versus inclusive societies, and their historical examples certainly back them up. My own experience in Africa, although not remotely comparable to my experience in Asia (I have made 15 or so trips to Africa over two decades, largely in a supervisory capacity connected with projects of the Harvard Institute for International Development) is consistent with their view that extractive regimes are a major part of the problem.

14. Jessica Cohen and William Easterly, eds., *What Works in Development? Thinking Big and Thinking Small* (Washington, D.C.: Brookings, 2009).

15. Robert Solow, "Technical change and the aggregate production function," *Review of Economics and Statistics* 39, no. 3 (August 1957), pp. 312–320.

16. For a methodological critique directly related to growth accounting estimates in East Asia, see Jesus Felipe, "A decade of debate about the sources of growth in East Asia. How Much Do We Know about Why Some Countries Grow Faster Than Others," *Estudios de Economia Aplicada* 24, no. 1 (2006), pp. 181–220. Critiques of the very concept of an aggregate production function go back to the famous Cambridge debate between MIT and Cambridge University economists.

17. Alwyn Young, "The Tyranny of Numbers: Confronting the Statistical Realities of the East Asia Growth Experience," *Quarterly Journal of Economics* 110, no. 3 (August 1995), pp. 641–680.

18. These data are from Economic Planning Board, *Handbook of Korean Economy 1980* (Seoul: Economic Planning Board, 1980), pp. 12–16.

19. See Jeffrey Williamson, "Why Do Koreans 'Save So Little'?," *Journal of Development Economics* 6, no. 3 (1979), pp. 343–362.

20. The GDP growth rates for the pre-1979 period are not the rates found in official publications. GDP was revalued in year 2000 prices that removed the large distortion caused by high state-set industrial prices prior to the 1990s that overweighted the rapidly growing industrial sector in the GDP calculations.

21. Young, "Tyranny of Numbers," p. 657. Young's data are for the years 1961–1966, so the match between growth, TFP, and the political changes is not exact.

22. Scott Baier, Gerald Dwyer, and Robert Tamura, "How Important are Capital and Total Factor Productivity for Economic Growth," *Economic Inquiry* 44, no. 1 (January 2006), p. 46. This study, like the work of Barry Bosworth and Susan Collins, *The Empirics of Economic Growth: An Update* (Washington, D.C.: Brookings, 2003), www.brookings.edu/research/papers/2003/09, estimates the growth accounting equations for a large number of countries. Of necessity,

this study uses a simplified calculation, since duplicating Young's methodology for 100 or more countries would take the better part of a lifetime. This simple approach is more than adequate for the uses we make of them here. Nonetheless, estimates dealing explicitly with the Sukarno period would have been helpful.

23. Pierre van der Eng, "Accounting for Indonesia's Economic Growth: Recent Past and Near Future," paper presented at University of Queensland, Brisbane, Australia, December 2006.

24. These data cover the years 1960–1994 and are from Barry Bosworth and Susan Collins, "Economic Growth in East Asia: Accumulation versus Assimilation," *Brookings Papers on Economic Activity* 2 (1996), pp. 135–191.

25. Khuong M. Vu, "Economic Reform and Performance: A Comparative Study of China and Vietnam," *China: An International Journal* 7, no. 2 (September 2009), pp. 189–226.

26. Lawrence Lau pioneered a quite different approach to growth accounting that pools data from a number of East Asian and European economies and estimates a pooled production function. The estimates in this equation attribute most of the growth to capital formation among the lower income East Asian economies in the sample, but this equation also indicates that there are very large aggregate economies of scale for these economies. We don't really have an understanding of what economies of scale at the aggregate production function level are, as contrasted to the individual firm production function, where they typically involve a large plant having lower costs per unit of production than a smaller plant. A plausible explanation at the aggregate level is that economies of scale involve external economies that occur as an economy expands in size. These external economies would appear in our growth accounting equations (where constant returns to scale are assumed) as a residual or a measure of TFP. Such external economies could include such things as major improvements in economic governance, etc. See, for example, Jong-Il Kim and Lawrence J. Lau, "The Sources of Asian Economic Growth," *Canadian Journal of Economics* 29, special issue (April 1996), pp. 448–454.

27. The education and labor force data for South Korea used to make this calculation were taken from Noel F. McGinn, Donald R. Snodgrass, Yung-Bong Kim, and Shin-Bok Kim, *Education and Development in Korea* (Cambridge, Mass.: Harvard University Council on East Asia Studies, 1980), p. 120.

28. One of the better known such growth equations that would substantially increase the contribution of education if growth accounting measures used it is in Robert Lucas, "On the Mechanics of Economic Development," *Journal of Monetary Economics* 22 (1988), pp. 3–42. This equation multiplies a standard growth equation with a variable designed to capture the external effects of education, but no one to my knowledge knows how to measure these external affects.

3. Government Intervention versus Laissez-Faire
in Northeast Asia

1. The well-known World Bank study attempted to draw general lessons from the experience of the more successful economies in both Northeast and Southeast Asia taken together; World Bank, *The East Asian Miracle* (New York: Oxford University Press, 1994). This chapter attempts to point out that there were major differences between the policies and performances not only of Southeast Asia relative to Northeast Asia but also within Northeast Asia, where the policies of Hong Kong had little in common with those of Japan or South Korea. There was no one model of East Asia growth, even when the discussion is confined to the more successful economies in the region. For earlier discussions of this see Dwight H. Perkins, "There are at Least Three Models of East Asian Development," *World Development* 22, no. 4 (1994), pp. 655–661 and K. S. Jomo, introduction to Jomo, *Southeast Asian Paper Tigers? From Miracle to Debacle and Beyond* (London: Routledge, 2003), pp. 1–18.

2. There was considerable government-led industrial development and trade policy in Europe even earlier, as well as considerable variation in the degree of government involvement in industry, but the broader subject of the history of industrial policy worldwide is far beyond the scope of this book. For those interested in the degree to which Japan's approach was similar or different from that on the European continent see David Landes, "Japan and Europe: Contrasts in Industrialization," in William W. Lockwood, ed., *The State and Economic Enterprise in Japan* (Princeton: Princeton University Press, 1965), pp. 93–182. For those interested in this subject, and the variation in European industrial policy in the first decades of industrialization more generally, see Alexander Gerschenkron, *Europe in the Russian Mirror* (Cambridge: Cambridge University Press, 1961).

3. There is a large literature on the economic development of Japan and its industrial development in particular, beginning with the Meiji Restoration in 1868 and ending with Japan's invasion of China in 1937. The classic is William W. Lockwood, *The Economic Development of Japan: Growth and Structural Change* (Princeton: Princeton University Press, 1954), on which this brief paragraph is based.

4. Henry Rosovsky, *Capital Formation in Japan* (Glencoe, Ill.: Free Press, 1961).

5. The best known work on the role of MITI during this period is Chalmers Johnson, *MITI and the Japanese Miracle: The Growth of Industrial Policy, 1945–1975* (Stanford: Stanford University Press, 1981).

6. This discussion of the Japanese economic system in the 1950s and 1960s is based in part on William W. Lockwood, "Japan's 'New Capitalism,'" in Lockwood, *The State and Economic Enterprise in Japan* (Princeton: Princeton University Press, 1965), pp. 447–522.

7. As late as 1962, total South Korean exports were a minuscule US$54.8 million (in current prices of 1962).

8. This is the value in 1975 factor cost (200.13 billion won) divided by the 1975 exchange rate of 483 won to the dollar; Economic Planning Board, *Handbook of Korean Economy 1980* (Seoul: Economic Planning Board, 1980), p. 19. In 2010 prices, this would be a bit over US$2 billion, still a very small figure for a country of 26 million people at the time.

9. See Jeffrey Williamson, "Why Do Koreans 'Save So Little'?," *Journal of Development Economics* 6, no. 3 (1979), pp. 343–362.

10. For a more in-depth look at the politics of this period of transition to an export-oriented development policy, see Stephan Haggard, *Pathways from the Periphery: The Politics of Growth in the Newly Industrializing Countries* (Ithaca: Cornell University Press, 1990), chap. 3.

11. Charles R. Frank, Kwang Suk Kim, and Larry E. Westphal, *Foreign Trade Regimes and Economic Development: South Korea* (New York: National Bureau of Economic Research, 1975), chap. 4.

12. It was undervalued in the sense that prices of exported products and most other tradables, except for a few protected sectors, were far below world prices (see discussion below of individual sector purchasing power exchange rates). It was not undervalued in the sense that Korea was running large trade surpluses. Korea ran trade deficits throughout the 1960s and 1970s even with numerous controls on imports. These trade deficits were structural, in that exports were virtually nonexistent at the beginning of the period and it took a long time for exporters to find foreign markets, produce goods appropriate for those markets, and thus gradually build market share. Korea did not run its first trade surplus until 1986, which was also the first year that the nominal Korean exchange rate appreciated.

13. The three key faculty members were Simon Kuznets, Robert Dorfman, and myself, with David C. Cole contributing as the organizer of the effort, working through the Harvard Development Advisory Service, later the Harvard Institute for International Development.

14. In the *Times* list of the top universities in the world in 2011, the Korean Advanced Institute of Science and Technology ranked number 79. Only seven universities in developing countries (two in Hong Kong, three in China, one other in Korea, and one in Singapore) were included.

15. This statement is based on discussions over the years with individuals who worked closely with President Park on economic matters.

16. This was one of the interviews done for the Korea Development Institute–Harvard University series of books on the Korean economy published in the early 1980s. See Leroy P. Jones and Sakong Il, *Government, Business, and Entrepreneurship in Economic Development: The Korean Case* (Cambridge, Mass.: Harvard Council on East Asia Studies, 1980).

17. Alice Amsden, *Asia's Next Giant: South Korea and Late Industrialization* (Oxford: Oxford University Press, 1989).

18. It is not possible to prove in a convincing fashion that the won was undervalued relative to what a free market would have produced because there were so many distortions in the Korean economy in the 1960s that it is not clear just what would have happened in a free market. What one can say is that Korean exporters faced little competition in their domestic market from imports thanks in part to the frequent devaluations of the won.

19. Frank, Kim, and Westphal, *Foreign Trade Regimes,* p. 208.

20. The data referred to here are in Frank, Kim, and Westphal, *Foreign Trade Regimes,* pp. 202–203 (these figures are the Corden average in table 10-5 in that source).

21. These data have the advantage over most such calculations by individuals in that they had the considerable support of the World Bank behind them, making it possible to spend considerable sums to ensure that the price comparisons were really for fully comparable products. The one weakness of these data, for my purposes, is that the prices in Korean won are mostly retail prices and thus include distribution costs, hence in that sense are not completely comparable to "border prices" (FOB or CIF prices at the port of exit or entry).

22. The high-priced sectors also included many sectors such as coffee, cocoa, spirits, tropical fruits, and the like that were treated as "luxuries" and taxed accordingly.

23. The household surveys in the first two decades after 1960 did not include families with incomes above a certain level (generally above about US$5,000 in current prices or perhaps US$35,000 in 2010 prices) that effectively excluded the top few percent of the highest earners.

24. It should be noted that Rosenstein-Rodan first developed this idea in the early 1940s, when there was good reason to believe that industries in most countries would have to rely on their domestic markets. Relying on exports had not been a realistic strategy from the beginning of World War I in 1914 through most years until after the end of World War II in 1945. Paul Rosenstein-Rodan, "Problems of Industrialization of Eastern and Southern Europe," *Economic Journal* 53 (1943), pp. 202–211.

25. For a discussion of the politics of the transition from import substitution to export orientation in Taiwan in the early 1960s, see Haggard, *Pathways from the Periphery,* chap. 4.

26. I heard him say this in speeches at Harvard and in a meeting with him in his office in Taipei.

27. The exchange rate had been substantially devalued in late 1958 from NT$24.58 per U.S. dollar (for exports) to NT$36.08 per dollar, and in early 1960 it was further devalued to NT$40.03 per U.S. dollar.

28. Manufactured exports by 1970 constituted 70 percent of Taiwan's total exports.

29. Robert Wade's influential book *Governing the Market: Economic Theory and the Role of Government in East Asia Industrialization* (Princeton: Princeton University Press, 1990) discusses the Taiwan model of this period. Wade's description is accurate for the time his research was done, but as will be made clear in the text, Taiwan's approach after the 1970s moved a long distance from the development model followed in the 1960s and 1970s.

30. See www.forbes.com/global2000.

31. Taiwan avoided the crisis because at the time of the crisis elsewhere, Taiwan was running current account surpluses, had large foreign exchange reserves, and limited foreign debt. Thus there was little danger of the central bank running out of foreign exchange and thus triggering a massive devaluation of the currency and large increases in foreign debt (expressed in NT dollars) as happened in Thailand, Korea, and Indonesia.

32. We don't have reliable GDP data for Hong Kong prior to the 1960s, so it is possible that high growth was already well under way at that time, but as pointed out in the text, Hong Kong, like the other three, had major adjustments to deal with in this period that would probably have slowed growth somewhat. Reliable GDP data for Singapore are also not available until the 1960s.

33. Dwight H. Perkins, "Corporate Governance, Industrial Policy, and the Rule of Law," in Shahid Yusuf, M. Anjum Altaf, and Kaoru Nabeshima, eds., *Global Change and East Asian Policy Initiatives* (Washington, D.C.: World Bank and Oxford University Press, 2004), pp. 293–336.

34. These figures are from Alan Heston, Robert Summers, and Betina Aten, *Penn World Tables 6.3 and 7.1* (Philadelphia: Center for International Comparisons of Production Income and Prices, University of Pennsylvania, August 2009 and July 2012), and are in 2005 international or U.S. prices.

35. Hong Kong accounted for 65.6 percent of foreign direct investment actually utilized in China in 1988 and 61.2 percent in 1989; National Statistical Office, *Zhongguo tongji nianjian 1990* [China Statistical Yearbook 1990] (Beijing: China Statistics Press, 1990), p. 654.

36. Government of Hong Kong SAR, Census and Statistics Department, 2011, www.centstatd.gov.hk/hong_kong_statistics. For a further discussion of this shift in the structure of Hong Kong's economy, see Zhigang Tao and Y C Richard Wong, *Hong Kong: From an Industrialized City to a Center of Manufacturing Related Services,* working paper, Hong Kong Institute of Economics and Business Strategy, 2001, www.hiebs.hku.hk/working_paper_updates /pdf.

37. Singapore Department of Statistics, www.singstat.gov.sg.

38. *Singapore Statistics Newsletter,* September 2010, www.singstat.gove.sg/pubn /papers.

39. See Transparency International, Corruption Perceptions Index 2010, www
.transparency.org/policy_research/survey_indices/cpi/2010/results.
40. These are PPP estimates in 2005 prices from Alan Heston, Robert Summers,
and Betina Aten, *Penn World Tables 6.3* and *7.1* (Philadelphia: Center for International Comparisons of Production Income and Prices, University of
Pennsylvania, August 2009 and July 2012). At the official exchange rate, Singapore's per capita GDP in 2009 was US$36,760, and it was US$51,600 in current prices in 2011 (www.singstat.gov.sg/stats).

4. Successes and Failures in Southeast Asia

1. World Bank, World Development Indicators, http://databank.worldbank.org
/ddp/home.do?Step=1.
2. The Indonesian legislature had to approve formal legislation, and members
could have some influence on specific elements in the legislation, but for the
most part, once the president had decided on an economic matter, that was
what was passed into law or put out as a Presidential Directive ("Inpres").
3. For an in-depth discussion of the broader political forces in Indonesia that
influenced economic policy from outside the government in the 1980s, see
Andrew McIntyre, *Business and Politics in Indonesia* (St. Leonards, Australia:
Allen and Unwin, 1991).
4. These officials included several whose training was in subjects such as accounting and who were allies, but not protégés, of Professor Widjojo or were
Ph.D. graduates of U.S. universities. At a dinner in Cambridge that I hosted as
head of the Harvard Institute for International Development for the then
minister of finance (Radius Prawiro) and the head of the Bank of Indonesia
(Arifin Siregar) they joked about how they were part of the "Rotterdam Mafia" since that was where they were educated.
5. Widjojo Nitisastro, *The Indonesian Development Experience: A Collection of
Writings and Speeches of Widjojo Nitisastro* (Singapore: Institute of Southeast
Asian Studies, 2011). The speech and writing selections in this book, however,
are mostly focused on particular crises that Indonesia faced rather than the
overall approach to development during noncrisis periods. Radius Prawiro,
who also played a key role in the development efforts of this period, first as
minister of finance and later as coordinating economics minister, has written
a book describing in more detail the many reform initiatives that comprised
the development strategy of the "technocrats." Radius Prawiro, *Indonesia's
Struggle for Economic Development: Pragmatism in Action* (Kuala Lumpur:
Oxford University Press, 1998).
6. See discussion in Wing Thye Woo and Anwar Nasution, "External Debt Management," in Jeffrey Sachs and Susan Collins, eds., *Developing Country Debt*

and Economic Performance (Chicago: University of Chicago Press, 1987), vol. 3, chap. 7.

7. In the early 1980s into the 1990s, the Harvard Institute for International Development managed a training program for the Ministries of Finance and Planning that involved placing many hundreds of students in American graduate programs in economics and management. This training program was directly connected to the economic reform efforts then under way.

8. World Bank, World Development Indicators, http://databank.worldbank.org/ddp/home.do?Step=1.

9. For a more complete discussion of Indonesian economic development through to the 1990s, see Hal Hill, *The Indonesian Economy* (Cambridge: Cambridge University Press, 2000).

10. It should be noted that 1996 was the year before the mismanagement of the economy led Indonesia into a deep recession during the 1997–1998 financial crisis. These indicators probably would have been higher in the 1980s and early 1990s. Doing Business, *Doing Business 2012* [and earlier years] (Washington, D.C.: World Bank, 2012 and earlier years).

11. For a more detailed discussion of Malaysia's economic policies and performance over the 50 years since independence, see Richard Leete, *Malaysia from Kampung to Twin Towers: 50 Years of Economic and Social Development* (Shah Alam: Oxford Fajar Sdn. Bhd., 2007).

12. Initially it also included Singapore, but Singapore was pushed out of the Federation in 1965.

13. Some individuals in the Harvard team in the Malaysian Economic Planning Unit (EPU) in 1968 and earlier felt that Tan opposed many of the EPU initiatives because he did not understand macroeconomics and hence opposed government-led investments designed to stimulate the economy. Just Faaland from Norway, Harvard's team leader in 1969, went back and read many of Tan's political speeches. This revealed that Tan knew quite clearly what he was doing by opposing many of these investment projects (particularly large-scale land settlement projects). They would be paid for by the Chinese business community, and he was also head of the main Chinese political party in the governing coalition led by the United Malay National Organization: his Chinese business constituency would receive few, if any, of the benefits of these programs.

14. I was one of the two other advisors involved in this exercise, and I wrote a first draft of a paper based on our discussions, but the final draft was done by the head of our project, Just Faaland, and he was the one who presented to Malaysian government officials at Frasers Hill. The other participant in these discussions was Donald Hoerr. For papers on related topics done at that roughly same time see Just Faaland, J. R. Parkinson, and Rais Saniman, *Growth and*

Ethnic Inequality: Malaysia's New Economic Policy (London: Hust, 1990), appendixes.

15. Chor Ching Go, "Family, Schooling, and Earnings: An Empirical Investigation for Malaysia" (Ph.D. diss., Harvard University, 1999).

16. The initial effort to force domestic non-Bumiputera firms to sell shares to Bumiputera ran into the problem that there were very few individual Bumiputera with sufficient funds to buy these shares, and when they were allocated shares at highly subsidized rates, they often simply sold them and pocketed the difference. This problem was dealt with by creating large unit trusts (mutual funds) that would hold these shares on behalf of all Bumiputera, who were then allocated shares from the unit trust.

17. For a discussion, among other things, of what it would take to increase Malaysia's rate of growth in the future, see Shahid Yusuf and Kaoru Nabeshima, *Tiger Economies under Threat: A Comparative Analysis of Malaysia's Industrial Prospects and Policy Options* (Washington, D.C.: World Bank, 2009).

18. Malaysia's oil boom began in the early 1970s, and production of oil and gas rose rapidly so that oil rents by the 1980s amounted to 17.5 percent of GDP, fell to 10.6 percent in the 1990s, and then rose and fell with the prices of petroleum but generally were above 11 percent of GDP and as high as 20 percent (in 2008).

19. G. William Skinner, *Chinese Society in Thailand: An Analytical History* (Ithaca: Cornell University Press, 1957).

20. Daron Acemoglu and James A. Robinson, *Why Nations Fail* (New York: Crown Business, 2012).

21. For an in-depth analysis of Philippines economic development see Arsenio M. Balisacan and Hal Hill, eds., *The Philippine Economy: Development Policies and Challenges* (Oxford: Oxford University Press, 2003).

22. For more discussion of the specific nature of industrial policies in Southeast Asia see Rajah Rasiah, "Manufacturing Export Growth in Indonesia, Malaysia, and Thailand," in K. S. Jomo, *Southeast Asian Paper Tigers: From Miracle to Debacle and Beyond* (London: Routledge, 2003), pp. 19–80.

5. From Command to Market Economy in China and Vietnam

1. They are closer in percentage terms in that $10,000 per capita is more than a third of the income of the average high-income country ($27,000 per capita according to the World Bank) but is ten or more times the level of the average low-income country.

2. National Statistical Office, *Xin Zhongguo 60 nian* [60 Years of New China] (Beijing: Statistics Press, 2009), pp. 608, 614.

3. These growth rates are derived from the official indexes for real growth in the primary, secondary, and tertiary sectors but using the sector weights for the

year 2000 in 2000 prices and then reconstructing the values of the three sectors back to 1952 or 1957 in 2000 prices and then adding the three sectors to get GDP in 2000 prices. See Dwight H. Perkins and Thomas G. Rawski, "Forecasting China's Economic Growth 2025," in Loren Brandt and Thomas Rawski, eds., *China's Great Economic Transformation* (Cambridge: Cambridge University Press, 2008), pp. 829–886 and appendixes on Dwight Perkins's Harvard Department of Economics website, www.economics.harvard.edu /faculty/perkins/files.

4. General Statistical Office, *Nien Giam Thong Ke 1993* [Statistical Yearbook 1993] (Hanoi: Statistical Publishing House, 1994), p. 218.

5. One of the best studies to comprehensively describe these reforms is Barry Naughton, *The Chinese Economy: Transitions and Growth* (Cambridge, Mass.: MIT Press, 2007) and *Growing Out of the Plan: Chinese Economic Reform, 1978–1993* (Cambridge: Cambridge University Press, 1995). For a detailed view from inside the reform process see Jinglian Wu, *Understanding and Interpreting Chinese Economic Reform* (Mason, Ohio: Thomson/Southwestern, 2005). For a less extensive but stimulating look at China's reforms see Justin Yifu Lin, *Demystifying the Chinese Economy* (Cambridge: Cambridge University Press, 2012).

6. These data are taken or derived from State Statistical Bureau, *Statistical Yearbook of China 1981* (Beijing; Statistics Press, 1981), pp. 357–358; National Statistical Office, *Xin Zhongguo 60 nian* [60 Years of New China], pp. 660–661; and National Statistical Office, *Zhonguo tongji zhaiyao 2011* [China Statistical Abstract 2011] (Beijing: Statistics Press, 2011), pp. 64–65.

7. These data are from Yun-wing Sung, *The China–Hong Kong Connection: The Key to China's Open-Door Policy* (Cambridge: Cambridge University Press, 1991), p. 19.

8. For a more in-depth analysis of the kinds of institutional changes brought about by the reforms in agriculture, see Yiping Huang, *Agricultural Reform in China: Getting Institutions Right* (Cambridge: Cambridge University Press, 1998).

9. This forecast first appeared in print in Dwight H. Perkins, "The International Consequences of China's Economic Development," in Richard Solomon, ed., *The China Factor: Sino-American Relations and the Global Scene* (New York: Prentice Hall, 1981), pp. 114–136. The essay got the approval of the Chinese press since it was more optimistic than most Chinese actually felt at the time (e.g. "Zhongguo gong nongye zongchanzhi wanquan keyi fanliangfan," [The gross output of China's industry and agriculture can quadruple], *Renmin ribao,* November 2, 1982, p. 6). The actual growth rate in 1979–1981 turned out to be 6.9 percent, but it soon accelerated to well above 8 percent as the reforms took hold and Zhao Ziyang with Deng Xiaoping's support moved beyond the conservative approach of Chen Yun, whose views had dominated many reform policies in those early years.

10. Different sources in China give different rates of increase in farm product purchase prices. The figure in the text is from National Statistical Office, *Zhongguo tongji nianjian 1990* [China Statistical Yearbook 1990] (Beijing: Statistics Press, 1990), p. 274, which also indicates that this purchase price index rose by 54.7 percent between 1978 and 1984. On the other hand, the Ministry of Agriculture's *Zhongguo nongye nianjian 1985* [China Yearbook of Agriculture 1985] (Beijing: Agriculture Press, 1985), p. 229, reports that the index for 1984 over 1978 was up 26.3 percent, but this figure appears to reflect only state-set prices, whereas the later national yearbook clearly attempts to measure the market prices actually paid to farmers.

11. These data are from National Statistical Office, *Zhongguo tongji nianjian 1985* [China Statistical Yearbook 1985] (Beijing: Statistics Press, 1985), p. 348. There are no reliable cultivated acreage data for this period, so per hectare figures were derived by assuming a cultivated acreage of 120 million hectares, a figure that is consistent with later estimates of China's total arable land.

12. One influential article by Justin Yifu Lin estimated that decollectivization, or a return to household production, accounted for nearly half of the growth in agricultural output (42 to 47 percent, depending on the methodology used) and the increase of farm product purchase prices relative to farm input prices accounted for another 16 percent in the six-year period (working through increases in inputs), 1979–1984. As for TFP, it accounted for 49 percent, most of which he estimated was due to the household responsibility system. Justin Yifu Lin, "Rural Reforms and Agricultural Growth in China," *American Economic Review* 82, no. 1 (March 1992), pp. 34–51.

13. For the disagreements over economic policy in this period between the more radical reformers led by Zhao Ziyang and supported by Deng Xiaoping and the more conservative reformers led by Chen Yun, see Ezra Vogel, *Deng Xiaoping and the Transformation of China* (Cambridge, Mass.: Harvard University Press, 2012), chaps. 14–16.

14. For an account of the debate over the dual-price system and many other aspects of the first phases of reform that was written by those involved in the process, see Sheng Hua, Xuejun Zhang, and Xiaopeng Luo, *China: From Revolution to Reform* (London: MacMillan, 1993).

15. Lawrence J. Lau, Yingyi Qian, and Gerard Roland, "Reform without Losers: An Interpretation of China's Dual-Track Approach to Transition," *Journal of Political Economy* 108, no. 1 (February 2000), pp. 120–143.

16. National Statistical Office, *Statistical Yearbook of China 1994* (Beijing: Statistics Press, 1994), p. 375.

17. For a more in-depth discussion of property rights in rural China in the 1980s and 1990s see Jean Oi and Andrew Walder, eds., *Property Rights and Economic Reform in China* (Stanford: Stanford University Press, 1999).

18. For another view of how China "solved" the property rights problem with respect to township and village enterprises, see Xu Chenggang and Martin Weitzman, "Chinese Township and Village Enterprises as Vaguely Defined Cooperatives," *Journal of Comparative Economics* 18, no. 2 (1994), pp. 121–145.

19. Economic Planning Board, *Major Statistics of Korean Economy 1987* (Seoul: Economic Planning Board, 1987), p. 195.

20. The Chinese data are all from National Statistical Office, *Xin Zhongguo 60 nian* [60 Years of New China] (Beijing: Statistics Press, 2009).

21. See reported records of meetings of these leaders in Zhang Liang, comp., and Andrew Nathan and Perry Link, eds., *The Tiananmen Papers* (New York: Public Affairs, 2001).

22. For a similar view based on a rich body of evidence see Ezra Vogel, *Deng Xiaoping and the Transformation of China*.

23. In 1974, 1978, and 1979 I accompanied Senator Henry M. Jackson of the state of Washington in meetings with Deng Xiaoping that focused on a wide range of strategic issues and lasted from two to five hours each.

24. Reinforcing this attitude was the fact that local political leaders had a major say in who became managers of the local branches of the major state-owned commercial banks.

25. A major work on the nature of the financial system at that time is Nicholas Lardy, *China's Unfinished Economic Revolution* (Washington, D.C.: Brookings Institution, 1998).

26. By 2010, politically directed lending by the state banks had been curtailed to a substantial although far from complete degree (e.g. large state bank lending for local investment in infrastructure during the global recession of 2008–2009 was a major exception).

27. National Statistical Office, *China Statistical Yearbook 1997* (Beijing: Statistics Press, 1997), p. 431.

28. In 2001, for example, state-owned enterprises in 33 of 37 industrial sectors were profitable sector-wide, and of the four sectors that were not profitable, only one, petroleum processing and coking, had significant losses (of 2.04 billion renminbi), probably because of state price controls on their products. This was one of the few sectors that had such controls.

29. National Statistical Office, *Zhongguo tongji nianjian 1987* [China Statistical Yearbook 1987] (Beijing: Statistics Press, 1987), pp. 604–605.

30. There are many studies of foreign direct investment in China. For a comprehensive analytical study see Yasheng Huang, *Selling China: Foreign Direct Investment during the Reform Era* (Cambridge: Cambridge University Press, 2003).

31. These comparisons are of PPP GDP as estimated in Alan Heston, Robert Summers, and Betina Aten, *Penn World Tables 7.1* (Philadelphia: Center for

International Comparisons of Production Income and Prices, University of Pennsylvania, July 2012).

32. This trade ratio uses the Chinese estimates of their foreign trade in renminbi and compares it with GDP in the same currency.

33. These data are from Economic Planning Board, *Major Statistics of Korean Economy, 1987,* p. 37, and Economic Planning Board, *Major Statistics of Korean Economy, 1993,* (Seoul: Economic Planning Board, 1993), p. 224.

34. As with the Korean data, these ratios are taken from the national accounts. The Taiwan data come from Directorate General of Budget, Accounting and Statistics, *Statistical Yearbook of the Republic of China, 1996* (Taibei: Directorate General of Budget, Accounting, and Statistics, 1996), pp. 152–153, and *Statistical Yearbook of the Republic of China, 2005* (Taibei: Directorate of Budget, Accounting and Statistics, 2005), pp. 154–155.

35. The official figures for 1986–1989 can be found in General Statistical Office, *Economy and Trade of Vietnam, 1986–1991* (Hanoi, 1992). For a more complete picture using both official and other sources, see Vo Nhan Tri, *Vietnam's Economic Policy since 1975* (Singapore: ASEAN Economic Research Unit, Institute of Southeast Asian Studies, 1990).

36. Vo Nhan Tri, *Vietnam's Economic Policy since 1975,* p. 221.

37. Vietnam received some foreign aid, notably from Sweden, but the amounts were small and did not increase when Soviet subsidies and aid were ended.

38. These price statistics are from General Statistical Office, *Ngiam Giam Thong Ke 1993,* p. 218, and *Economy and Trade of Vietnam, 1986–1991,* p. 160.

39. These figures are based on a rural population in 2000 of 807.39 million people and 4.2 members per household in 2000. The cultivated acreage figure is for 2010 at 121.72 million hectares (National Statistical Office, *Zhongguo tongji zhaiyao 2011,* p. 5). Some of the earlier estimates of China's cultivated acreage understated the total amount, so I used the most recent figure available.

40. Dao Duy Tung, "How Doi Moi Began," *Vietnam Economic Times,* October 1994/January 1995, pp. 30–31, and Dao Duy Tung, "Cong cuoc doi moi cua Viet Nam bat nguon tu dau," in *Thoi su kinh te.*

6. The End of High Growth Rates

1. Because Vietnam started its economic high-growth period later than the others, GDP per capita rose only 2.4 times by 2010 (over 1988).

2. Herman Kahn, *The Emerging Japanese Superstate: Challenge and Response* (New York: Prentice Hall, 1971) and subsequent books by Kahn and coauthors.

3. These figures are in U.S. dollars in the prices of the year (2000 or 1973). Japan's GDP did continue to grow fairly rapidly by international standards after

1973 until the years of stagnation of the 1990s and beyond, but at roughly half the rate of the two decades prior to 1973.

4. I first noticed this pattern of GDP growth deceleration when Thomas Rawski and I were attempting to forecast when the Chinese economy was likely to slow down and wanted to see what happened in economies similar to that of China that had already achieved high-income status (i.e. Japan, South Korea, and Taiwan). The similarity of the deceleration point was striking, and later in a study with Kwanho Shin and Barry Eichengreen we decided to see if a similar pattern prevailed in other high-income countries, leading to the results presented in Figure 6.1 that are based on the data in the study of Korea. Dwight H. Perkins and Thomas G. Rawski, 2008, "Forecasting China's Economic Growth to 2025," in Loren Brandt and Thomas G. Rawski, eds., *China's Great Economic Transformation* (Cambridge: Cambridge University Press, 2008), table 20.6, p. 856; and Barry Eichengreen, Dwight H. Perkins, and Kwanho Shin, *From Miracle to Maturity: The Growth of the Korean Economy* (Cambridge, Mass.: Harvard Asia Center, distributed by Harvard University Press, 2012), figure 2.6 and table 2.

5. Countries such as Kuwait or Brunei that have high income almost entirely because of large oil reserves were not included in the data used to derive figure 6.1.

6. Eichengreen, Perkins, and Shin, *From Miracle to Maturity.*

7. Barry Eichengreen, Dwight H. Perkins, and Kwanho Shin, *From Miracle to Maturity: The Growth of the Korean Economy* (Cambridge, Mass.: Harvard Asia Center, distributed by Harvard University Press, 2012).

8. Per capita PPP GDP is calculated by first estimating the prices in local currencies of locally made products and comparing these local prices to international prices for the exact same item in dollars. By using urban prices for local products, one is using prices higher than the average for the country as a whole. That has the effect of lowering the ultimate estimate of local output when measured in international prices or dollars.

9. For a thought-provoking discussion of where China is heading see Edward S. Steinfeld, *Playing Our Game: Why China's Rise Doesn't Threaten the West* (Oxford: Oxford University Press, 2010).

10. There are economists who challenge the reliability of this figure for China (taken from National Statistical Office, *Zhongguo tongji zhaiyao 2012* [China Statistical Abstract 2012] (Beijing: Statistics Press, 2012), p. 36), but it is consistent with the national household surveys and with other data. If there is a significant downward bias in these estimates of household consumption, therefore, it is unlikely that the bias is large enough to change the analysis here. To change the analysis here, household consumption would have to be underestimated by 20 percent or more.

11. China's military expenditure data are widely believed to exclude major weapons development and procurement expenditures that probably are included in the investment/gross capital formation data. These unpublished military expenditures may be something like 2 percent of GDP.

12. In economics this is called the accelerator effect. Investment (other than depreciation) is needed when incomes and consumption expenditures rise (or when there is an expectation that consumption expenditures will rise), but it is not needed when there is no increase in consumption expenditures or when there is a decline in such expenditure. The precise level of investment will also be influenced by the cost of capital.

13. The real consumption figure was derived by dividing the increase in consumption in current prices by the consumer price index (a price index for government expenditures was not available, so the consumer price index was used for government expenditures as well).

14. These are crude estimates based on estimates of the real rate of consumption increase in 2000 over 1999 and 2010 over 2009 as a share of GDP times the average incremental capital-output ratio during 2001–2010 (=3.75). There could be considerable error in these estimates, but no plausible figures would raise the investment share required more than a few percentage points. If the net capital-output ratio were used (the gross ratio minus the component representing depreciation) the investment share of GDP would be smaller.

15. I multiplied the per capita living space in National Statistical Office, *Xin Zhongguo 60 nian* [60 Years of New China] (Beijing: Statistics Press, 2009), p. 628, by three to get these estimates.

16. This is comparing a gross value figure with GDP, which is the total of value added in the economy. The comparison is valid in this context because by using the gross value figure one is also including in gross construction the cost of all materials used and other costs that would be included in other sectors of GDP but would nevertheless be part of building construction's share of GDP.

17. Albert Keidel, *South Korean Regional Farm Product and Income 1910–1975* (Honolulu: University of Hawaii Press, 1981).

18. These gross and net housing construction figures are rough estimates. The Chinese figures are derived from data on the increase in the per capita housing in the urban and rural areas together with the increase in the officially registered urban population and the small decline in the registered rural population. The Japanese figures for per capita housing are from Edward Lincoln, *Japan Facing Economic Maturity* (Washington, D.C.: Brookings Institution Press, 1988), p. 52. The U.S. estimates are based on an average construction of housing of 1.5 million units a year (Council of Economic Advisors, *Economic Report of the President 2010* [Washington, D.C.: Government Printing Office, 2010], table B-56) and an estimated living unit size of 175 square me-

ters, a figure adjusted downward from the average single-unit house of 200 square meters.

19. This figure is a very crude estimate based on meeting the housing needs of 400 million migrants at 20 square meters per migrant. The statement that most of this will need to be public housing (or subsidized private housing) is based on the fact that migrant incomes are much too low to purchase apartments on the commercial market, at least in the larger cities, where land prices are very high. Actual migration may be larger than this, but some of the migrants will be able to purchase housing on the commercial market or will choose to continue residence in the rural areas and live only temporarily in the cities.

20. Estimates by Victor Shih suggest that the true figure might be twice this official estimate (personal communication).

21. Chinese report wage data in a way that is not ideal for my purposes here, because they lump together the wages of the skilled and unskilled in a particular sector and thus some of the increase in wages represents increases in the skill levels of the labor force in that sector and not a real wage increase for workers of a given skill. Official wage indexes for unskilled workers as a group or by industry do not exist, however, or at least none were available to me.

Acknowledgments

This book is an expansion of the Edwin O. Reischauer Lectures, which I gave at Harvard University in April 2009. These lectures were in turn based on the course I taught during my final 10 years of lecturing at Harvard University. Titled "Economic Development in East Asia," the course covered topics relevant to the economic history and contemporary development of East and Southeast Asia. This book, the Reischauer Lectures, and the course were based on what I believe I have learned about economic development in East and Southeast Asia over a half century of research, writing, consulting, and advising in the region. This book and the lectures that preceded them, however, are not a memoir of my experiences, although I do draw on them to a limited degree in this book. They are instead my attempt to explain how so many countries at the eastern end of the Asian continent were to varying degrees able to transform their economies in the short span of less than half a century. The book does not attempt to define an "East Asian model of economic development" because no single model describes accurately what the 10 most successful economies in the region did to achieve this transformation. In most of the countries, in fact, more than one model or approach to development was tried as the conditions within as well as between the countries changed. There were common themes, however, and the countries that started the transformation later learned from those that went ahead.

My interest in East Asia began in the early 1950s at Cornell University, when I took a course on Chinese history from Professor Knight Biggerstaff, who is responsible more than any other person for my focusing my career on East Asia. I then majored in "Far Eastern Studies," the one and only major in that subject in my class at Cornell, and began my up-and-down study of the Chinese language and courses that covered Southeast as well as East Asia. After two years in the U.S. Navy I returned to graduate school in economics at Harvard University in 1958. I first traveled to Asia in 1961–1962, and in the winter of 1963 I taught my first course at Harvard on the economy of China. I have been at Harvard ever since, as a teacher in the Department of Economics and as an active participant in the rich array of Asian programs the university offers. I began my direct involvement with the People's Republic of China when I made my first trip to Beijing in 1974 as an aide to then senator Henry M. Jackson.

Critical for the writing of this book and for my understanding of economic development more generally, however, was when I began to work with what initially was called the Harvard Development Advisory Service and later became the Harvard Institute for International Development. I spent two summers on either side of an academic year in Japan with the Advisory Service working in the Economic Planning Unit of the Government of Malaysia. The second summer immediately followed the election and resulting riots that led to the New Economic Policy, which still shapes Malaysian policy to some degree today. That summer was followed with summers working with the Korea Development Institute in Seoul, first helping that major institution get started and later working with it through joint research that has produced a series of volumes on Korean development, work that has also continued to this day. In 1980, through a series of fortunate accidents, I became director of the Harvard Institute for International Development and stayed in the position until 1995. In that capacity I had the privilege of working with some of the ablest economic policy-makers in Asia, particularly in Indonesia but also in Vietnam, Korea, China, and elsewhere. I have continued many of those relationships in the 17 years since I left the directorship of the institute.

Along the way I have accumulated a very large number of debts, even if I limit it to the people who helped shape this book. The list includes the professors who taught me at Cornell and Harvard, the many more people I have had as colleagues at Harvard, the students, from whom one learns as well as teaches, and many government officials and academics in countries in Asia (and Africa and Latin America). Most of all I owe the largest debt of gratitude to my wife, Julie Rate Perkins, who has accompanied me on all of my longer journeys to Asia and who has brought a different perspective and found different relationships in the region that have enriched my understanding.

More immediately, in the production of this book I am deeply grateful to Magnus Feldman, Malcolm McPherson, and David Dapice for reading and critiquing earlier drafts of the manuscript. Their comments were invaluable in the major revisions I then undertook.

Finally I am grateful to Kathleen McDermott of Harvard University Press for shepherding this manuscript through the publication process, to production editor Brian Ostrander, and to Martha Ramsey for her able copyediting.

Index